The Economics of Biological Invasions

The Economics of Biological Invasions

Edited by

Charles Perrings

Professor of Environmental Economics and Environmental Management, University of York, UK

Mark Williamson

Professor Emeritus of Biology, University of York, UK

and

Silvana Dalmazzone

Post-doctoral Research Fellow, University of York, UK and Research Fellow, ICER – International Centre for Economic Research, Turin, Italy

Edward Elgar
Cheltenham, UK • Northampton, MA, USA

Published by
Edward Elgar Publishing Limited
Glensanda House
Montpellier Parade
Cheltenham
Glos GL50 1UA
UK

Edward Elgar Publishing, Inc.
136 West Street
Suite 202
Northampton
Massachusetts 01060
USA

Reprinted 2003

A catalogue record for this book
is available from the British Library

Library of Congress Cataloguing in Publication Data
The economics of biological invasions / edited by Charles Perrings, Mark Williamson, Silvana Dalmazzone.
    Includes bibliographical references.
        1. Biological invasions—Economic aspects. 2. Non-indigenous pests—Control.   I. Perrings, Charles.   II. Williamson, M. H. (Mark Herbert)
III. Dalmazzone, Silvana.

    QH353 .E36   2000
    577'.18—dc21

                                                                            00–026460

ISBN 1 84064 378 1

Typeset by Manton Typesetters, Louth, Lincolnshire, UK.
Printed and bound in Great Britain by Biddles Ltd, *www.biddles.co.uk*

Contents

Figures

Tables

Contributors

Edward B. Barbier   Department of Economics and Finance, University of Wyoming, Laramie, Wyoming 82071–3985, USA.

Silvana Dalmazzone   International Centre for Economic Research, Turin, Italy. E-mail: <silvana.dalmazzone@unito.it>

Doriana Delfino   Environment Department and Department of Economics and Related Studies, University of York, Heslington, York YO10 5DD, UK. E-mail: <dd109@york.ac.uk>

Peter M. Dowling   New South Wales Agriculture, Australian Centre for Weed Research and Cooperative Research Centre for Weed Management Systems, Orange Agricultural Institute, Forest Road, Orange, NSW 2800, Australia.

Robert P. Freckleton   Schools of Environmental and Biological Sciences, University of East Anglia, Norwich NR4 7TJ, UK.

David Greathead   International Institute of Biological Control, CABI Bioscience, Ascot, Berkshire SL5 7TA, UK.

Barry Heydenrych   Botany Department, University of Cape Town, Private Bag, Rondebosch 7701, South Africa.

Garry Hill   International Institute of Biological Control, CABI Bioscience, Ascot, Berkshire SL5 7TA, UK. E-mail: <g.hill@cabi.org>

Victor Kasulo   National Economic Council, P.O. Box 30136, Lilongwe 3, Malawi. E-mail: <vkasulo@hotmail.com>

Duncan Knowler   School of Resource and Environmental Management, Simon Fraser University, 8888 University Drive, Burnaby, British Columbia, Canada V5A 1S6. E-mail: <djk@sfu.ca>

Jon C. Lovett   Environment Department, University of York, Heslington, York YO10 5DD, UK. E-mail: <jl15@york.ac.uk>

Harold A. Mooney   Department of Biological Sciences, Stanford University, Stanford, CA 94305, USA. E-mail: <hmooney@jasper.stanford.edu>

Geraldine Newton-Cross   Environment Department, University of York, Heslington, York YO10 5DD, UK. E-mail: <ganc100@york.ac.uk>

Charles Perrings   Environment Department, University of York, Heslington, York YO10 5DD, UK. E-mail: <cap8@york.ac.uk>

Jason F. Shogren   Department of Economics, University of Wyoming, Laramie, Wyoming 82071–3985, USA. E-mail: <JRamses@UWYO.EDU>

Peter J. Simmons   Department of Economics and Related Studies, University of York, Heslington, York YO10 5DD, UK. E-mail: <ps1@york.ac.uk>

Jane Turpie   Percy FitzPatrick Institute of African Ornithology, University of Cape Town, Rondebosch 7701, South Africa. E-mail: <jturpie@botzoo.uct.ac.za>

Andrew R. Watkinson   School of Environmental and Biological Sciences, University of East Anglia, Norwich NR4 7TJ, UK. E-mail: <a.watkinson@uea.ac.uk>

Piran C.L. White   Environment Department, University of York, Heslington, York YO10 5DD, UK. E-mail: <pclw1@york.ac.uk>

Mark Williamson   Department of Biology, University of York, Heslington, York YO10 5DD, UK. E-mail: <mw1@york.ac.uk>

Preface   The Global Invasive Species Program (GISP)*

Harold A. Mooney

During the period between 1982 and 1988 the Scientific Committee on Problems of the Environment (SCOPE) engaged a large number of scientists in an effort to document the nature of the invasive species 'problem'. The results of this effort appeared in a number of books and as a synthesis in 1989 entitled *Biological Invasions: A Global Perspective* (Drake et al., 1989). This synthesis clearly established that invasive species could have major impacts on ecosystem functioning and that virtually all ecosystems were impacted by them, even those under preservation management. It was also clear that we are on the way to establishing a whole new biotic order on the Earth due to the massive breakdown of biogeographic barriers to migration. Although the SCOPE programme was quite successful scientifically it did not offer much to managers except to inform them they were not alone in the world dealing with these problems.

SCOPE, along with partners from UNEP (United Nations Environment Program), IUCN (International Union for the Conservation of Nature) and CABI (Commonwealth Agricultural Bureau International), is embarking on a new programme on invasive species, this time with the explicit objective of providing new tools for understanding as well as dealing with invasive species. This venture is called the Global Invasive Species Program, or GISP. This effort differs substantially from the previous programme in that it will engage the many constituencies that are involved with the problem including natural and social scientists, educators, lawyers, resource managers, and people from both industry and government.

The programme has 11 elements. Each of these will contribute to building the comprehensive approach that is needed for dealing with invasive species. Four elements deal with synthesizing our current knowledge on invasive species. These include the ecology of invasive species (led by David Richardson

* This preface appeared in *Biological Invasions*, **1**: 97–8, 1999. Reprinted here with kind permission from Kluwer Academic Publishers.

and Marcel Rejmánek), the current status of invasive species and new methods for assessing their changing distributions and abundance (Mark Lonsdale
and Richard Mack), how society views and values invasive species (Jeff
McNeely) and how global change will impact the success of invaders (Richard Hobbs and Harold Mooney).

A major effort of GISP will be the development of new tools and approaches for dealing with invasives. These include the development of a
global early warning system for the most serious invasive species (Mick
Clout), an analysis of the changing pathways of trade as they provide vectors
for invasives (James Carlton and Greg Ruiz), new approaches for developing
risk analyses dealing with the introduction of new biotic material into ecosystems (David Andow), assessment of the best practices for management and
control of invasives (Jeff Waage), the development of new approaches for
educating the general public on the potential dangers of invasive species
(Alan Holt), the economic consequences of invasive species (Charles Perrings
and Mark Williamson), and an analysis of the legal and institutional frame-
works for dealing with invasives (Lyle Glowka).

All of these elements will have one or more workshops with specific
products. All of these activities will be synthesized at a summary workshop
in Capetown, South Africa, in September 2000.

Whereas the original SCOPE project was satisfied with production of a
scientific synthesis volume as a final product, GISP has much broader objectives. The focus is on the production of new tools, the evaluation of best
management practices, and the articulation of a new strategy for addressing
the issues. Specific products would include management and educational
packages, summaries for policy makers, and importantly, a popular volume
describing all that was learned during this programme.

Post-GISP efforts would put this strategy into action. GISP is funded by
the Global Environment Facility (GEF), UNEP, the United Nations Educa-
tional, Scientific, and Cultural Organization (UNESCO), the National
Aeronautics and Space Administration (NASA), the International Council for
Science (ICSU), La Fondation Total, the John T. and Catherine D. MacArthur
Foundation, and the Norwegian government.

For more information about GISP contact Véronique Plocq-Fichelet, SCOPE
Secretariat, 51, bd de Montmorency, 75016 Paris, France (e-mail:
scope@paris7jussieu.fr). The Website is http://jasper.stanford.edu/GISP/.

REFERENCE

Drake, J.A., H.A. Mooney, F. di Castri, R.H. Groves, F.J. Kruger, M. Rejmánek and
    M. Williamson (eds) (1989), *Ecology of Biological Invasions: A Global Perspec-
    tive*, SCOPE 37, New York: John Wiley.

1. Introduction

Charles Perrings, Mark Williamson and Silvana Dalmazzone

---

1 THE PROBLEM OF BIOLOGICAL INVASIONS

A large share of the attention attracted by biological invasions has been motivated, until recently, by the impact on crops of alien species that became pests. Living organisms have always been transported beyond their original range; however, because of the enormous growth in the international transport of people and commodities in the last quarter to half a century, invasions now have unprecedented environmental and economic effects.

In addition to their impact in terms of forgone output in agriculture, forestry and fisheries, pest control and health care, invasive species have proved to be one of the main drivers behind biodiversity loss in a wide range of ecosystems. The factors that have evolved with them and that control their population and spread in their native range are generally not present in their new habitats. Native species may not possess defence mechanisms that allow them to compete successfully for vital resources and may therefore be driven to extinction. Indeed, invasives are sometimes said to be the second most important cause of biodiversity loss, after habitat destruction (Glowka et al., 1994). They are certainly a major threat on oceanic islands. The extinctions due to cats, rats, goats, the snail *Euglandina rosea* and the brown tree snake *Boiga irregularis* are all well known (Williamson, 1996). On continents, the threat of invasives to biodiversity is variable. It is better known in developed countries than developing ones, but Mack (1997) notes invasives affecting whole landscapes in parts of the USA, Central America from Mexico to Panama, Venezuela, Brazil, Argentina, Iceland and many other smaller islands, South Africa, Madagascar, India, Myanmar, Australia and New Zealand, which is a mix of most types of economies. In the United States, invasives have been shown to be the major threat to imperilled species after habitat destruction (Wilcove et al., 1998). Czech and Krausman (1997), though, claimed that this is primarily an island effect; of 305 species endangered by non-natives, only 115 are on the mainland, but 190 are on Hawaii and Puerto Rico, both oceanic islands.

Many ecological functions are supported at any one moment in time by a relatively small number of species. Their removal can induce a transformation of the ecosystem (Holling, 1992; Heywood, 1995). The level of biodiversity in an agroecosystem determines its capacity to respond to external shocks, whether market or environmental. From an ecological perspective, biodiversity protects ecosystem resilience by underwriting the provision of ecosystem services over a range of environmental conditions (Holling et al., 1995). Certain species have greater ecological value under one state of nature than others, but species that are 'passengers' under one state of nature may have a key structuring role to play under other states of nature. The ecological impact of biodiversity loss depends on the link between the species and the functions of the system. Whether the deletion of some species affects a given function depends on the number of alternative species that can support the function if the ecosystem is perturbed (Schindler, 1990; Lawton and Brown, 1993). Invasive species may be critical in undermining the buffering role played by ecological redundancy.

Invasive species have a great variety of impacts, of which swamping of other species, diseases and new top trophic species (predators such as cats, herbivores such as goats) are generally the most severe (Williamson, 1996). Impacts have been measured in a great variety of different ecosystems, terrestrial, fresh-water and marine, animal, plant and microbe (Parker et al., 1999) and have a great variety of economic and ecological effects (Williamson, in press). Impacts vary more or less continuously from negligible to severe and each type of impact has its own spectrum of species, each species its own spectrum of impacts (Williamson, 1998). There is clearly a need for more modelling of impacts, and more experimental and observational research on the relation of different impacts and the ways of measuring them (Parker et al., 1999). Some of the remarkable variety of impacts are described, in a semi-scientific way, by Bright (1999) and Devine (1998) and the cases studies in this book, Chapters 5–11, give further instances.

With the growth of global economic activity, there will be many new impacts by invasives that will not be predicted (Williamson, 1999 and in press), but measures can be taken to avoid a repeat of old impacts in new areas, to forestall new impacts and to manage efficiently, both economically and ecologically, those species that cannot be eradicated. That is the contribution of this book to the Global Invasive Species Project.

2   THE GLOBAL INVASIVE SPECIES PROJECT

The chapters of this book are based on presentations at a symposium on the economics of invasive biological species held in York, England, in March

1999. The symposium was part of the Global Invasive Species Project, itself a programme of SCOPE, the Scientific Committee (of ICSU, the International Council for Science) on Problems of the Environment. GISP is funded from many sources but primarily by GEF, the Global Environment Facility of the United Nations. A major aim of the project is to improve implementation of Article 8(h) of the Convention on Biological Diversity which exhorts the Contracting Parties to 'prevent the introduction of, control or eradicate those alien species which threaten ecosystems, habitats or species'. The Convention on Biological Diversity (CBD) was signed by more than 150 governments at the 1992 Earth Summit in Rio de Janeiro, and became effective as international law in December 1993. It is the first international agreement which commits governments to a comprehensive protection of the Earth's biological resources. As of November 1999, 176 countries have ratified the agreement.[1] At the core of the Convention is the recognition that diversity must be maintained, if only because failure to do so would threaten human existence. This is achievable only through sustainable use and a fair and equitable distribution of the benefits derived from the use. By signing the CBD, participating governments have agreed, among other things, to pursue policy measures such as creation of national plans for the protection of biodiversity, identification of ecosystems, species and genomes crucial for conservation, monitoring of biological diversity and of any factors that might have an impact on it, establishing systems of protected areas, rehabilitating damaged ecosystems, and taking measures for *ex-situ* conservation. The Convention comprises 42 articles concerning its objectives, the practical obligations of the signatories, the policies to be followed and the use of terms.[2]

GISP intends, *inter alia*, to provide advice about invasive species, and how to implement Article 8(h). Its audience includes decision makers responsible for health, agriculture, forestry, fisheries and the environment. That advice should include information on how to identify and estimate the economic effects of invasives, and on their prevention, control and mitigation. The symposium reported here is a first major step towards formulating and codifying such advice.

3   THE ECONOMICS OF INVASIVES

The core problems in the economics of invasives are, first, to understand the causes, consequences and economic forces behind invasions; and second, how to achieve an efficient allocation of resources to the prevention, control and mitigation of invasives, given socioeconomic and environmental conditions, and given the objectives of the decision makers.

Valuation is a part of this problem. Although economists recognize that the market prices of species and ecological services are poor indicators of their value to humanity, they have only recently begun to grapple with the problem of the valuation of biodiversity (Pearce and Moran, 1994). There is some consensus that the most appropriate methods for the valuation of non-marketed biological resources focus on their local opportunity cost – their impact on the range of services provided by the affected ecosystem (Heywood, 1995). To arrive at an appropriate valuation, therefore, requires an appropriate specification of the underlying physical problem and the attendant risks. It depends on getting the science of invasions right.

This requires that we are able to understand, measure, explain and predict invasions – a field recently reviewed by Williamson (1999). There are many biologists who would like to think that invasions can in principle be predicted, particularly from the general properties of species or habitats or both. The evidence, unfortunately, is that this is not and will not be possible. Part of the problem is that there seem to be no general laws governing biological invasions. Lawton (1999, p. 180) argues that 'if we need, or want, to predict in detail the population dynamics of a particular species in a particular habitat, then there is no alternative but to study that species in detail in the place or habitat of interest'. Law et al. (in press) make a similar point: namely that understanding invasions depends as much on detailed knowledge of idiosyncratic biological interactions as on general properties of community structure. The advice of Kareiva et al. (1996) is that models and short-term experiments are inadequate predictors of invasions, so new situations will require extensive monitoring. In practice this means studying previous invasions by the same species. This approach was found by Williamson (1999) to be the only predictor other than propagule pressure that could be called 'quite good'. Even though prediction is so difficult, explanations of the behaviour of invasives can be found by appropriate ecological studies (ibid.). That is sufficient to inform the economics of invasions. But the limitations of biological explanation and prediction need to be borne in mind when formulating economic protocols.

Whereas the management of pests in agriculture, forestry and fisheries has been extensively researched, there has been little systematic economic analysis of the broader problem of invasives. The economics of pest and disease control is the basis for most existing estimates of the cost of invasives. It is certainly the area in which data are most reliable. There are, for example, reasonably good estimates of the relative costs of herbicide control for different plant species in Britain (Williamson, 1998). There are estimates of the damages and/or the control costs also for a few other invaders. Bioeconomic or ecological–economic models have been employed to estimate the economic impact and the control costs of a potential invasion of Australia by the

Old World screwworm fly, *Chrysomya bezziana* (Anaman et al., 1994); the benefits from clearing alien species from Fynbos ecosystems in South Africa (Higgins et al., 1997b; Turpie and Heydenrych, Chapter 9, this volume); the impact of Knapweed and Leafy Spurge on the economy of several US states (Hirsch and Leitch, 1996; Bangsund et al., 1999); the damages to North American and European industrial plants from the zebra mussel and other invaders (Khalanski, 1997); the impact of the green crab *Carcinus maenas* on the North Pacific Ocean fisheries (Cohen et al., 1995); and the control costs for water hyacinth and rabbit, both discussed in chapters in this volume.

Many of these studies suffer from data limitations when dealing with the economic aspect of the problem, and most concentrate on estimates of costs and benefits, without developing decision models or theoretical analyses. Among the very few exceptions, Sharov and Liebhold (1998) and Sharov et al. (1998) develop an economic analysis of decisions about eradication, stopping, or slowing the spread of invasive species in North American ecosystems. They apply it to case studies of the gypsy moth *Lymantria dispar*. Higgins et al. (1997a) provide an ecological–economic model for the analysis of alternative strategies for control and conflict resolution in the case of environmental weeds whose eradication is resisted by parties who utilize them.

There are few attempts to aggregate the economic costs of invasions, and those that do exist vary very widely. Two estimates of the costs of invaders to the American economy, for example, are US OTA (1993) and Pimentel et al. (1999). The US OTA estimates damage costs of $96 994 million from 79 particularly harmful species over 85 years. Pimentel et al. estimate damage costs of $122 639 million per year from all species – a difference of two orders of magnitude (despite the apparent precision of both). Given this level of uncertainty about the severity of the problem, it is important to investigate the difficulties facing decision makers who deal with invasives, and how many resources should be committed to prevention, control and mitigation.

Part of the difficulty in producing estimates is that the aggregate cost of invasions is made up of innumerable components, most of which are subject to considerable errors of measurement that are compounded in the summation. In addition, none of the available estimates considers all the relevant components. One that is often neglected, for example, is the globally important loss of genetic information. There are few estimates of the magnitude of these costs but all indicate that the sums involved are not trivial (Heywood, 1995; Pearce and Moran, 1994). Most cultivated crop varieties and some livestock strains contain genetic material recently incorporated from related wild or weedy species, or from more primitive genetic stocks still used and maintained by traditional agricultural peoples. It has been estimated that at least half of the increase in agricultural productivity achieved in the last hundred years is attributable to artificial selection, recombination and intraspecific gene transfer procedures (Perrings et al., 1995). The value of genetic diversity in this case lies in the fact that it provides the raw material for desirable genetic traits in crops. Genetic resources have been used to boost productivity of meat, milk and wool, impart resistance to pests, and help adapt animals to harsh environments. Traditional varieties are the result of millennia of selection by farmers, and are a major source of genetic diversity in agriculture and of genetic resources for plant breeding. 'Natural' habitats may contain wild populations of existing crops and these wild genepools are a valuable resource for crop improvement. Displacement of such genetic resources is a major cost of invasions in agroecosystems.

Aside from the direct costs of the prevention, control or mitigation, the economic cost of invasives also includes their indirect ecological consequences. Invasives may lead to changes in ecological services that are locally important, by disturbing the operation of the hydrological cycle including flood control and water supply, waste assimilation, recycling of nutrients, conservation and regeneration of soils, pollination of crops and so on (Daily, 1997). These services have both current-use value and option value – the potential value of such services in the future. As an example, an estimate of the indirect benefits of forest conservation in Korup National Park, Cameroon (Ruitenbeek, 1989) found the net benefits of watershed protection, flood control and soil fertility maintenance to be roughly comparable to the forgone benefits from timber production. A further example, described in this book, is the role of acacia species in the hydrological cycle in the South African Fynbos. A change in the biodiversity of the Fynbos induced by the establishment of an invasive species has changed water supplies to the whole community (Turpie and Heydenrych, Chapter 9, this volume). One aim of this book is to clarify how the direct and indirect costs of invasions may be assessed.

Agricultural pests, epidemic diseases, and the establishment of wild species in unmanaged ecosystems are all part of the same general problem. In many cases the introduction and establishment of new species is an external effect of market activities. Although the destruction of crops and harvests is usually reflected in the market prices of agricultural, fishery, or forestry commodities, these costs are not borne by the source of the introductions. They are in the nature of externalities – costs which a given activity unintentionally imposes on another, without the latter being able to exact a compensation for the damage received. The biodiversity loss caused by habitat destruction (but not that caused by poaching, for example) also falls in that general conceptual category.

There is, however, a notable difference between biological invasions and externalities as conventionally understood in economics. The generally accepted notion of external effect implies that, in order to persist, the damage must be associated with a continuing flow of output from the source. Biological invasions, on the other hand, once set in motion are largely self-perpetuating. Even if the source of the introduction ceases its activity, damages from the invasives continue and generally increase over time. For this reason the policies developed to deal with conventional externalities and applied in the literature on general biodiversity loss – taxes and subsidies, the establishment of well-defined property rights, and possibly even permits and quotas – in all likelihood are ill-suited to deal with the problem of invasions. Consider, for example, the recent invasion of the North American Great Lakes by the fishhook waterflea (*Cercopagis pengoi*), expected to infest the entire ecosystem and to seriously disrupt sport and commercial fisheries (Mittelstaedt, 1999). Even if the cargo responsible for the introduction could be induced by an economic policy instrument to never return again to the region, the flow of damages would not be extinguished. Moreover, the identification of the pathways of introduction is a well-known problem among experts of invasions as well as policy makers – and so is the prediction of which species are a potential source of trouble. Indeed, the problems associated with uncertainty, monitoring and enforcement are all more severe than they are in the presence of conventional externalities.

4   THE STRUCTURE OF THE BOOK

The book is divided into two parts. The first part is concerned with the general theoretical and methodological issues raised by the problem of invasive species. The second part comprises case studies that collectively lead to important empirical generalizations about invasions. Both approaches are important and both will be needed to develop decision rules, tools and protocols for the effective management of invasive biological species. Chapter 12 offers some conclusions.

The evaluation of costs associated with invasive species and benefits of control strategies by no means exhausts the potential for an economic analysis of the problem of biological invasions. An economic approach can be aimed also at understanding mechanisms and relationships, at investigating causes and possible policies. It is important, for example, to identify the institutional and policy conditions that predispose countries to biological invasion. In the first part of this volume, the chapter by Dalmazzone (Chapter 2) is an initial step in that direction. Based on data concerning established alien plant species in 29 different countries in different continents, and a large number of economic variables – the composition of a country's trade flows, its regulatory regimes, the importance of agriculture, livestock, tourism sectors and so on – the chapter investigates the empirical support for the hypothesis of economic activities as determinants in the recent changes in the rate of alien species introductions. The analysis constitutes a preliminary study of which economic activities are likely to play a role, and of their relative importance in explaining a country's susceptibility to biological invasions. It also aims at investigating the relative importance of disturbance (which may undermine the ability of ecosystems to resist to invasions) versus introductions of alien species as determinants of biological invasions.

From a different perspective, Delfino and Simmons (Chapter 3) regard infectious diseases as invasives into the human species and look at how the invasive disease interacts with the economy in which it occurs. Having outlined the invasive nature of the major infectious diseases, they look at the dynamic epidemiology of the human population. Then they explore how economically motivated mechanisms to control the disease affect the population dynamics. Finally they look at the main reasons for a regulatory control of human behaviours that may affect patterns of introduction and spread of the disease.

Shogren (Chapter 4) focuses on the risks that exotic invaders pose to both ecological and economic systems by disrupting traditional production systems. Societies reduce the risks posed by invaders through private and collective mitigation or adaptation or both. Mitigation reduces the odds that bad events happen; adaptation reduces the consequences when a bad event does occur. The chapter develops an analytical framework to capture how a society can mix mitigation and adaptation strategies to reduce the risk from exotic invaders. Using the economic theory of endogenous risk, three implications are considered – the interaction of biological and economic factors to assess risk, the value of risk reduction, and the impact of additional risk of damages.

The last two chapters in Part I apply models to particular case studies. Knowler and Barbier (Chapter 5) offer a conceptual framework for looking at the costs imposed by unintended species introductions. They develop a model of an introduction with consequences for an indigenous harvested species, whose population dynamics are altered by the invader. After discussing the general implications and costs associated with this event, they proceed to a case-study application of a particular variant of the model. The Black Sea offers one of the most interesting examples of a large commercial harvesting loss due mainly to an invading species – the comb-jelly *Mnemiopsis leidyi*, introduced in the early 1980s. The chapter contains a model of the population dynamics of the Black Sea anchovy, integrating the influence of the invasive as a structural change in the anchovy stock–recruitment relationship; it assesses the economic impact of this structural change using a dynamic discrete time bioeconomic model; and it provides estimates of the losses involved.

Annual weeds are present in all but the most intensively managed agricultural systems. In agricultural systems worldwide, many of these species are not native but have invaded from elsewhere. Watkinson, Freckleton and Dowling (Chapter 6) outline how classical ecological models can be used to address some of the problems of invasive weeds, including (i) prediction of the numbers of weeds and the yield losses that result from their presence; (ii) the use of sensitivity analysis of population models in order to target key areas of the life cycle at which control will be most effective; and (iii) exploration of the general determinants of invasions. When information on the responses of populations to management and the cost of management are available, their approach feeds the predictions of ecological models into an economic analysis and predicts the optimum management strategies. These principles are illustrated with reviews of two case studies based on the invasion of Australian farming systems by weeds from Europe.

The chapters in Part II focus on five representative case studies. White and Newton-Cross (Chapter 7) focus on rabbits – Australia's most serious vertebrate pest. Rabbit grazing causes considerable economic damage to agriculture and forestry and also has adverse effects on the native flora and fauna. Their chapter assesses the market and non-market values associated with the introduction of rabbit calicivirus disease (RCD), officially released throughout Australia in October 1996, as a biological control agent for rabbits. The market values include costs and benefits accruing to the public sector, agriculture, forestry, the commercial rabbit industry and pet owners. The non-market values include costs and benefits to the wider ecosystem including native fauna and flora. Based on current scientific knowledge, the benefits of the introduction of RCD appear to exceed the costs considerably. However, some uncertainty remains about key aspects such as the long-term stability of RCD itself.

The impact of invasive plant species in tropical rain forests is a much debated issue. Lovett (Chapter 8) argues that, in that domain, concerns over the impact of invasive species are often not articulated within an ecological or a financial economic reasoning. Rather they are the result of a perceived change in the rain forest from an undisturbed *Urwald*, to a derived secondary type of forest. Lovett sees the arrival of new species in ecosystems as a normal process that has led to the accumulation of biological diversity. The main reason for concern is then perceived in terms of existence values or citizens' preferences for a particular state of nature. This point of view is illustrated using the case of *Maesopsis eminii*, a tree considered as an invasive in the Eastern Arc rain forests of Tanzania, an area listed as one of the Earth's most important biodiversity hotspots.

The South African Cape Floral Kingdom, with its characteristic Fynbos vegetation, is the smallest but richest of the world's six floral kingdoms. While facing a number of threats, its integrity is most severely threatened by the invasion of alien plants which rapidly transform natural areas into monospecific stands. These invasions, which already affect 66 per cent of the remaining Fynbos area in the Western Cape, not only reduce biodiversity and scenic beauty, but alter ecosystem functioning. Turpie and Heydenrych (Chapter 9) argue that Fynbos mountain catchments are extremely valuable in terms of their water yield, and this service is reduced significantly by alien invasions. While there has been some previous research on Fynbos's contribution to the hydrological cycle, this study also provides estimates of the value it yields in the form of consumptive use benefits, non-consumptive use value and option and existence values. The incentives to clear invasive aliens are evaluated depending on location (mountain ecosystems, agricultural land and so on) and property right regime (protected areas, private property, public property). The chapter reviews also the internationally funded Working for Water Project, initiated by the South African government in 1995 as a result of research which demonstrated the water benefits of alien eradication. That project has also turned alien clearing into a source of poverty relief through the creation of jobs, in addition to its value in terms of biodiversity conservation.

Kasulo (Chapter 10) analyses the ecological and socioeconomic impact of invasive species in African lakes. The focus is on introduced fish species and water weeds – in particular, the chapter analyses the biological and economic implications of the introduction of Nile perch, the Tanganyika sardine, and water hyacinth into Lakes Victoria, Kyoga, Nabugabo, Kariba, Kiw, Itezhi-tezhi and Malawi. The introduction of Nile perch has increased profits from commercial fishing and contributed to the generation of foreign exchange. However, the Nile perch is believed to have caused the extinction of numerous endemic species. The introduction of the sardine also resulted in an increase in productivity, with less dramatic impact on the lakes' ecosystem. The water hyacinth, introduced in Africa as an ornamental plant, has proliferated explosively in most African lakes, obstructing water passages and displacing native aquatic plants, fish and invertebrates by cutting out light and depleting dissolved oxygen. The weed is also believed to harbour disease-carrying organisms, and has little potential for economic utilization.

In Chapter 11, Hill and Greathead are concerned with biological control as a tool to counteract invasions. Approximately 10–15 per cent of some five thousand classical biological control introductions against arthropods have proved completely successful. Against weeds, about 30–40 per cent of some nine hundred introductions have achieved their objective. While most attempts at classical biological control are failures, a review of 27 economic analyses of successful programmes shows that they are extremely profitable, so much so that the successes may comfortably cover the costs of the failures. Research and fund managers need better tools to assist them in increasing the ratio of successes to failures, thereby increasing further the return on investment in biological control. In this regard, decision support tools incorporating economic and technical parameters are needed for *ex-ante* analyses to help assess the economic and non-economic impact of invading species and the probability of successful biological control.

We are a long way from a comprehensive and consistent economic theory of biological invasions. Whereas invasive species are attracting increasing scientific attention as many countries' budgets for control measures are on the rise, the economics of the problem has so far attracted little attention. The chapters in this volume represent a first coordinated attempt in that direction, provide a few of the essential building blocks, and – we hope – improve our understanding of the economic mechanisms behind biological invasions relative to what it was before.

NOTES

1. The Convention has not been ratified by Afghanistan, Azerbaijan, Kuwait, Liberia, Malta, Thailand, the United Arab Emirates, the United States of America and the Federal Republic of Yugoslavia.
2. For a comprehensive guide to the CBD, see Glowka et al. (1994). A concise account is, for example, Gaston and Spicer (1998, pp. 94–105).

REFERENCES

Anaman, K.A., M.G. Atzeni, D.G. Mayer and J.C. Walthall (1994), 'Economic assessment of preparedness strategies to prevent the introduction or the permanent establishment of screwworm fly in Australia', *Preventive Veterinary Medicine*, **20**(1–2): 99–111.

Bangsund, D.A, F.L. Leistritz and J.A. Leitch (1999), 'Assessing economic impacts of biological control of weeds: the case of leafy spurge in the northern Great Plains of the United States', *Journal of Environmental Management*, **56**: 35–43.

Bright, C. (1999), *Life out of Bounds*, London: Earthscan.

Cohen A.N., J.T. Carlton and M.C. Fountain (1995), 'Introduction, dispersal and potential impacts of the green crab *Carcinus maenas* in San Francisco Bay, California', *Marine Biology*, **122**(2): 225–37.

Czech, B. and P.R. Krausman (1997), 'Distribution and causation of species endangerment in the United States', *Science*, **277**: 1116–17.

Daily, G. (ed.) (1997), *Nature's Services: Societal Dependence on Natural Systems*, Washington, DC: Island Press.

Devine, R. (1998), *Alien Invasion*, Washington, DC: National Geographic Society.

Gaston, K.J. and J.I. Spicer (1998), *Biodiversity: An Introduction*, Oxford: Blackwell Science.

Glowka, L., F. Burhenne-Guilmin and H. Synge (1994), *A Guide to the Convention on Biological Diversity*, Gland: IUCN.

Heywood, V. (ed.) (1995), *Global Biodiversity Assessment*, Cambridge: Cambridge University Press.

Higgins, S.I., E.J. Azorin, R.M. Cowling and M.J. Morris (1997a), 'A dynamic ecological–economic model as a tool for conflict resolution in an invasive alien-plant, biological control and native-plant scenario', *Ecological Economics*, **22**(2): 141–54.

Higgins, S.I., J.K. Turpie, R. Costanza, R.M. Cowling, D.C. LeMaitre, C. Marais and G.F. Midgley (1997b), 'An ecological economic simulation model of mountain Fynbos ecosystems: dynamics, valuation and management', *Ecological Economics*, **22**(2): 155–69.

Hirsch, S.A. and J.A. Leitch (1996), *The Impact of Knapweed on Montana's Economy*, Department of Agricultural Economics, North Dakota State University, Fargo, North Dakota, Agricultural Economics Report 355, July.

Holling, C.S. (1992), 'Cross-scale morphology, geometry and dynamics of ecosystems', *Ecological Monographs*, **62**: 447–502.

Holling, C.S., D.W. Schindler, B.W. Walker and J. Roughgarden (1995), 'Biodiversity in the functioning of ecosystems: an ecological primer and synthesis', in C.A. Perrings, K.-G. Mäler, C. Folke, C.S. Holling and B.-O. Jansson (eds), *Biodiversity Loss: Ecological and Economic Issues*, Cambridge: Cambridge University Press: 44–83.

Kareiva, P., I.M. Parker and M. Pascual (1996), 'Can we use experiments and models in predicting the invasiveness of genetically engineered organisms?', *Ecology*, **77**: 1670–75.

Khalanski, M. (1997), 'Industrial and ecological consequences of the introduction of new species in continental aquatic ecosystems: the zebra mussel and other invasive species', *Bulletin Français de la Pêche et de la Pisciculture*, 344–5: 385–404.

Law, R., A.J. Wetherby and P.H. Warren (in press), 'On the invasibility of persistent protist communities', *Oikos*, **88**.

Lawton, J.H. (1999), 'Are there general laws in ecology?', *Oikos*, **84**: 177–92.

Lawton, J.H. and V.K. Brown (1993), 'Redundancy in ecosystems', in E.-D. Schulze and H.A. Mooney (eds), *Biodiversity and Ecosystem Function*, Ecological Studies No. 99, Berlin: Springer Verlag: 255–270.

Mack, R. (1997), 'Plant invasions: early and continuing expressions of global change', in B. Huntley, W. Cramer, A.V. Morgan, H.C. Prentice and J.R.M. Allen (eds), *Past and Future Rapid Environmental Changes: The Spatial and Evolutionary Responses of Terrestrial Biota*, NATO ASI Series I: Global Environmental Change, Vol. 47: 205–16.

Mittelstaedt, M. (1999), 'Asexual flea threatens Great Lakes', *The Globe and The Mail*, 22 November: A3.

Parker, I.M., D. Simberloff, W.M. Lonsdale, K. Goodell, M. Wonham, M. Williamson, B. Von Holle, P.B. Moyle, J.E. Byers and L. Goldwasser (1999), 'Impact: toward a framework for understanding the ecological effects of invaders', *Biological Invasions*, **1**: 3–19.

Pearce, D.W. and D. Moran (1994), *The Economic Value of Biodiversity*, London: Earthscan.

Perrings, C., K.-G. Mäler, C. Folke, C.S. Holling and B.-O. Jansson (eds) (1995), *Biological Diversity: Economic and Ecological Issues*, Cambridge: Cambridge University Press.

Pimentel, D., L. Lach, R. Zuniga and D. Morrison (1999), 'Environmental and economic costs associated with non-indigenous species in the United States', College of Agriculture and Life Sciences, Cornell University, Ithaca, NY. URL: http://www.news.cornell.edu/releases/Jan99/species_costs.htm.

Ruitenbeek, H.J. (1989), *Economic Analysis of Issues and Projects Relating to the Establishment of the Proposed Cross River National Park (Oban Division) and Support Zone*, London: World Wide Fund for Nature.

Schindler, D.W. (1990), 'Experimental perturbations of whole lakes as tests of hypotheses concerning ecosystem structure and function', Proceedings of 1987 Crafoord Symposium, *Oikos*, **57**: 25–41.

Sharov, A.A. and A.M. Liebhold (1998), 'Bioeconomics of managing the spread of exotic pest species with barrier zones', *Ecological Applications*, **8**(3): 833–45.

Sharov A.A., A.M. Liebhold and E.A. Roberts (1998), 'Optimizing the use of barrier zones to slow the spread of gypsy moth (Lepidoptera: Lymantriidae) in North America', *Journal of Economic Entomology*, **91**(1): 165–74.

US OTA (1993), *Harmful Non-Indigenous Species in the United States*, Washington, DC: Office of Technology Assessment, United States Congress.

Wilcove, D.S., D. Rothenstein, J. Dubow, A. Phillips and E. Losos (1998), 'Quantifying threats to imperiled species in the United States', *Bioscience*, **48**(8): 607–15.

Williamson, M. (1996), *Biological Invasions*, London: Chapman & Hall.

Williamson, M. (1998), 'Measuring the impact of plant invaders in Britain', in S. Starfinger, K. Edwards, I. Kowarik and M. Williamson (eds), *Plant Invasions: Ecological Mechanisms and Human Responses*, Leiden: Backhuys: 57–70.

Williamson, M. (1999), 'Invasions', *Ecography*, **22**: 5–12.

Williamson, M. (in press), *Quantifying the Ecological and Economic Risks of Invaders and GMOs*, Proceedings of the Workshop on Plant Health in the New Global Trading Environment: Managing Exotic Insects, Weeds and Pathogens, Canberra.

PART I

Analysis

2. Economic factors affecting vulnerability to biological invasions

Silvana Dalmazzone*

1 INTRODUCTION

The contribution of human activities to biological invasions is generally acknowledged. The movement of people and goods is usually taken to be the main driver of the process. Even though, from the very early stages of agriculture, crops and animals have been intentionally transported from one region of the world to another, the rate of species introduction by humans has increased sharply in recent years. Figure 2.1 presents two estimated trends in the establishment of alien plant species in California over the last 300 years. Since its colonization by Europeans there has been an exponential increase in established aliens. Available data would be consistent with both an exponential and a logistic regression, should there be an inflection point above the data. Increasing trends may be seen in many other countries.

It has been claimed (Lövei, 1997; Vitousek et al., 1997; Mooney, 1999; and others) that the introduction of alien species is a significant component of human-induced global change, and one of the most serious threats to biodiversity. The unprecedented mobility of people and commodities brought about by the globalization of the world economy is progressively breaking down the genetic isolation of communities of co-evolving species of plants and animals. Such isolation has been essential for the evolution and maintenance of the Earth's biological diversity (Clout et al., 1996). If this view is correct it follows that invasions may be among the most significant external effects of market activities.[1]

This chapter considers whether the available data support the hypothesis that economic activities are correlated with changes in the rate of alien species introductions. It considers which activities are likely to have played a role either as pathways ('vectors') for the introduction of invasives or as causes of a country's susceptibility to biological invasions.

This is a very preliminary study, not only because the problem has not been addressed before, but also because a well-specified and generally

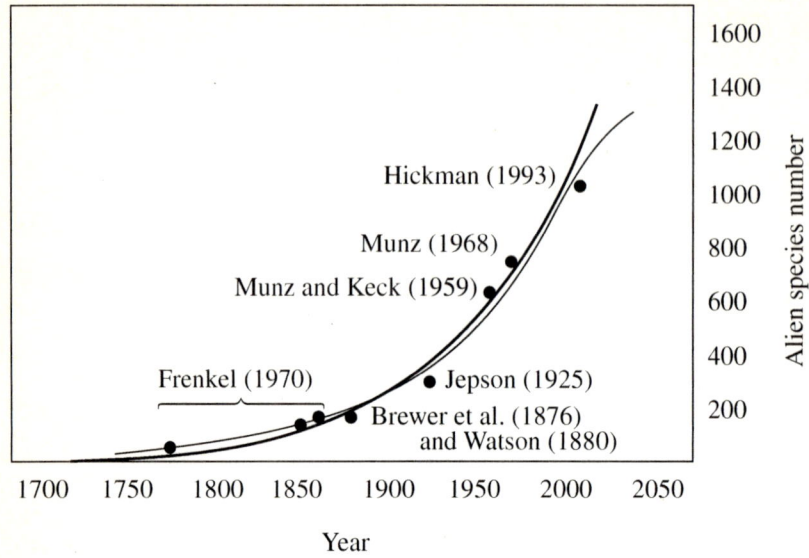

Source: Rejmánek and Randall (1994).

Figure 2.1   *Number of alien species of vascular plants in California flora,*
              1700–1993

accepted econometric model of invasions is not available. The aim of the study is simply to identify some of the forces at work as these are revealed by the empirical data. A more rigorous analysis will have to await further research.

2   THEORY

Since this is a preliminary investigation the theory is really nothing more than a set of primitive hypotheses about stock relationships. Among a number of possible alternatives, the dependent variable that has been retained is the ratio of established alien to native species – the odds that any randomly chosen species in a given country is an alien.

   The key biological priors are the following. The biological literature recognizes the sensitivity to biological invasions of island ecosystems. Their endemic species, having generally evolved in isolation over a long period of time, are often rare and particularly vulnerable to extinction through competition from introduced species. One prior is that there should be a higher proportion of alien species on islands than in continental countries. The literature on invasions also tells us that the incidence of biological invasions on continents increases from north to south until one reaches dry subtropical regions; it is relatively low in the tropics, and increases again in south temperate areas (Vitousek et al., 1997). A second prior reflects this finding.

There are two primitive hypotheses about the relation between economic activities and biological invasions. The first of these is that invasions are an increasing function of the extroversion of an economy – its openness to the movement of goods and services (trade) and of people. There are no readily available cumulative measures of this variable. The chapter therefore relies on proxies of extroversion (trade as a share of the gross domestic product (GDP), for example, or the volume of imports, the number of tourists, and so on) to explain the differences in the way various countries are affected by invasions. In this view, commerce and tourism would be the channels for the introduction of non-native species. However, it should be noted that none of these adequately captures the cumulative effects of historical trends.

The second primitive hypothesis is that invasions are an increasing function of the degree to which natural habitats are disturbed in the course of economic activity. Many studies underline disturbance as a key factor explaining invasibility. Disturbance creates 'open space' that may allow alien species to get established – it may in other words undermine the ability of ecosystems to resist invasions.[2] Intermediate levels of disturbance, particularly, offer invaders an edge against the better-adapted and therefore usually competitively stronger native species. When the level of disturbance is low the best competitors dominate the space, while at high levels of disturbance most alien species may simply be unable to get established. Intermediate levels of disturbances can make open space available to invasive species before the native ones are given enough time to dominate again the entire ecosystem (Connell, 1978; Rejmánek, 1984; 1989; Lodge, 1993; Etter and Caswell, 1994; Pyšek et al., 1998; Shigesada and Kawasaki, 1997 and references therein). The higher frequency of alien species in disturbed sites, however, may simply reflect the fact that disturbed areas are those where rates of introduction through economic activities are higher (Crawley, 1987; Usher, 1988; and Williamson, 1996). It has not been shown yet, in other words, how important disturbance is as a determinant of invasibility – of the chances to get established that a given area offers to an alien species. Proxies for the disturbance associated with human activities include population density and the level of GDP per capita. More importantly they include direct measures: the percentage of agricultural land, that of wood and forests, and the proportion of a country's territory permanently used as pastures.

3 DATA

Previously published ecological data on established alien plant species were assembled for 26 countries in Africa, Europe, North and South America, and Australia. These data cover a period that ranges from the early 1960s to the early 1990s.[3] The economic data are obtained from the FAO's Statistical Database (*FAOSTAT* 1997) and the World Bank's *World Development Indicators 1998*, as well as from the CIA (US government) (*The World Factbook, 1998*) and from other publicly available databases. Data on economic variables include GDPs, trade flows and their composition, tourism and rates of economic growth. Key structural data comprise the amount of land devoted to agriculture and to livestock production, along with the proportion of a country's territory preserved as forest and woods. Key demographic data include population density and growth. Policy and institutional variables include indirect measures of openness to trade, especially import duties.[4]

It should be made clear from the outset that the data are severely limited. The ecological data sets used are not homogeneous in quality, or in the definition of variables. The ideal ecological variable would be a flow – the rate of change in the occurrence of alien species in the last decade – rather than a stock – absolute numbers of species present at a specific point in time. Available data reflect the cumulative result of historical introductions (before the economic variables entering the empirical analysis may have had an effect). To accommodate this, as far as possible, the economic data are similarly selected to reflect the cumulative outcome of historical activity or policy. Ideally, we are interested in the relation between biological invasions in different countries and conformable economic data (timed so as to match the ecological data). New quantitative information on recent changes in species introductions for a large enough sample of countries would make it possible to test the impact of current policies.

A further fundamental problem is the mismatch between biologists' and economists' definitions of the relevant areas: ecological data – the numbers of alien and native species – in most cases are available by region or natural reserves, whereas the relevant economic data are typically classified by country. This is the main factor constraining the present sample size.

Tables 2.1 and 2.2 present the data set that was used to perform the final regression analysis. The data for demographic and land-use variables correspond for each country to the year of the ecological data, that is, to the year when the species count was made, whereas for the economic variables a five-year lag was built in: for each country, GDP, imports and other economic variables are those for the fifth year preceding the corresponding ecological variables.

Table 2.1   Ecological data[1]

Country	Area km^2	Natives	Aliens	Aliens/natives	Island	Data source
Australia	7 686 848	15 638	1 952	0.1248	0	Hnatiuk (1990)
Bahamas	14 500	1 104	246	0.2228	1	Correll and Correll (1982)
Belize	22 965	3 023	107	0.0354	0	Dwyer and Spellman (1981)
Bermuda	54	165	303	1.8364	1	Britton (1918)
Canada	9 976 139	3 270	940	0.2875	0	Scoggan (1978–79)
Cayman Islands	259	536	65	0.1213	1	Proctor (1984)
Chile	756 600	4 437	678	0.1528	0	Marticorena and Quezada (1985)
Cuba	114 500	5 790	376	0.0649	1	Borhidi (1991)
Djibouti	23 000	641	44	0.0686	0	Lebrun et al. (1989)
Egypt	1 000 250	2 015	86	0.0427	0	Roessler and Merxmüller (1976)
Finland	338 145	1 250	247	0.1976	0	Tutin et al. (1993)
France	549 619	4 350	480	0.1103	0	Tutin et al. (1964–80)
Greenland^2	410 449	427	86	0.2014	0	Bay (1993)
Guadeloupe and Martinique	2 620	1 668	360	0.2158	1	Fournet (1978)
Guam	583	327	185	0.5657	1	Lee (1974)
Namibia	824 293	3 159	60	0.0190	0	Merxmüller (1966–72)
New Zealand	268 575	2 449	1 623	0.6627	1	Atkinson and Cameron (1993)
Norway	323 878	1 195	580	0.4854	0	Fremstad et al. (1994)
Panama	77 082	7 123	263	0.0369	0	D'Arcy (1987)
Peru	1 285 200	17 900	314	0.0175	0	Barko and Zarucchi (1993)
Poland	312 680	2 250	275	0.1222	0	Kornas (1990)
Puerto Rico	8 897	2 741	356	0.1299	1	Francis and Logier (1991)
Rwanda	26 338	2 500	93	0.0372	0	Troupin (1978–88)
Swaziland	17 366	2 715	110	0.0405	0	Kemp (1983)
Uganda	236 040	4 848	152	0.0314	0	Vitousek et al. (1997)
Coterminous USA	7 844 400	17 300	2 100	0.1214	0	Kartesz (1994), USDA (1982)

Notes:
1.   The table is based on information in Rejmánek and Randall (1994), Vitousek et al. (1997) and other selected sources.
2.   The figure for land area refers to area free of ice. The total area is 2 166 086 km^2 (Statistics Greenland, 1999).

21

Analysis

Table 2.2   Economic and demographic data

Country	P.c. GDP[1]	M. imports[2]	% Duties[3]	% Agr.[4]	% Pasture[5]	Pop. dens.[6]
Australia	11 518	12.00	9	60	55	2.00
Bahamas	6 427	59.00	18	1	0	20.98
Belize	1 838	55.20	14	4	2	6.40
Bermuda	18 105	55.40	–	0	–	1 220.00
Canada	10 425	22.50	6	7	3	2.47
Cayman Islands	10 000	23.08	–	8	8	115.83
Chile	3 926	11.70	–	23	18	14.88
Cuba	1 400	15.30	–	52	24	92.87
Djibouti	1 000	66.00	–	56	56	15.82
Egypt	900	3.00	28	3	–	33.80
Finland	15 641	21.60	2	8	0	16.25
France	9 716	18.08	9	59	22	93.17
Greenland	14 952	34.00	–	1	1	0.16
Guadeloupe and Martinique	3 000	44.79	–	36	16	249.00
Guam	5 000	–	–	34	15	151.00
Namibia	1 500	57.00	23	47	22	1.00
New Zealand	13 968	16.78	5	65	46	12.00
Norway	16 073	23.65	1	3	52	14.00
Panama	4 294	32.90	9	24	0	27.00
Peru	3 706	16.00	15	24	19	16.00
Poland	3 641	15.25	9	61	21	122.00
Puerto Rico	6 000	56.00	–	52	13	385.00
Rwanda	610	10.66	27	65	38	223.00
Swaziland	1 375	71.00	25	74	28	31.00
Uganda	645	10.00	16	31	65	56.00
Coterminous USA	17 968	9.40	4	55	9	27.00

Notes:
1. Per capita GDP expressed at purchasing power parity, current international dollars.
2. Merchandise imports as a share of GDP.
3. Import duties as a percentage of imports.
4. Agricultural area as a share of total land area.
5. Land used as permanent pasture as a share of total land area.
6. People per square kilometre.

Sources: FAO (1997), World Bank (1998), CIA (1998).

4 ANALYSIS

The primitive hypotheses were tested in a linear regression model in which the independent variable is the share of alien versus native plant species in each country. In the final version of the model, island status, population density, land use, GDP per capita, merchandise imports and import duties were used as regressors.

In Table 2.3, three alternative specifications are reported in which all models include the islands dummy, population density and the variables concerning land use, whereas they differ by the inclusion or exclusion of GDP per capita, merchandise imports and import duties:

Model 1

$$A_t = \alpha_1 + \alpha_2 ISL + \alpha_5 POP_t + \alpha_6 GDP_{t-5} + \alpha_7 AGR_t + \alpha_8 PAS_t + u_t;$$

Model 2

$$A_t = \alpha_1 + \alpha_2 ISL + \alpha_4 DUT_{t-5} + \alpha_5 POP_t + \alpha_7 AGR_t + \alpha_8 PAS_t + u_t;$$

Model 3

$$A_t = \alpha_1 + \alpha_2 ISL + \alpha_3 M_{t-5} + \alpha_5 POP_t + \alpha_6 GDP_{t-5} + \alpha_7 AGR_t + \alpha_8 PAS_t + u_t.$$

These regression models explain, respectively, 84.2 (model 1), 80.7 (model 2), and 84.4 (model 3) per cent of variation in the share of alien versus native species.

The analysis rejected the first primitive hypothesis, at least given the proxies of extroversion used as independent variables. Neither trade as a share of GDP nor tourism turned out to be statistically significant explanations of vulnerability to plant invasions. Marginal improvements were obtained if, instead of total trade flows, imports were considered; and if merchandise imports were used instead of total imports of goods and services. The coefficients for merchandise imports and for import duties are of the expected sign, positive and negative, respectively (although *t*-ratios for the former are low).

However, the analysis confirmed the second primitive hypothesis. Measures of disturbance do turn out to be significant explanations of invasions. The proportion of land used as permanent pasture is significant. Livestock production and alien plant invasions are positively correlated: a 10 percentage points increase in pasture areas as a proportion of total land is associated with an increase of about 0.04 in the share of alien versus native species. The

Table 2.3   Overview of model results: multiple regression coefficients and t-ratios (in parentheses)[1]

Predictors	Abbreviations	Model 1	Model 2	Model 3
Island*	ISL	0.08719 (1.128)	0.10062 (1.186)	0.07963 (1.004)
Merchandise imports % GDP	M	–	–	0.00117 (0.650)
Import duties % GDP	DUT		-0.01359 (-2.599)	–
Population density	POP	0.00100 (6.592)	0.00114 (6.893)	0.00097 (6.100)
GDP per capita	GDP	0.00002 (3.521)	–	0.00002 (3.516)
% Agricultural area	AGR	-0.00247 (-1.634)	0.00319 (-1.952)	-0.00251 (-1.636)
% Permanent pasture	PAS	0.00398 (2.007)	0.00391 (1.793)	0.00421 (2.061)
Intercept	α_1	-0.06979 (-0.569)	0.25725 (2.657)	-0.11135 (-1.054)

Note: 1.   Critical *t*-ratios ($\alpha = 0.05$): Models 1 and 2 (19 df (degrees of freedom)): one-tailed (*) 1.328, two-tailed 1.729; Model 3 (18 df): one-tailed (*) 1.330, two-tailed 1.724.

24

proportion of land committed to arable production is also significant, but the coefficient on this variable is negative: the proportion of land used for agriculture is inversely related to invasions.[5] The intuitive explanation for this is that agriculture involves a simplification of the ecosystem and alien plants and insects are frequently eradicated (as weeds or pests) to support arable production. An additional hypothesis, investigated in Shigesada (1999), is that the heterogeneous environments generated by segmenting an original habitat into a regularly striped or criss-crossed pattern beget unfavourable conditions for invading species.

The coefficient estimates for GDP per capita and for population density are significant and of the expected sign. A 500 US dollars increase in per capita GDP is associated with an increase of 0.01 in the share of alien versus native species. As mentioned earlier, invasions increase for ecological and climatic reasons as we move south – whereas levels of income generally move in the opposite direction. It is noteworthy that, this notwithstanding, the per capita GDP variable remains significant. An increase in population density of about 10 people per square kilometre is similarly associated with an increase of 0.01 in the share of alien species.[6]

In the sample of countries considered, the island status raises on average by 0.09 the odds that a species picked at random is non-native.[7] The coefficient's moderate significance is likely to result from the fact that island states are overrepresented in the sample, and the continental countries for which ecological data were available are among those with more-than-average invasive species problems.

Given the weakness of our various proxies for the extroversion of the economy, several variants of the regression model have been estimated. It was expected that there would be a high correlation between imports and GDP and between imports and import duties. However, there turned out to be a high correlation between import duties and GDP – possibly due to a correlation between a country's income and its participation in trade agreements. Excluding GDP from the analysis, import duties prove significant. It would be interesting to understand how import duties influence invasions other than by reducing imports. A possible explanation is that duties exert a selective effect on the composition of imports, rather than just affecting the volume of imports. To test such a hypothesis, it would be necessary to distinguish imports by country of origin. If invasives came mostly from distant countries and trade agreements tended to group contiguous countries, then trade duties would indeed exert a discriminating influence.

5   CONCLUSIONS AND DISCUSSION

Although the issues investigated in this chapter call for an improvement in the data set, it is clear that economic variables do play an important role in explaining a country's susceptibility to biological invasions. Specifically, the variables affecting the recipient environment (land tenure, level of GDP, population density) are responsible for explaining a high proportion of the variation in the share of alien species in different countries. This would support the hypothesis that the disturbances associated with human activities are important determinants of the vulnerability of a given country to invasions – the *disturbance* hypothesis. Although probably all ecological communities are invasible, economic activities appear to have an influence in making some of them more prone to invasions than others.

Variables related to trade flows – particularly imports of merchandise and raw materials and import duties – have a less strong although still significant impact on the share of alien species hosted by any given country. This suggests a potentially interesting extension of existing work on the negative externalities associated with trade.[8] It also prompts us to consider ways of controlling for the effect of imports and of other indicators of openness to reduce biological invasions. The benefits of international commerce are significant enough that any policy implemented to reduce biological invasions should be designed in such a way as to minimize the adverse effects of these policies on international trade. The policy problem is thus one of unbundling importations from invasive species – allowing for a growing volume of imported goods and services, while keeping the introductions of alien species at a minimum. This implies looking for ways of making monitoring through licencing, inspections, quarantines, and so on, as unobstrusive as possible.

The present analysis also adds some insight into the problem of biological invasions on islands. Island ecosystems are generally considered highly susceptible to invasions because of a particularly vulnerable native biodiversity. But island states are also typically, on average, small open economies, often geared to the production of primary products. The average percentage of merchandise imports as a share of the GDP, in the sample considered, is about 43 per cent for island countries, against an average 32 per cent for the whole sample, and 26.8 per cent for continental countries. There appear to be economic reasons, in addition to the ecological ones, for the incidence of invasives on islands.

Further extensions of the present study would be possible by considering other variables such as migration rates, temporary transborder movements of people and the labour force, or the ethnic mix of the human population in any given country (a cumulative measure) as additional indexes of the degree of extroversion of that country's economy; and indicators of capital stock such as kilometres of road per unit area.

Generally, the association of biological invasions with a number of economic variables implies that at least in principle invasions would be responsive to all the factors that affect the incentives to undertake or not a particular course of action: taxes, subsidies, permits and so on. Because of the self-perpetuating nature of the externalities associated with biological invasions, however, the implications of the conventional economic approach to dealing with external effects cannot be applied mechanically. As discussed in the Introduction to this volume, the issue calls for an *ad hoc* analysis. An economic perspective on the problem and on the policies that can be designed to tackle it can represent an addition to the study of biological invasions that goes beyond the evaluation of the monetary and non-monetary costs associated with invasives.

NOTES

* I would like to thank Giovanni P. Baiocchi, Albert Breton, Charles Perrings and Mark Williamson for a number of valuable suggestions. Remaining errors are my sole responsibility.

1. Although by no means market activities alone. An important component of the migrations that have taken place in the world, for example, has been and continues to be driven not by market forces, but by religious and political persecutions.
2. An open space, to an organism, can be defined as 'a space which when invaded will allow reproductive growth' (Shigesada and Kawasaki, 1997, p. 114). Examples are areas that recently underwent a forest fire, flood, or clearing because of commercial logging, construction works, road building, and so on; territorial vacuum left when previously resident organisms are displaced (by local eradication or extinction); and so on.
3. The available data do not allow me to single out *unintentional* introductions of non-native species, let alone those that have become pests. While it is evident that not all the established alien plants in any given country are a source of net negative externalities, the aim of the present study, given the current availability of quantitative information, is limited to exploring the relationship between a country's ratio of alien to native species and possible economic determinants of that ratio.
4. The classification of variables into categories is always somewhat arbitrary. For example, population density is, from some points of view, a demographic variable. However, population density is *ceteris paribus* a function of the demand for land relative to its supply and therefore an indirect function of the price of land. Demand for land, in turn, depends on the intensity of human activity in a given area. As such, population density is a straightforward economic variable in addition to being a proxy for the disturbance associated with human activities. The same is true, *mutatis mutandis*, of the fraction of land devoted to agriculture and to livestock and of other like variables.
5. Other studies found a positive correlation between weed invasions and increase in agricultural activities (for example, irrigation in arid areas). See Stadler et al. (1998).
6. The association of higher population densities with plant invasions is found also in studies on the determinants of the occurrence of alien species in urban flora (Pyšek, 1998). It should be noted, however, that the very high *t*-statistics of the demographic variable in the present analysis partly reflects the influence of the extremely high population density on the

  Bermuda Islands, which is also the country with the highest share of alien versus native species in the sample.

7. In evaluating the magnitude of the island coefficient, however, it should be taken into account that, besides vulnerability, such a coefficient is also likely to reflect a statistical artifact due to the general presence of fewer native species in island ecosystems (Williamson, 1996).

8. Recent studies on this issue include Bhagwati and Hudec (1996), and Vogel (1995).

REFERENCES

Atkinson, I.A.E. and E.K. Cameron (1993), 'Human influence on the terrestrial biota and biotic communities of New Zealand', *Trends in Ecology and Evolution*, **8**: 447–51.

Barko, L. and J.L. Zarucchi (1993), *Catalogue of the Flowering Plants and Gymnosperms of Peru*, St. Louis, MI: Missouri Botanical Garden.

Bay, C. (1993), 'Taxa of vascular plants new to the flora of Greenland', *Nordic Journal of Botany*, **13**: 247–52.

Bhagwati, J. and R.E. Hudec (1996), *Fair Trade and Harmonization: Prerequisites for Free Trade?*, Cambridge and London: MIT Press.

Borhidi, A. (1991), *Phytogeography and Vegetation Ecology of Cuba*, Budapest: Akadémiai Kiadó.

Brewer, W.H., S. Watson and A. Gray (1876), *Geological Survey of California*, Botany, Vol. I, Cambridge, MA: Welch, Bigelow & Co. University Press.

Britton, N.L. (1918), *Flora of Bermuda*, New York: Charles Scribner's Sons.

Central Intelligence Agency (CIA) (1998), *The World Factbook 1998*, URL: http://www.cia.gov/cia/publications/factbook/.

Clout, M., S. Lowe and the IUCN/SSC Invasive Species Specialist Group (1996), *Draft IUCN Guidelines for the Prevention of Biodiversity Loss Due to Biological Invasion*, URL: http://weeds.merriweb.com.au/IUCN-inv.htm.

Connell, J.H. (1978), 'Diversity in tropical rainforests and coral reefs', *Science*, **199**: 1302–10.

Correll, D.S. and H.B. Correll (1982), *Flora of the Bahama Archipelago*, Vaduz: J. Cramer.

Crawley, M.J. (1987), 'What makes a community invasible?', in A.J. Gray, M.J. Crawley and P.J. Edwards (eds), *Colonization, Succession and Stability*, Oxford: Blackwell Science, 429–543.

D'Arcy, W.G. (1987), *Flora of Panama. Checklist and Index*, St. Louis, MI: Missouri Botanical Garden.

Dwyer, J.D. and D.L. Spellman (1981), 'A list of Dicotyledoneae of Belize', *Rhodora*, **83**: 161–235.

Etter, R.J. and H. Caswell (1994), 'The advantages of dispersal in a patchy environment: effects of disturbance in a cellular automaton model', in K.J. Eckelbarger and C.M. Young (eds), *Reproduction, Larval Biology and Recruitment in the Deep-Sea Benthos*, New York: Columbia University Press: 285–305.

FAO (1997), *FAOSTAT 1997*, CD ROM, Food and Agriculture Organization of the United Nations.

Fournet, J. (1978), *Flore Illustrée de Phanerogames de Guadelupe et de Martinique*, Paris: Institut d'Elevage et de Médicine Vétérinaire des Pays Tropicaux.

Francis, J.K. and H.A. Logier (1991), *Naturalized Exotic Tree Species in Puerto*

Rico, General Technical Report SO-82, US Department of Agriculture, Forest Service, Southern Forest Experimental Station, New Orleans.

Fremstad, E., R. Elven, and S.B.A. Tømerå (1994), *Introduksjoner av Fremmde Organismer til Norge*, Trondheim: Nork Institutt for Naturforskning.

Frenkel, R.E. (1970), *Ruderal Vegetation along some Californian Roadsides*, Berkeley, CA: University of California Press.

Hickman, J.C. (ed.)(1993), *The Jepson Manual*, Berkeley, CA: University of California Press.

Hnatiuk, R.J. (1990), *Census of Australian Vascular Plants*, Australian Government Publishing Service, Canberra: AGPS Press Publications.

Jepson, W.L. (1925), *A Manual of the Flowering Plants of California*, Berkeley, CA: University of California Press.

Kartesz, J.T. (1994), *A Synonymized Checklist of Vascular Flora of the United States, Canada, and Greenland*, Portland: Timber Press.

Kemp, E.S. (1983), 'A flora checklist for Swaziland', Occasional Paper No. 2, Lobamba: Swaziland National Trust Commission.

Kornas, L. (1990), 'Plant invasions in Central Europe: historical and ecological aspects', in A.J. Gray, M.J. Crawley and P.J. Edwards (eds), *Colonization, Succession and Stability*, Oxford: Blackwell Science: 429–543.

Lebrun, J.P., J. Audru and J. Cesar (1989), *Catalogue des Plantes Vasculaires de la République de Djibouti*, Paris: Institut d'Elevage et de Médicine Vétérinaire des Pays Tropicaux.

Lee, M.A.B. (1974), 'Distribution of native and invader plant species on the Island of Guam', *Biotropica*, **6**: 158–64.

Lodge, D.M.(1993), 'Biological invasions: lessons for ecology', *Trends in Ecology and Evolution*, **8**: 133–7.

Lövei, G.L. (1997), 'Global change through invasion', *Nature*, **388**, 14 August, 627.

Marticorena, C. and M. Quezada (1985), 'Catalogo de flora vascuala de Chile', *Gayana Botanica*, **42**: 1–157.

Merxmüller, H. (1966–72), *Prodromus einer Flora von Südwestafrika*, Lehre: Cramer.

Mooney, H.A. (1999), 'Species without frontiers', *Nature*, **397**, 25 February: 665–6.

Munz, P.A. (1968), *A California Flora and Supplement*, Berkeley, CA: University of California Press.

Munz, P.A. and D.D. Keck (1959), *A California Flora*, Berkeley, CA: University of California Press.

Proctor, G.R. (1984), *Flora of the Cayman Islands*, Kew, UK: Royal Botanic Gardens.

Pyšek, P. (1998), 'Alien and native species in Central European floras: a quantitative comparison', *Journal of Biogeography*, **25**: 155–63.

Pyšek, P., K. Prach and B. Mandák (1998), 'Invasions of alien plants into habitats of Central European landscape: an historical pattern', in U. Starfinger, K. Edwards, I. Kowarik and M. Williamson (eds), *Plant Invasions: Ecological Mechanisms and Human Responses*, Leiden, Netherlands: Backhuys Publishers: 23–32.

Rejmánek, M. (1984), 'Perturbation-dependent coexistence and species diversity in ecosystems', in P. Schuster (ed.), *Stochastic Phenomena and Chaotic Behaviour in Complex Systems*, Berlin: Springer-Verlag: 220–30.

Rejmánek, M. (1989), 'Invasibility of plant communities', in J.A. Drake, H.A. Mooney, F. Di Castri, R.H. Groves, F.J. Kruger, M. Rejmánek and M. Williamson (eds), *Biological Invasions: A Global Perspective*, SCOPE 37, New York: Wiley: 269–383.

Rejmánek, M. and J.M. Randall (1994), 'Invasive alien plants in California: 1993 summary and comparison with other areas in North America', *Madroño*, **41**: 161–77.

Roessler, H. and H. Merxmüller (1976), 'Nachträge zum Prodromus einer Flora von Südwestafrika', *Mitteilungen der Botanisches Staatssammlungen München*, **12**: 361–73.

Scoggan, H.J. (1978–79), *The Flora of Canada*, Vols 1–4, Ottawa: National Museum of Natural Sciences.

Shigesada, N. (1999), 'Biological invasions into fragmented environments: reaction-diffusion models', paper presented at the Workshop 'Local Interaction and Global Phenomena in Vegetation and Other Systems', 19–23 April, Institute for Mathematics and Its Applications, University of Minnesota.

Shigesada, N. and K. Kawasaki (1997), *Biological Invasions: Theory and Practice*, Oxford: Oxford University Press.

Stadler, J., G. Mungai and R. Brandl (1998), 'Weed invasion in East Africa: insights from herbarium records', *African Journal of Ecology*, **36**(1): 15–22.

Statistics Greenland (1999), URL: http://www.statgreen.gl/English/IndexUK.htm.

Troupin, G. (1978–88), *Flore du Rwanda, Spermatophytes*, Vols 1–4, Tervuren, Belgique: Musée Royal de l'Afrique Centrale; Butare, République Rwandaise: Institut National de Recherche Scientifique.

Tutin, T.G., V.H. Heywood, N.A. Burges, D.H. Valentine, S.M. Walters and D.A. Webb (1964–80), *Flora Europaea*, Vols 1–5, Cambridge, UK: Cambridge University Press.

Tutin, T.G., V.H. Heywood, N.A. Burges, D.H. Valentine, S.M. Walters and D.A. Webb (1993), *Flora Europaea*, Vol. 1, 2nd edn, Cambridge, UK: Cambridge University Press.

United States Department of Agriculture (USDA) (1982), *National List of Scientific Plant Names*, Washington, DC: US Government Printing Office.

Usher, M.B. (1988), 'Biological invasions of nature reserves: a search for generalisation', *Biological Conservation*, **44**: 119–35.

Vitousek, P.M., C.M. D'Antonio, L.L. Loope, M. Rejmánek and R. Westbrooks (1997), 'Introduced species: a significant component of human-caused global change', *New Zealand Journal of Ecology*, **21**(1): 1–16.

Vogel, D. (1995*), Trading Up: Consumer and Environmental Regulation in a Global Economy*, Cambridge, MA: Harvard University Press.

Watson, S. (1880), *Geological Survey of California. Botany*, Vol. II, Cambridge, MA: Welch, Bigelow & Co. University Press.

Williamson, M. (1996), *Biological Invasions*, London: Chapman & Hall.

World Bank (1998), *World Development Indicators 1998*, CD ROM, International Bank for Reconstruction and Developemnt/World Bank.

3. Infectious diseases as invasives in human populations

Doriana Delfino and Peter J. Simmons

---

1 INTRODUCTION

Invasives are typically thought of as a species of plant or animal that enters a local ecosystem. The way the new species interacts with the existing environment may lead to its rapid growth and, sometimes, to a sharp and major reduction in the biodiversity of the existing environment. The invasive may take over the environment either directly or indirectly through its initial impact on other species in the environment, which in turn then take off to become invasives (Burdon and Leather, 1990). We argue that infectious disease in human and animal populations can be thought of as an invasive force in the population. For example, the introduction of myxomatosis decimated the rabbit population; in much the same way the medieval plague decimated the populations of many European countries. Here the invasive is regarded as the disease germ itself; its invasive effects occur indirectly through infected individuals interacting with healthy individuals, infecting them so that the disease takes over the population. Our focus is on the nature of infectious diseases as invasives in human populations and then the ways in which the economy in question interacts with the invasive disease on a global scale. Once we have established a framework for this, we analyse how the invasive disease can be controlled and whether public policy is necessary to implement the control.

2 NATURE OF INFECTIOUS DISEASE

Infectious diseases have had important effects in reducing human population growth either through altering fertility and mortality rates or in influencing directions of migration. Until the nineteenth century, infectious diseases were the major cause of human mortality and in developing countries they still remain so (Davey et al., 1995).

Examples of infections in Europe are the tuberculosis epidemics at the end of the last century and the Black Death of 1348. In India it was calculated that in 1930 about a hundred million people were infected with malaria and that about two million deaths per annum occurred. Enteric infections together with respiratory infections are the 'giant-complex' of early childhood in warm climate countries so that mortality rates in infants are largely determined by their prevalence. Infantile gastro-enteritis in England and Wales in 1911 caused the death of 40 000 children. Examples to illustrate the interaction between host and parasite can be found in infectious diseases such as measles and smallpox that can have catastrophic effects on malnourished and immunosuppressed populations. During the 1970s, measles is documented to have been the cause of death in 80 per cent of children in Bolivia and 70 per cent in the northeast of Brazil; exceptional outbreaks of measles occurred also in areas such as Fiji, the Hudson Bay region and Terra del Fuego (Cruickshank et al., 1976). Smallpox among the indigenous population who had no immunity facilitated the European conquest of Mexico and the rest of the North American continent; similar epidemics occurred also in South America and later on among the aborigines in Australia (Burnet and White, 1972). A recent example of infectious disease is given by the worldwide reoccurrence of tuberculosis stimulated mainly by two factors: the outbreak of multidrug-resistant tuberculosis and the emergence of acquired immune deficiency syndrome (AIDS). As estimated by the World Health Organization (WHO, 1999), every year approximately 8 million cases of tuberculosis arise from this infected pool (95 per cent in developing countries) leading to 3 million deaths (99 per cent in developing countries). Given this evidence, preventive and control measures are demanded.

Prevention and treatment require understanding of the dynamics between the infectious disease and the human species. Infectious disease, whether in humans or animals or plants, is the result of the invasion of the host by a parasite. The parasites that are responsible for infectious diseases in humans are: bacteria, viruses, protozoa, fungi and worms (Boycott, 1971; Burnet and White, 1972).

Bacteria are unicellar plants that multiply most rapidly at the body temperature of the host; they also reproduce at lower temperatures but at a lower rate. All bacteria are killed by exposure to 45°C with the exception of a few species that by assuming a 'spore form' can survive at extremes of heat and cold. Among the most common human bacterial diseases there are those caused by various types of cocci (Staphylococcus, Pneumococcus, Meningococcus, Streptococcus, Escherichia Coli): diphtheria, scarlet fever, typhoid fever, tuberculosis, cholera, plague, psittacosis, trachoma, syphilis and gonorrhoea.

Viruses multiply only within the cells of the host. The viral cell has a central core of nuclei acid that is covered by an envelope of protein to protect it while the cell is outside the host. The number of infectious diseases caused by viruses is quite high and every year previously unknown virulent epidemics appear. Examples are different types of influenza, measles, rubella, hepatitis A and B, herpes, smallpox and the more recent Ebola and Marburg viruses.

Protozoa are unicellular organisms generally found in every situation that can provide both water and food supply of smaller microorganisms. Infections caused by protozoa are widespread in tropical and subtropical regions and very rare in temperate climates. The more relevant protozoa diseases can be divided into two categories: infectious disease transmitted directly from person to person (for example, amoebic dysentery) and infectious diseases in which the parasite is transferred by an insect intermediary (for example, malaria, sleeping sickness, kala azar).

Fungi and worms play only a small part in causing diseases in humans. Both present a great variety of morphology and habits. Among the most relevant worms are Filaria, which produces tropical elephantiasis, and Schistosoma, which is one of the more widespread plagues in Africa. Candida, meningitis and ringworm are caused by fungi.

Parasites may enter the human host at the following main sites (Cruickshank et al., 1976; Hardy, 1993; Mims, 1987; Robinson, 1985; Warin et al., 1980). The skin acts as a natural barrier to microorganisms but can be either directly infected (vaccinia, scabies, impetigo) or penetrated at the site of breaks in its continuity, whether microscopic (leptospirosis, erysipelas) or macroscopic (wound infections, burn sepsis) or by injection (virus B hepatitis, septicaemia). Small or large bites are also important sites for entry of microorganisms. Biting arthropods such as mosquitoes, mites, ticks, fleas and sandflies penetrate the skin during feeding and can introduce pathogenic agents into the human body (malaria, typhus, plague). Virus in the saliva of infected biting mammals such as dogs, wolves and vampire bats may transmit infectious diseases, for example, rabies. Airborne infections normally enter by the respiratory tract. Once established in the respiratory tract, infection may either stay localized (whooping cough, pulmonary tuberculosis) or affect distant tissues (diphtheria, scarlet fever, non-pulmonary tuberculosis) or spread throughout the body (measles, chickenpox). Infections present in the bowel excreta of an infected individual can be ingested by a host. Transmission may be either direct via infected fingers, eating utensils, clothing and toilets or indirect via food and water where the microorganism undergoes a further period of multiplication. Once established, infection may either stay localized in the bowel (gastroenteritis, dysentery, salmonellosis) or disseminate throughout the body (typhoid, brucellosis, Q fever) or may produce distant toxic effects (botulism).

Whether a parasite spreads epidemically in a community will depend essentially on the level of specific antibodies in the community as a whole.

Once an epidemic has begun the population may be divided into: susceptible individuals; latent individuals (incubation period); infected individuals (detected or not); and immune individuals (naturally immune, vaccinated or recovered). The more individuals there are in the first three classes the more rapidly the disease will spread. The more there are in the last class the less likely is an epidemic.

Other factors influence the probability of the spread of diseases (Burnet and White, 1972). Human susceptibility to infectious diseases is generally influenced by the genetic features of the host. Examples include pulmonary tuberculosis spreading from resistant Europeans to previously unexposed and highly susceptible Africans and North American Indians. Yellow fever, originating in Africa, was transmitted to the Americas on the slave ships and affected genetically more susceptible people of Central and South America together with Europeans. Different responses to the disease are also due to differences in age. Generally susceptibility is greater in infancy and old age than during the adult life. Nevertheless, there are some viral infections, such as yellow fever, that can cause serious and fatal disease in adults but have only mild effects in young individuals. Whooping cough, measles, scarlet fever and diphtheria were all serious infectious diseases especially among children. Until 1954, polio was the one important infectious disease of developed countries which had failed to respond to the general medical improvement and higher living standards. Starting in 1887 in one of the more advanced countries, Sweden, polio proved to be an age-related disease. From about 1920, polio epidemics had a major incidence among children less than five years old. There is also an interrelationship between infection and nutrition (Cruickshank et al., 1976). A deficiency of protein and vitamins in the diet limits the production of antibodies and depresses the defensive mechanisms of the body. Kwashiorkor, a disease due to protein deficiency in many parts of Africa, is associated with increased susceptibility to many common infectious diseases. The death rate from measles in Zambia is as high as 30 per cent whereas in London it is less than 1 per cent. Among different factors that influence the course of infectious diseases, poor hygienic conditions merit particular mention. McKeown (Davey et al., 1995) identifies major infections as contributing to the nineteenth-century mortality decline that were recognized as preventable because they were directly contagious and associated with unsanitary conditions. In Australia the "gold rushes" resulted in serious outbreaks of typhoid fever as a consequence of the extremely primitive sanitary arrangements. Another classical example of a serious spread of typhoid fever in a population living under crowded and unsanitary conditions (caves and air-raid shelters) can be found in the history of Naples in December 1943 when it was occupied by allied troops. Beef, infected by polluted water while being canned in Argentina, caused the spread of typhoid fever in Aberdeen in 1968.

Aggravating these problems is the phenomenon of rural–urban migration which has recently assumed massive proportions; it aggravates the existing unfavourable conditions in housing, nutrition, employment and health (Stephens, 1995).

Even though many old infections have been eradicated from developed countries, numerous diseases, either in an endemic or epidemic form, have taken their place. Attempts to limit or eliminate an epidemic may take several forms. The plague in Europe over the five hundred year period from 1350 was largely controlled by segregation and quarantine measures. Many infectious diseases declined following general improvements in living conditions (Davey et al., 1995). Most of the decline in mortality due to tuberculosis had taken place before the beginning of the present century, following an improvement in housing and living conditions. Mortality due to measles in England and Wales fell rapidly and continuously from about 1915 while targeted specific measures have only recently been introduced in the form of immunization. Treatments against cholera introduced in the 1930s had little effect on the spread of the disease as most of the improvement occurred in the late nineteenth century mainly following improvements in hygienic conditions. However, reduction in the spread of infectious diseases was also accelerated by the development of medical innovations (vaccines and antibiotics for sick or both sick and healthy). The control of disease by specifically targeted policies such as vaccination, used on a large scale, has greatly contributed to the eradication of infectious diseases. In the United States, measles has mostly been eliminated from the country by a widespread programme of vaccination. Many other infections, for example, smallpox and poliomyelitis, have receded following a vaccination programme.

3   THE EPIDEMIOLOGICAL PROCESS

To develop a framework within which we can examine the ways in which some of the different control mechanisms work, we have to first specify the epidemiology of the population. We think of a population N_t of individuals in a given area at instant t. Generally individuals can be in one of two states: susceptible but healthy or actively infected and infectious. In the sequel sometimes we allow for recovery from the disease. Let x_t be the number of healthy susceptibles at instant t and y_t the number of actively infected and infectious individuals. We suppose that the net growth rate of susceptibles (that is, the birth rate minus the mortality rate) is constant at α and that the death rate of the infected sick is constant at ω.

We have to model the process of infection in the system; that is, how does the invasive disease spread? The physical interpretation of the transmission mechanism is that a given healthy person has a chance of infection given by

Pr(becoming infected) = Pr(meeting a sick person and the meeting leads to
                              infection)
                      = Pr(meeting a sick person Pr(the meeting leads to
                              infection)

since these events are generally taken as independent. The chance of infection from an encounter between a sick and a healthy person is usually assumed
to be a constant, β. For different diseases it may depend on individual characteristics (for example, the age of the healthy person) or characteristics of the
meeting (for example, the plague often spread apparently through fleas pass-
ing from one person to another in multioccupied beds). In common with the
literature we abstract from this and assume homogeneity within population
groups. Given x_t healthy people and this transmission mechanism, the average number of new cases of infection at t is then

Pr(meeting a sick person) Pr(the meeting leads to infection) x_t.

With equally likely meetings between any two people this probability is
given by the chance of a meeting with anyone multiplied by the chance that
this meeting is with a sick person: the latter is given by the proportion of sick
in the population, $y_t/(x_t + y_t)$. Hence, treating β as the combination of the
chance of infection spreading given a meeting between a sick and a healthy
person and the chance of a person meeting anyone else, with β being a pure
number, the equations are:

$$\begin{cases} \dot{x}_t = \alpha x_t - \beta x_t y_t /(x_t + y_t) \\ \dot{y}_t = \beta x_t y_t /(x_t + y_t) - \omega y_t \end{cases} \tag{3.1}$$

In fact this approach has been taken by May and Anderson (1989) in exploring
the dynamics of human infection virus (HIV) and (AIDS). Define $p_t = y_t/x_t$ and
rewrite the dynamic equations in terms of just p_t and x_t as

$$\begin{cases} \dot{p}_t = \beta p_t /(1 + p_t) - \omega p_t - p_t[\alpha - \beta p_t /(1 + p_t)] = (\beta - \alpha - \omega)p_t \\ \dot{x}_t = [\alpha - \beta p_t /(1 + p_t)]x_t \end{cases} \tag{3.2}$$

where α, β and ω are constants.

In this pure demographic system we can solve as follows: first the equation
in p_t has the solution

$$p_t = p_0 \exp[(\beta - \alpha - \omega)t]. \tag{3.3}$$

Putting this back into the equation for x_t gives

$$\dot{x}_t = \alpha x_t - \beta x_t \frac{p_0 \exp[(\beta - \alpha - \omega)t]}{1 + p_0 \exp[(\beta - \alpha - \omega)t]} \qquad (3.4)$$

which has solution

$$x_t = x_0 \exp(\alpha t)\{1 + p_0 \exp[(\beta - \alpha - \omega)t]\}^{-\beta/[(\beta-\alpha-\omega)y_0]} \qquad (3.5)$$

and so

$$y_t = p_0 x_0 \exp[(\beta - \omega)t]\{1 + p_0 \exp[(\beta - \alpha - \omega)t]\}^{-\beta/[(\beta-\alpha-\omega)\omega_0]} \qquad (3.6)$$

In the pure demographic system the ratio p_t either rises or falls to zero, depending on whether the infection rate is greater than the combined net growth rate of the healthy and death rate of the sick. There are no stationary or steady states of the system. On the other hand, the number of healthy individuals may not be monotonic: the growth rate $\dot{x}_t / x_t$ from (3.4) may vary in sign starting negative and then becoming positive if $\alpha < \beta p_0/(1 + p_0)$. A typical example is shown in the phase diagrams of Figure 3.1 in which we take $(\beta - \alpha - \omega) < 0$ and Figure 3.2 in which $(\beta - \alpha - \omega) > 0$. In the first case the parameters are $\alpha = 0.08$, $\beta = 0.2$ and $\omega = 0.13$ with $(\beta - \alpha - \omega) < 0$; the effect is that p_t continuously falls for any initial condition. Initially both the numbers of healthy and of sick may fall, but, for most initial conditions, once the population of both groups is fairly low, the infection process becomes unimportant (there are few sick and healthy to interact) and growth of the healthy becomes dominant. The disease is not actually eliminated but remains at a low endemic level in the population while the numbers of healthy grow at a near constant rate. In the second case the parameters are $\alpha = 0.08$, $\beta = 0.25$ and $\omega = 0.13$ and so $(\beta - \alpha - \omega) > 0$. For any initial condition the ratio of sick to healthy rises, but initially the number of healthy individuals may rise before reaching a maximum, after which the infection process becomes dominant and the numbers of sick continue to rise while the numbers of healthy fall. Then once the healthy stock is small enough so that there are relatively few left to infect, the number of sick also starts falling as deaths of the sick dominate new infections. Eventually this drives the population to zero.

This extreme dynamic behaviour is not inconsistent with the history of the plague in the thirteenth century in England or Italy (whole villages were eliminated whereas other communities emerged relatively unscathed from an initial infection), or the plague in Egypt or the effects of smallpox in mid-America (Watts, 1997). We shall use this basic demographic structure in the next section.

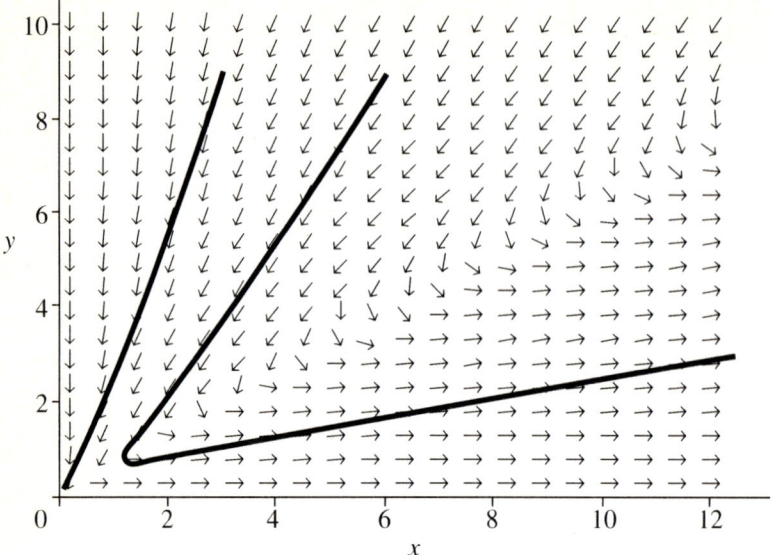

Figure 3.1   Pure demographic system: $(\beta - \alpha - \omega) < 0$

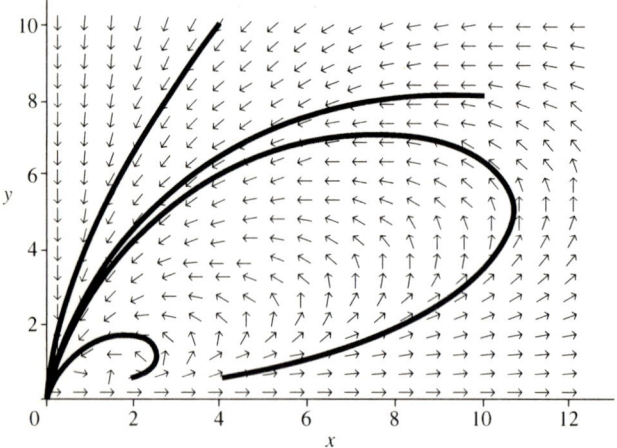

Figure 3.2   Pure demographic system: $(\beta - \alpha - \omega) > 0$

4 CONTROL MECHANISMS

Controlling the spread of diseases is important both to understand why historically the extinction case of Figure 3.2 has not commonly been observed and also to limit the economic and social cost of the disease. In the past the process of control has been varied; possibilities are:

1. Specific targeted control policies. We can think of these as either preventive or curative measures. The main preventive measures might be enforced segregation, for example, by quarantine (in European and especially Italian responses to the plague and in responses to leprosy until the eighteenth century there was an enforced policy of isolation of infected individuals) or medical treatments such as vaccination programmes. Curative policies could involve research and development into cures or the delivery of existing cures generally through the provision of hospital-style facilities. Generally the medically based policies have required some prior medical innovation into understanding the transmission mechanism of the disease and innovations such as vaccines in disease control or cures.
2. Rising economic prosperity bringing changes in the basic immune system of individuals and in the general infrastructure of the economy.
3. Changes in individual human behaviour within existing technology and endowments.

In this section we look at each of these in turn, giving examples of the effects of the control mechanism which are generally calibrated on the extinction example of Figure 3.2. The idea is to see to what extent the different control mechanisms can change the dynamics from one involving extinction of the population to one involving either elimination of the invasive disease or its control to a low endemic level in the population.

4.1 Medical Control: Vaccination

The most common form of prevention is vaccination, which can give either permanent and certain protection against the disease or a partial reduction in the chance of infection, where this partial reduction may itself be random. Geoffard and Phillipson (1997) consider the case of permanent certain immunity in the context of a Lotka–Volterra-style framework (Lotka, 1925; Volterra, 1926) for the interaction of the sick and healthy and model the effect of vaccination as a reduction in the net birth rate of susceptibles. The immune vaccinated individuals just drop out of the susceptible class. One of their main points is that typically the presence of a vaccine will not lead to elimination of the invasive disease. In the case of a vaccine provided on private markets this is because the demand for vaccination may fall too fast as the incidence of the disease decreases and individuals perceive that the risk of infection is becoming negligible. In the case of a state-provided vaccine, since the programme is highly unlikely to be able to achieve 100 per cent vaccination, there will most probably always be an endemic level of the disease. Geoffard and Phillipson do not analyse the effect of vaccination on the dynamics of the population structure but focus on the unique steady state of their system. The analogy to their analysis in the framework that we are using is that a once-and-for-all increase in vaccination will lead to a once-and-for-all reduction in α which paradoxically leads to an increase in the growth rate of p_t. It is possible that vaccination causes the sign of $(\beta - \alpha - \omega)$ to switch from negative to positive – a somewhat perverse effect. In a related paper (Delfino and Simmons, 1999b), we consider the dynamic effects of alternative vaccination policies in this permanent and certain immunity case. We find that vaccinating when the prevalence is low produces dynamic time paths that have less disease in general than vaccinating when the prevalence of the disease is high. In that paper we also consider the partial immunity case in which vaccination reduces but does not eliminate the risk of infection. We find there that a high prevalence policy of vaccination is preferable. It can lead to a near constant population structure at about the same stationary prevalence level as pre-vaccination but without the epidemic cycles.

With the epidemiological system that we are using here, the partial immunity case can be modelled as a reduction in β, the chance of infection of a susceptible. We can contrast the effects of three alternative vaccination policies on the dynamics of the population. For approximately the same economic cost we can compare:

1. a continuous vaccination policy that shifts β downwards to a constant new level β_C;
2. a high prevalence policy in which vaccine is administered only when prevalence is high (for the sake of argument we define high prevalence by $y_t > x_t$) leading to a reduction of β at such instants to β_L;
3. a low prevalence policy in which vaccine is administered only when $y_t < x_t$; again we take the post-vaccine level of β to be β_L.

Here $\beta_L < \beta_C < \beta$. As examples we start with $\beta = 0.25$ and set $\beta_C = 0.175$, $\beta_L = 0.1$; the high or low prevalence policies are in force approximately half as often as the constant policy so these parameter values allow the intermittent policies to reduce β twice as much as the constant continuous policy. With these parameter values, if the cost of changing β is linear in the reduction in β, then the total cost of the continuous or intermittent policies will be approximately equal. In Figure 3.3 we have the constant policy (without the vaccine we would be in the dynamics of Figure 3.2 again). In this example the constant policy gives a strong enough reduction in β to switch the dynamics from extinction to the case in which the disease drops to an endemic level. Figure 3.4 shows the dynamics of the high prevalence policy; as soon as $y_t >$ x_t the vaccine policy switches on and the system switches from the extinction case to the case in which the disease would become endemic at a low level. The effect is that for any initial condition we would expect to see the system settle down in a vicinity of the region in which the policy is on the margin of coming into force. In the example in Figure 3.4, this is the 45° line; exactly where the system settles on this line is determined by the initial conditions. Conversely Figure 3.5 shows the low prevalence policy that makes the system relatively unstable; partly this is due to the notion of low prevalence.

Comparing these policies, the best form depends on whether vaccination has a sufficiently strong effect in reducing β to switch the dynamics from the extinction case of Figure 3.2 to the endemic disease case of Figure 3.3. If it does, then constant vaccination may be best. If it does not, then the low prevalence policy will lead either to extinction or to growth of both the healthy and sick depending on initial conditions. The high prevalence policy of Figure 3.4 will tend to generate a stable population structure with the scale of the overall population set by initial conditions.

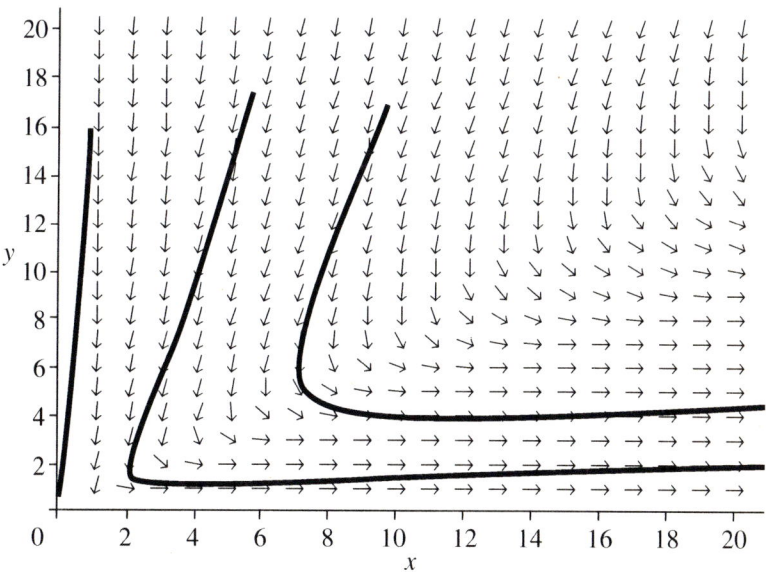

Figure 3.3   Vaccination: constant policy

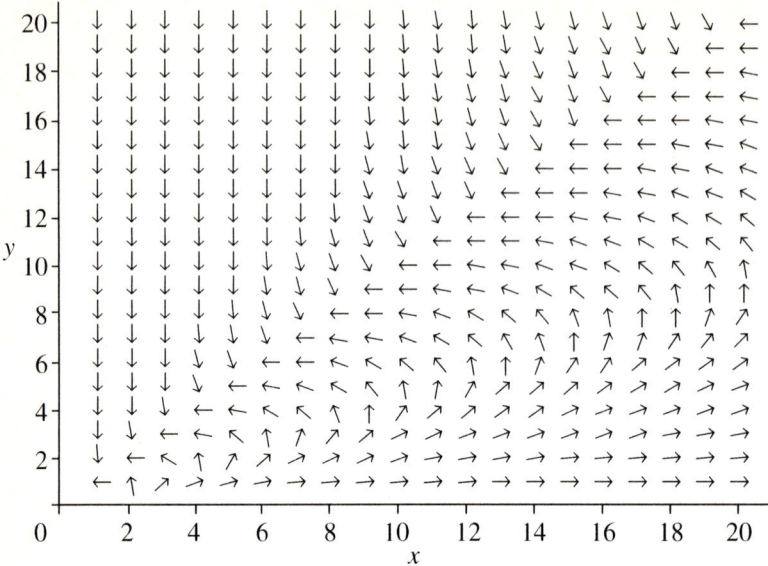

Figure 3.4   Vaccination: high prevalence policy

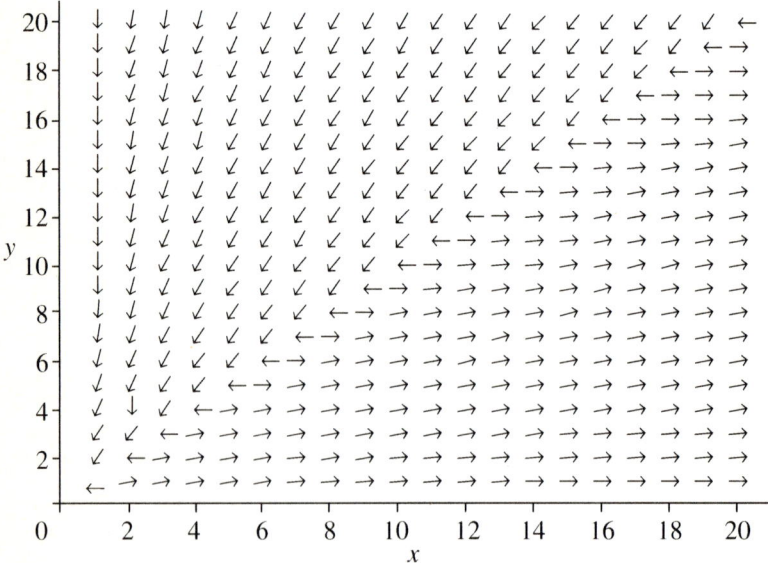

Figure 3.5   Vaccination: low prevalence policy

4.2   Medical Control: Cure of the Disease

Recovery from the disease may take alternative forms when it is possible at all; for some diseases like tuberculosis, individuals who recover from the disease develop immunity. In this case we would have three groups in the population: those who are healthy but susceptible to infection, those who are immune and those who are sick. The basic equations of the system thus become

$$
\begin{cases}
\dot{x}_t = \alpha x_t - \beta x_t y_t / (x_t + y_t + r_t) \\
\dot{y}_t = \beta x_t y_t / (x_t + y_t + r_t) - \omega y_t - \rho y_t \\
\dot{r}_t = \rho y_t - \gamma r_t
\end{cases}
\tag{3.7}
$$

where ρ is the recovery rate of the sick and γ is the net death rate of the recovered individuals. The recovered form a class of their own here; the dynamics of the healthy and sick are exactly like those of Figures 3.1 and 3.2 but with an increase in the 'decay' rate of the sick to $\rho + \omega$. The effect is that a model that without recovery had $(\beta - \alpha - \omega) > 0$ may, with recovery, have $(\beta - \alpha - \omega - \rho) < 0$. Therefore the discovery of a cure can switch the epidemiology from a case where the disease is taking over and driving the population to extinction to a case in which the disease drops to a low endemic level.

Alternatively, if the cured individuals do not develop immunity then the equations can be written as

$$
\begin{cases}
\dot{x}_t = \alpha x_t - \beta x_t y_t / (x_t + y_t) + \rho y_t \\
\dot{y}_t = \beta x_t y_t / (x_t + y_t) - \omega y_t - \rho y_t
\end{cases}
\tag{3.8}
$$

In terms of p_t these equations imply

$$
\dot{p}_t = (\beta - \alpha - \omega - \rho)p_t - \rho p_t^2
\tag{3.9}
$$

The pure demographic system represented by the $p = 0$ equation now has the solution

$$
p_t = p_0 \bigg/ \left\{ \left[\frac{\rho}{(\beta - \alpha - \omega - \rho)} p_0 \right. \right.
$$
$$
\left. \left. + \left[1 - \frac{\rho}{(\beta - \alpha - \omega - \rho)} p_0 \right] \exp[-t(\beta - \alpha - \omega - \rho)] \right\}
\tag{3.10}
$$

The equation has stationary points at $p = 0$ and $(\beta - \alpha - \omega - \rho) = \rho p$ (the latter only makes sense if $(\beta - \alpha - \omega - \rho) > 0$. At $p = 0$, x_t grows at the rate α and

Analysis

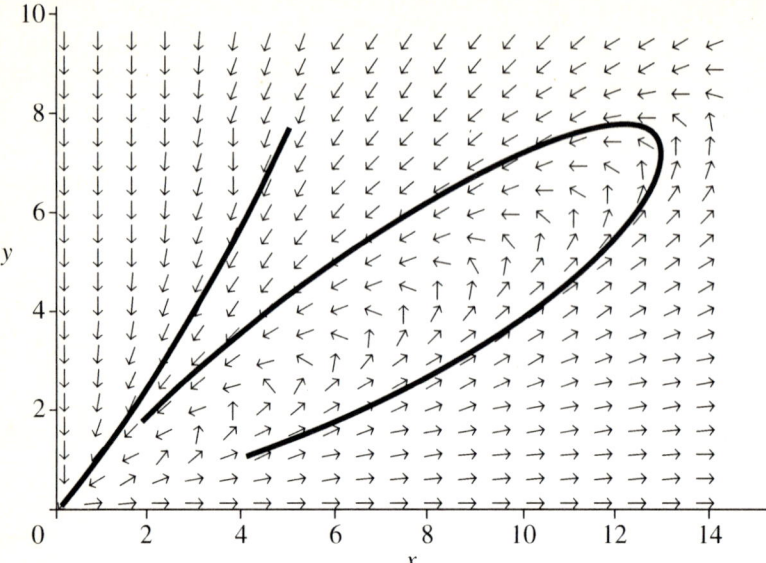

Figure 3.6   Medical control: low cure rate case ($\rho = 0.02$)

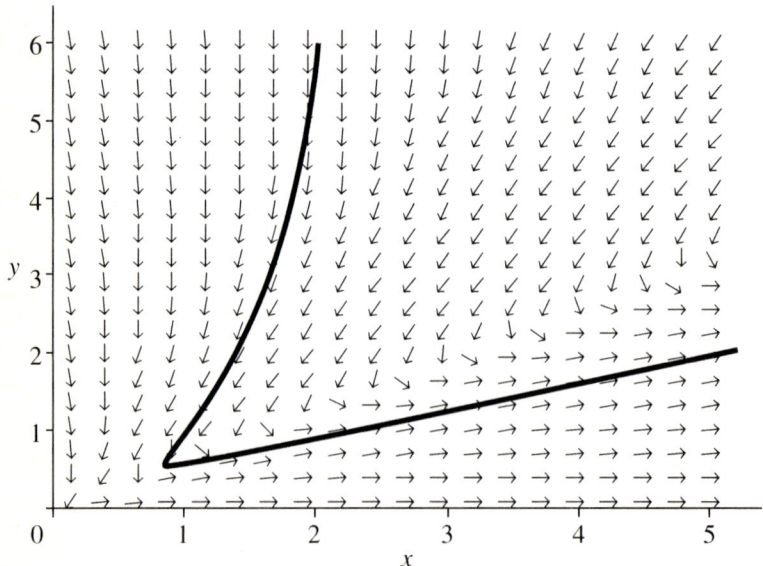

Figure 3.7   Medical control: high cure rate case ($\rho = 0.03$)

there is no disease; at $p = (\beta - \alpha - \omega - \rho)/\rho$, x_t and y_t grow or fall at the common rate $[(\omega + \rho)(\alpha + \omega) - \beta\omega]/(\beta - \alpha - \omega)$. On the other hand, there is a unique stationary point in (x_t, y_t) at the origin. The dynamics of the system is similar to that in Figures 3.1 and 3.2. In Figure 3.6 a case is given in which $\alpha = 0.08$, $\beta = 0.25$, $\omega = 0.13$ and $\rho = 0.02$ so that $(\beta - \alpha - \omega - \rho)/\rho = 1$; along the 45° line x_t and y_t decay linearly to the origin; above the 45° line x_t falls with y_t; below the 45° line x_t first rises and then falls.

However, it is possible to have $(\beta - \alpha - \omega - \rho) > 0$ but $(\omega + \rho)(\alpha + \omega) - \beta\omega > 0$; an example is given in Figure 3.7 where $\alpha = 0.08$, $\beta = 0.25$, $\omega = 0.13$ and $\rho = 0.03$. The effect is that, if the cure rate is high enough but still below $(\beta - \alpha - \omega)$, it is possible for the disease prevalence p_t to remain roughly constant while the total population grows.

4.3   Economic Growth

Rising prosperity leads to improvements in diet and housing (in particular less overcrowding, cold and damp) which can slow the transmission process both through increasing disease resistance and reducing involuntary interpersonal contact arising from congestion. In addition, rising prosperity is probably associated with medical innovation and education of the population at large about the transmission process. It also leads to a view that the government has public health responsibilities in a variety of public good areas such as the water supply and sewage systems (for example, the control of cholera in India has largely come through these routes). It also possibly changes the birth and death rates of the different population groups. In terms of the demographic model, α, β and ω are functions of economic prosperity; there are a variety of ways of measuring this. We choose to regard the demographic parameters as functions of the productive inputs of the economy (the labour force and/or the capital stock). This will be consistent with demographics depending on consumption or income of the economy. However, we also want to model the causes of economic growth; there is some evidence that there are feedback effects of the infectious disease on the ability of the economy to provide growth through debilitating the labour force. For example the import of smallpox to Mid-America in the sixteenth century among the local population who had no immune resistance to the disease led to their decimation which in turn eliminated the local labour force for working the silver mines. The plague in the Middle East had the effects of reducing the productive workforce so heavily that localized famines emerged (Watts, 1997).

A natural economic approach would be to assume that infected individuals cannot work; the production possibilities of the economy depend on the productive labour force *inter alia*. Hence, if there is a high proportion of infected then output and economic prosperity is low *ceteris paribus*. Since economic prosperity affects demographics, with low prosperity the net birth rate of susceptibles falls; the death rate of the infected rises and the infection rate rises. So with a high proportion of infected and a low labour force, the infection rate rises, the death rates rise and the net birth rate of the susceptibles falls. This leads to a fall in the productive labour force, which in turn leads to a fall in consumption per capita. A vicious cycle emerges. Hence, it would appear that if output depends on susceptible labour alone, the system with endogenous economic effects reinforces instability.

To see how this works we take economic prosperity at time t, W_t, to depend on x_t : $W_t = f(x_t)$, a function which is increasing and concave. Then as prosperity rises we assume that the infection rate β and the mortality rate of the infected fall while initially we assume that the birth rate of the healthy α rises with W. Effectively this means that the demographic parameters become functions of x_t with $\alpha'(x_t) > 0$, $\beta'(x_t) > 0$ and $\omega'(x_t) > 0$. If we select functional forms for the dependence of the demographic parameters on x_t and parameter values which generate the case in which the population is extinguished by the disease in the absence of prosperity effects on disease control (that is, $\alpha(0)$, $\beta(0)$ and $\omega(0)$ have the values underlying Figure 3.2), then the dynamics of the system switches into that of Figure 3.8. The effect is that so long as there is a finite value of x at which $(\beta - \alpha - \omega) = 0$, there is a stationary point that satisfies the equations

$$(\beta(x^*) - \alpha(x^*) - \omega(x^*)) = 0$$

and

$$y^* = \frac{\alpha(x^*)}{\omega(x^*)} x^*$$

Locally this is a saddle point. Some of the unstable trajectories corresponding to the saddle (those with a low level of susceptibles) converge towards the origin thus involving asymptotic extinction. However, the system is not actually defined at the origin. For low initial values of x_t the invasive leads to extinction of the population. But if initially there are sufficient healthy individuals to give enough prosperity to impact on the demographic parameters then the number of healthy individuals grows and the disease dies away. So there are elements of a vicious cycle; but it can be offset if the initial conditions are favourable.

In this example we have set

$$\alpha(x_t) = 0.08[1.2 - 0.2\exp(-2x_t)] \qquad (3.11)$$

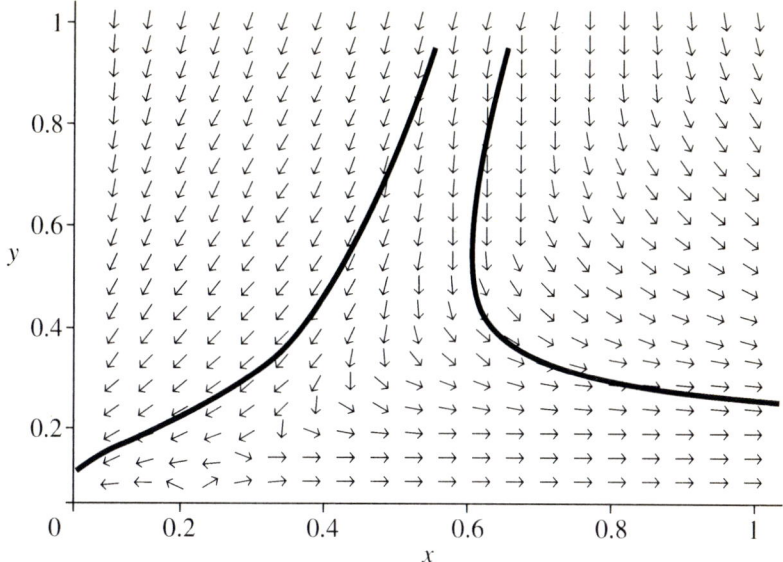

Figure 3.8   Economic growth

$$\beta(x_t) = 0.12[(1 + 2\exp(-2x_t)] \qquad (3.12)$$

$$\omega(x_t) = 0.13[(0.8 - 0.2\exp(-2x_t)] \qquad (3.13)$$

In the absence of prosperity effects, with these parameter values, the healthy population net growth rate is 8 per cent but this rises to an upper limit of 9.6 per cent with prosperity. The baseline infection rate is 25 per cent but this falls to a lower limit of 12 per cent with prosperity. The mortality rate of the sick is at a base of 13 per cent but falls to 10.4 per cent with sufficiently high prosperity. Again the parameters have been set at the baseline of Figure 3.2 in the absence of prosperity effects.

However, this treatment ignores the possibility of investment in productive capital that together with healthy workers can raise output and so prosperity. The capital effect will generally reinforce the beneficial effects of rising prosperity so long as increases in the capital stock increase the productivity of healthy workers. In two related papers (Delfino and Simmons, 1999a, 1999c), we explore this more formally. In one paper we use the epidemiological process used here together with controlling the system for an optimal rate of capital accumulation through time. In the other paper we use a slightly different epidemiological process and find that the presence of productive capital and the economic system reduces the amplitude of demographic cycles.

48

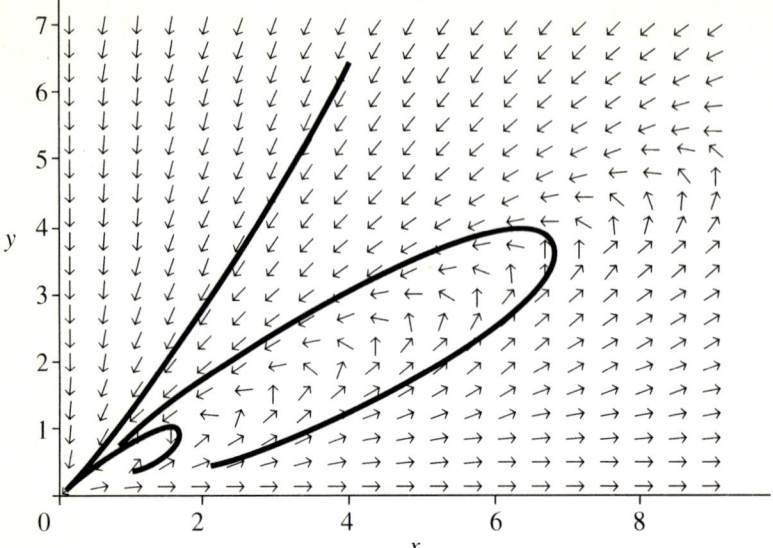

Figure 3.9   Individual adaptive behaviour: ($\beta_0 = 0.2$, $\beta_1 = 0.05$)

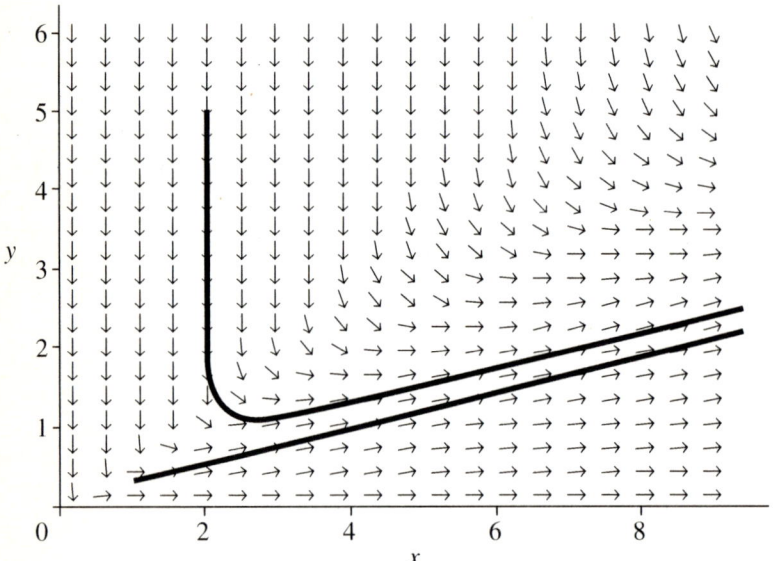

Figure 3.10   Individual adaptive behaviour: ($\beta_0 = 0.1$, $\beta_1 = 0.15$)

4.4   Individual Adaptive Behaviour

Since infection depends primarily on interpersonal contact and on the form
the contact takes, individuals may independently adapt their modes of interpersonal contact as the prevalence of the disease varies (for example, in
medieval England the rich would flee the cities during outbreaks of the
plague to live in their country houses). In addition, market incentives to use
available preventive medicine vary with the prevalence of the disease.

   Probably the most important area for allowing adaptive behaviour by individuals in the population is through the infection rate β. In accounts of the
plague in England the rich could take preventive segregation measures by
physically moving out of a city which had plague outbreaks. To allow for this
we could take $\beta = \beta\,(p_t)$ with $\beta' < 0$. From a biological perspective this is
often considered as density dependent effects on the interaction process
between the two subpopulations. The effect is that there may be a non-zero
value of p_t at which $\dot{p}_t = 0$; this will then give a ray in the $x - y$ plane of either
proportional decay or growth of the sick and healthy. As an example we take

$$\beta(p_t) = \beta_0 + \beta_1 \exp(-p_t) \tag{3.14}$$

so that the base level of the infection rate is given by $\beta_0 + \beta_1$ when $p_t = 0$, but
preventive action can reduce this rate to β_0 as $p_t \rightarrow \infty$. The effects on the
dynamics of x_t and y_t depend very much on parameters and the responsive-
ness of the infection rate to p_t. If we select $\beta_0 = 0.2$ and $\beta_1 = 0.05$ we get the
results of Figure 3.9 whereas if we select $\beta_0 = 0.1$ and $\beta_1 = 0.15$ we get the
results of Figure 3.10 (again both these are calibrated on the extinction case
of Figure 3.2).

   Note that in both cases the baseline infection rate without individual adaptation is 0.25, giving us the basic parameters underlying Figure 3.2, but the
difference is in the sensitivity of the infection rate to prevalence. With enough
sensitivity the disease settles down to an endemic level, while when there is
little sensitivity we are in the extinction case.

4.5   Population Movement

Thinking of the Middle Ages in Europe with the plague or the situation of
many developing countries with tuberculosis, the prevalence of infection is
quite different in various regional locations, for example, cities or villages.
Primarily this is because the mobility between centres in such societies is
restricted by a poor transport infrastructure and so the chances of infection in
relatively healthy areas by contact with actively infected from the relatively
sick areas is minimal.

Consequently, susceptible individuals living in a particular location face a migration choice. They can stay where they are and enter into the risks of infection in their present location; or they can move to another region which may have higher or lower risks of infection. Locations differ in infection risk but also in non-health-related attributes, for example, in the available distributions of income through differing employment opportunities. A stylized paradigm might have cities that are dangerous from the health aspect but which offer higher income prospects as compared with rural areas – a version of the Todaro model (Todaro, 1976). Healthy susceptible individuals will then trade off the benefits from a higher mean distribution of income and a higher risk of infection in urban areas against a low risk of infection and lower income prospects in rural areas. One would expect to find more risk-averse individuals or those with a higher preference for mean levels of health as opposed to income living in rural areas. Those with a more urgent need for income will live in city areas, balancing this off against the higher risk of infection.

On the other hand, those who are already infected will have a different tradeoff. With most of the diseases we are thinking of, infected individuals cannot work; their only concern is with the available health facilities reflected in the recovery and death rates of the actively infected. So sick individuals will move to areas where the recovery chances are greatest or the death rates of infected are lowest. In a migration equilibrium if there is sufficient diminishing returns in the recovery and death processes of the infected, there will be an extensive margin. This will equate the chances of recovery/death of the infected in each region (this obviously depends on the form of preferences of the infected between recovery and death). For the marginal susceptible it will equate the expected utility between regions arising from the differential income and health opportunities. Within this scenario segregation is one possible equilibrium: because the infected are interested only in their health care and survival prospects (they cannot work) if one region is unambiguously better than another in its survival chances or its health care, then all the infected will gather there. If the income prospects of that region are insufficient to compensate for its greater health risk all the susceptibles will move out. This then supports a segregation equilibrium. The full range of dynamic solutions to the migration process in response to tuberculosis is an open question that we are currently examining.

Historically, public control of population movement has been important in disease control (Watts, 1997); quarantine and isolation regulations are still in force today in the United Kingdom for some communicable diseases, such as smallpox. When segregation by health state has occurred, it has generally been as the result of conscious policy and the consensus in the literature seems to be that it has been a highly effective if somewhat draconian method of control when it has been implemented rigorously.

5   NEED FOR REGULATION

The question here is to what extent is conscious policy intervention necessary, once the economic and ecological interactions have been recognized. A *laissez-faire* approach would argue that privately motivated individuals will seek out their own best solutions to the threat of invasion which affects individual utility as well as social welfare. An important issue here is then whether it is plausible that the individual response on its own is powerful enough to control the disease without policy intervention. A further issue is whether the private incentives to undertake preventive activity match the social incentives – there is an obvious externality in that individuals who become infected damage not only their own health and welfare but also that of those with whom they subsequently interact. There are also strong distributional considerations since typically the market price of prevention or cures can be high either because a new product has just been innovated and the development costs are being recouped or because the willingness to pay for treatment shoots up during an epidemic. We provide a summary discussion of the main factors that are likely to lead to a need for regulation.

5.1   Dynamic Externalities

If individuals use their private utility payoffs to determine whether to take costly preventive action such as vaccination, they ignore the dynamic externality effect that this can have on the future risks of infection for other individuals. In these circumstances the market solution will typically lead to too low a level of prevention. In the same way, if one of the public benefits from economic growth is an improvement in social and health infrastructure which reduces the chance of infection, then individuals making their private savings decisions will ignore the public beneficial effects of the increase in capital stock that their savings allow. So again a market solution will tend to lead to too low a level of saving.

5.2   Distributional Issues

Several of the control mechanisms are costly to the individual if they are privately provided. Vaccines typically show a falling price profile through time, being initially introduced at a very high price (which may be the result of price discrimination between users by the supplier) but becoming cheaper as their use widens and as substitutes are developed. Similarly, moving is costly; in medieval times, escape to the rural areas was easier for the rich both because of the transport cost and because they often had a second country home. In many contemporary societies there are fixed costs of moving due, for example, to the way in which the housing market works or to the uncertainty of finding employment quickly in the new area. For reasons such as these we would expect high-income or high-wealth individuals to have better control against invasive diseases than the less prosperous. In itself this may give distributional grounds for public subsidies on control mechanisms. The exception is the extent to which rising general prosperity provides control freely for everyone; an efficient civic sanitation system has non-excludable and non-rival effects.

5.3   Information

There are various informational problems with privately provided control solutions. First, if individuals are heterogeneous in their risks of infection in a way that is unobservable to the provider then adverse selection problems may arise where only the high-risk individuals are willing to buy the vaccine. Second, individuals may wrongly perceive the risk of infection – the phenomenon of cognitive dissonance (Akerlof and Dickens, 1982) – or the effects of infection, typically underestimating both. This then leads to a demand for control that is below the social optimum.

5.4   Non-cooperative Behaviour

Some similar control processes would have a static externality in the disease transmission chance; if there is for example a personal hygiene variable Z_i for individual i then the infection risk depends on total personal hygiene effort $\beta = \beta(\Sigma Z_i)$. Suppose that each individual i has income m_i that can be spent either on consumption c_i or on preventive activity Z_i with the relative price of the preventive expenditure being π, so that $c_i + \pi Z_i = m_i$. For example, in the case of tuberculosis it could be a face mask, or in the case of cholera improved sanitation. For the ith susceptible expected utility is given by

$$EU_i = \beta(\Sigma Z_i)u(I, c_i) + [1 - \beta(\Sigma Z_i)Y]u(S, c_i) \qquad (3.15)$$

where $u(I, c_i)$ measures the utility of being infected with consumption c_i and $u(S, c_i)$ measures the utility of being a healthy susceptible with consumption c_i. Maximizing EU_i, subject to the budget constraint over Z_i and c_i, gives the ith susceptible's demand for Z_i as the solution to

$$E\partial u(\cdot)/\partial c_i = -\partial \beta/\partial Z_i[u(S, c_i) - u(I, c_i)] \qquad (3.16)$$

in the form

$$Z_i = Z_i(Y, \pi, m_i, \overline{Z}), \qquad (3.17)$$

where $\bar{Z}$ is the aggregate preventive expenditure of other susceptibles. Combining the reaction curves in Z for all susceptibles gives Nash equilibrium values of preventive expenditure that will vary with π and the distribution of income. Obviously this solution fails to be Pareto optimal because each susceptible ignores the effect of his/her own preventive activity on the infection risk faced by others. In the Nash equilibrium we then have $\beta = \beta(\pi, m_1, \ldots, m_s)$ where s is the current number of susceptibles.

5.5 Monopoly

If the control mechanism is supplied through a market system with monopoly or imperfections in competition in the supply, then as usual there will be distortion of consumer and producer prices. Suppliers will restrict supply and price above marginal cost leading to underprovision of the control. Major reasons for monopoly to be a likely occurrence are the relatively heavy fixed costs of research and development associated with medical innovation which can lead to natural monopoly conditions, and also the workings of the legal patent system.

6 CONCLUSIONS

The point of this chapter is to argue that infectious diseases in human populations can fruitfully be modelled using concepts from the literature on biological invasions. Infectious diseases act indirectly as invasives, dividing the population into at least two groups (the infected and the healthy susceptibles). Interaction between the two groups leads to the spread of the invasive. We outline the physical nature of a variety of infectious diseases and chart their historical trends. By adopting a formal predator–prey-type model of the dynamic interaction of the two groups we can analyse the evolution of the invasive and the population structure. We adopt a scenario where there are two qualitative types of behaviour possible: either the infectious disease is so strong that eventually both the infected and the susceptible groups become extinct or, if conditions are suitable, the invasive can be accommodated by the system and, while the disease is not eliminated, it reaches a low endemic level in the population and the susceptibles keep multiplying.

Once this framework has been laid out we can identify points at which different types of control mechanisms impact on the dynamics of the invasive disease. In turn we consider medical control in the form of preventive vaccination giving either total or partial immunity and medical cures. In the total immunity case, vaccination can have perverse effects on the structure of the population. In the context of vaccination giving partial immunity, we consider the effects of different dynamic vaccination policies, for example, vaccinating at a constant rate versus vaccinating at a rate that depends on the prevalence of the disease. Depending on how much immunity the vaccine gives, we find that generally either a high prevalence policy or a constant policy is more effective in controlling the disease.

Next we examine the interaction between economic prosperity and the health structure of the population. There is a two-way interaction: there is quite a lot of evidence that rising prosperity and the improvements in the social infrastructure that this brings are instrumental in controlling the infective power of the disease. On the other hand, infected people cannot work and so cannot contribute to rising economic prosperity. There is a watershed: if there is an insufficient number of susceptible workers, then prosperity is too low to control infection and the population converges to extinction; conversely, with sufficient initial susceptible workers prosperity can rise sufficiently to control the disease at an endemic level in the population.

Next we analyse the extent to which individual adaptation of behaviour in the form of taking care to avoid contact with the infected or physically moving to safe rather than high-risk areas can control the disease without regulation. We find that the results depend very much on parameter values. For example, one settlement pattern solution that is possible is that individual location choice leads to segregation with all the infected in one region and all the susceptibles in another region.

An important issue is whether individual incentives are sufficient for control of the invasive to appear naturally without need for public policy. There are several reasons for supposing that policy intervention is necessary. One basic factor is associated with the static and dynamic externalities that the disease causes: in taking preventive action individuals look only at their own welfare from staying healthy and ignore the risk that their infection poses for further infection of susceptibles. A second basic factor is concerned with distributional issues: typically control is costly to the individual (vaccination fees, migration costs, costs of cure) and the historical evidence is that it is the richer economies which have managed to eliminate some of the major diseases. There are also other reasons for market failure in this area, such as the information problems individuals face in selecting preventive behaviour; they may not know who is infectious, or the nature of the disease. Because medically based prevention or cure is typically the result of medical innovation emerging from costly research and development, there are likely to be problems of monopoly in the supply of medical control facilities. So it is likely that control carried out in the context of public policy will be more effective than the *laissez-faire* solution.

Some of the results we find are qualitative and would appear to be robust to particular parameter values; in some cases we can define the various outcomes that are possible but what will actually happen depends on parameter values. We have also selected a particular epidemiological structure; there are many versions of the basic predator–prey interaction and some of our conclusions may not hold under other variants of the epidemiology. This highlights the need for empirical testing in the context of specific disease invasives.

REFERENCES

Akerlof, G.A. and W.T. Dickens (1982), 'The economic consequences of cognitive dissonance', *American Economic Review*, **72**: 307–19.

Boycott, J.A. (1971), *Natural History of Infectious Disease*, London: Edward Arnold.

Burdon, J.J. and S.R. Leather (eds) (1990*), Pests, Pathogens and Plant Communities*, Oxford: Blackwell Scientific Publications.

Burnet, Sir Macfarlane and D.O. White (1972), *Natural History of Infectious Disease*, Cambridge: Cambridge University Press.

Cruickshank, R., H.B.L. Russell and K.L Standard (1976), *Epidemiology and Community Health in Warm Climate Countries*, Edinburgh: Churchill Livingstone.

Davey, B., A. Gray and C. Seale (eds) (1995), *Health and Disease: A Reader*, Buckingham and Philadelphia: Open University Press.

Delfino, D. and P.J. Simmons (1999a), 'Infectious disease and economic growth: the case of tuberculosis', Discussion Paper, 99/23, Department of Economics and Related Studies, University of York.

Delfino, D. and P.J. Simmons (1999b), 'Infectious disease control by vaccines giving full or partial immunity', Discussion Paper, 99/32, Department of Economics and Related Studies, University of York.

Delfino, D. and P.J. Simmons (1999c), 'Optimal control of infectious diseases by capital accumulation', mimeo, Department of Economics and Related Studies, University of York.

Geoffard, P.Y. and T. Philipson (1997), 'Disease eradication: private versus public vaccination', *American Economic Review*, **87**(1), March: 222–30.

Hardy, A. (1993), *The Epidemic Streets. Infectious Disease and the Rise of Preventive Medicine 1856-1900*, Oxford: Clarendon Press.

Lotka, A.J. (1925), *Elements of Physical Biology*, Baltimore, Hopkins & Williams.

May, R.M. and R.M. Anderson (1989), 'The transmission dynamics of human immunodeficiency virus', in S.A. Levin and T.G. Hallam (eds), *Applied Mathematical Ecology*, Berlin: Springer-Verlag: 263–311.

Mims, C.A. (1987), *The Pathogenesis of Infectious Disease*, London: Academic Press.

Robinson, D. (ed.) (1985), *Epidemiology and the Community Control of Disease in Warm Climate Countries*, New York: Churchill Livingstone.

Stephens, C. (1995), 'The urban-environment, poverty and health in developing countries', *Health Policy and Planning*, **10**(2): 109–21.

Todaro, M.P. (1976), *Internal Migration in Developing Countries*, Geneva: International Labour Organization.

Volterra, V. (1926), 'Variazioni e fluttuazioni del numero di individui in specie animali conviventi', *Memorie Academia Nazionale dei Lincei*, **2**: 31–113.

Warin, J.F., A.G. Ironside and B.K. Mandal (1980*), Lecture Notes on the Infectious Diseases*, Oxford: Blackwell Scientific Publications.

Watts, S. (1997), *Disease, Power and Imperialism*, New Haven, CT, and London: Yale University Press.

World Health Organization (1999), *Global Tuberculosis Control*, WHO Report.

4. Risk reduction strategies against the 'explosive invader'

Jason F. Shogren

---

1 INTRODUCTION

Organisms that move beyond their traditional natural range can have undesirable ecological and economic consequences. Scientists have documented numerous examples of exotic plants and animals causing unacceptable damages, both monetary and non-monetary. Exotic deer and livestock, for instance, have altered the structure and composition of native vegetation in the Nahuel Huapi National Park in Argentina (Veblen et al., 1992). Nile perch (*Lates niloticus*) released into Africa's Lake Victoria has caused mass extinction of native fish, and water quality problems. Field bindweed (*Convolvulus arvensis*) is estimated to cause over $40 million in crop damages in Kansas every year (FICMNEW, 1998). Zebra mussels (*Dreissena polymorpha*) in the Great Lakes have led to serious biotic and abiotic effects, for example, greatly diminished phytoplantkton biomass and biofouling of manmade structures (MacIsaac, 1996).

These 'explosive invaders' pose a risk to society (Elton, 1958). Understanding the nature of this risk and potential risk reduction strategies is crucial for better management of exotic species. Assessing the risk–benefit tradeoffs accurately requires a consistent analytical framework to guide the information gathering on the determinants of risk, values and costs to protect society from the accidental or planned introduction of a non-native species. This chapter uses the economics theory of endogenous risk to develop such an analytical model, which frames the ecological and economic tradeoffs with undesirable invasive species.

We consider a representative policy maker who allocates scarce resources to reduce the risk from invasive species. He/she reduces the risks by mitigating or adapting or some combination. Mitigation actions take effect when people change the pattern of species distribution, and thereby reduce the odds that bad events happen. Adaptation occurs when people make adjustments in practices, processes or structures of systems, thereby reducing the consequences when a bad event does occur. In the language of endogenous risk, mitigation is 'self-protection' – actions to reduce the probability of a bad state; adaptation is 'self-insurance' – actions to reduce the severity of a bad state if realized (Ehrlich and Becker, 1972). And although mitigation and adaptation are likely to be intertwined at many levels, it is useful to keep the choice of action separate to keep the problem tractable. This presumption can be relaxed in future work.

The rationale for our framework is that economic behaviour matters more for invasive species policy than many people think. By economic behaviour, we mean the allocation of scarce resources across both market and non-market goods for the overall benefit of society. We take the position that an ecologically sound risk reduction strategy will be much more effective if economic circumstance such as relative prices and wealth are taken into account (also see Dudgeon, 1992; Viscusi, 1992; Shogren et al., 1999). Herein we (i) provide a framework to organize the collection of economic and ecological information for strategic and effective risk reduction, (ii) argue why economic circumstances should be included in risk assessment scenarios, (iii) discuss why the value of risk reduction depends on both collective and private risk reduction strategies, and (iv) consider how increased risk in invasive species affects these two risk reduction strategies. We recognize that integrating economic behaviour into the ecological theory of invasion will be a challenge. Assessing whether the net benefits of integrating economic circumstances into biological theory is an empirical question, and one well worth examining if our goal is to provide better invasive species policy at less expense.

2　RISK REDUCTION STRATEGIES

Despite the dramatic stories of the damage caused by exotic species, the evidence suggests that most invaders never become established in new territory, and those that do often do not become a pest (Kareiva, 1996). Less than 0.1 per cent (200–250) of all known plants, for example, are considered to be exotic pests in world agriculture (FICMNEW, 1998). And in many cases exotic species provide a livelihood through unique recreational opportunities and commercial benefits. Exotic species may or may not create undesirable risks, and the evidence thus far suggests that the odds of a calamity are low. But the fear is that with increased world trade, more habitat fragmentation and easy mobility, these risks are going up – not down (see Soulé, 1990; Cohen and Carlton, 1998).

We can protect ourselves from this mounting risk through mitigation and adaptation. We mitigate risk by curtailing and eradicating species to lower the likelihood that bad states of nature occur; we adapt to risk by changing production and consumption decisions to reduce the severity of a bad state if it does occur. Both mitigation and adaptation jointly determine the risks and the costs to reduce them. And since private citizens have the liberty to adapt on their own accord, a policy maker must consider these adaptive responses when choosing the optimal degree of public mitigation. Otherwise, policy actions will be more expensive than need be with no additional reduction in invader risk.

While most people would agree with this logic – mitigation and adaptation are linked – the full implication is not always appreciated in risk reduction policy. If mitigation and adaptation are linked, then economic and environmental systems are simultaneously determined. Human actions and reactions affect nature just as nature affects our actions and reactions. And just as good public policy-driven economics must include the biophysical circumstances from the natural sciences into risk management, so should the natural sciences include the prevailing economic circumstances in their models of risk assessment.

This realization challenges the traditional risk reduction perspective which habitually and artificially separates risk assessment from risk management. This fragmentation of risk policy essentially presumes that economic and environmental systems are not jointly determined. But this assumption might not be useful for many environmental risks. Consider the risk to biodiversity as a motivating example. Conservation biologists often maintain that establishing the threshold of species endangerment is strictly a biological question as determined by the present sizes, trends and distributions of its populations and their likely interactions with the stochastic forces of nature. These stochastic events are said to be separable from human actions. This perspective is overly narrow if it does not address economic circumstances. The odds of species' survival depend on the economic forces of today as revealed by relative prices and wealth because these parameters drive land-use decisions today and into the future. Assessing the risk to species and setting a minimum acceptable probability of survival is as much an economic question as it is a biological one. Our choice to create and avoid risk is endogenous (see Shogren and Crocker, 1991).

The endogenous risk perspective captures the notion that people invest resources to reduce the risks they confront or create. We know that people routinely act and react to risk. Examples of endogenous decision making by people to counter environmental risk abound. Farmers and ranchers alter cropping and pest control strategies purposefully to increase the odds that they will not suffer from the invasion of exotic species. People buy bottled water, if they can afford it, to protect themselves from suspect drinking water supplies – a choice that directly affects the perceived risk of poor health. Parents apply lotion with sunblock to protect themselves and their children from the sun – an action that reduces skin cancer risk. Landowners modify land-use plans to either enhance or reduce the likelihood that resident wildlife survive another year.

The same logic holds for the case of exotic invaders – the risk of introduction and establishment of a pest is both a biological and an economic question. In considering whether a species poses a risk, a strict disciplinary perspective might give biased estimates of risk if people's actions and reactions to risk are not addressed explicitly. People like nature, and that leads them to protect species both privately and collectively. The ability of a biological system to absorb these species is affected by these choices, helpful and harmful, which are driven in part by the economic circumstances of the region. Risk assessment that does not account for heterogeneous wealth and land prices faced by private citizens and communities, affecting this provision of habitat, will underestimate risks in some regions and overestimate them in others. The precision of species risk assessment and implementation of collective action can thus be increased by using both biological and economic parameters as determinants of endangerment (Shogren et al., 1999).

The economic theory of endogenous risk builds on the seminal models of choice under uncertainty developed over the past half century (for example, von Neumann and Morgenstern, 1944; Savage, 1954; de Finetti, 1974; Drèze, 1987). A person has preferences over outcomes and preferences over the lotteries that define those outcomes, and makes choices to secure those more preferred lotteries. These choices are usually categorized as either mitigation, Q, *ex-ante* efforts to reduce probability, or adaptation, x, *ex-ante* efforts to reduce the realized severity. Some actions could affect both the odds and severity of the risk of a pest making a new home; we save that complication for another day.

For invasive species, mitigation methods take the form of quarantine, trade and transport regulations to reduce the risk of introduction; or if established, mitigation efforts include poisoning, shooting, trapping, weeding, spraying, uprooting, biocontrol agents, viral disease and sterile insects. In addition, several national and international conventions have been approved to control the introduction of exotic species. These conventions include the 1973 Code of Practices from the International Council for the Exploration of the Seas, and the Convention on Biological Diversity adopted at the 1992 United Nations environmental summit in Rio de Janeiro, and so far ratified by more than 150 nations. Adaptation activities include changing the choice of a crop or seedling, which reduces the severity of a pest invasion.

Suppose a manager selects his/her mitigation, Q, and adaptation, x, efforts to maximize expected social welfare, EU, of his/her nation.

$$\text{Max}_{x,Q}(\int_a^b \{p(Q;\theta)V_0[m - c(x, Q)] + [1 - p(Q;\theta)]V_1[m - D(x;\theta)$$
$$-c(x, Q)]\}dF(\theta;\beta))$$

We withhold the nation-specific subscript to reduce notational clutter. The details of the manager's problem that need to be defined and understood are as follows:

- $p(Q; \theta)$ is the probability that a good state of nature is realized, that is, no damage from an invasive species; $1 - p(Q; \theta)$ is the probability that a bad state of nature is realized, that is, invasive species damage the native system. The probability is assumed to be a function of economic behaviour, mitigation and biological factors – including biotic and abiotic variables that affect the odds that the invader becomes a pest. This form of the probability function says that both economic and biological factors count in risk assessment. It also suggests that one should view the *tens rule* as an exogenous baseline, subject to change due to both economic and biological conditions. The tens rule suggests that for a variety of British species, one in ten species imported appears in the wild, one in ten of those introduced becomes established, and one in ten of those established becomes a pest (Williamson, 1996). Understanding exceptions to the tens rule will require more than just biological information within this endogenous risk framework.

- $D(x; \theta)$ is the money equivalent of realized damages if a bad state of nature is realized. The damages are a function of adaptation or self-insurance, and the stochastic variable. Damages could also be presented by non-monetized ecological damages such as changes to the structure and composition of native vegetation. In this case, the manager would be required to assess the social welfare impacts of a change in the quantity of ecosystem services or functions.

- x is the manager's investment in adaptation. Adaptation is assumed to be a private good – exclusive and rival in consumption.

- Q is the manager's investment in mitigation to increase the odds that no damage will occur. Mitigation is assumed to be a public good – non-exclusive and non-rival in consumption. Assume that mitigation is represented by a weak-link public good technology, $Q = \min (Q_1, Q_2, ..., Q_n)$, which implies that the least successful mitigation effort drives the odds to reduce the likelihood that the community will realize a bad state of nature (see Hirshleifer, 1983).

- θ is a random variable that reflects the basic scientific uncertainty about the impact of invasive species. This variable is crucial because it reflects the state of knowledge about the causes and effects of exotic invaders. But numerous additional questions arise here: can we truly recognize a native from an invasive species, or does another more muddled category exist – a cryptogenic species (Carlton, 1996)? Which factors matter the most for establishment and diffusion and transformation into a pest – biotic or abiotic factors (Moyle and Light, 1996)? How do invasive species behave shortly after they arrive in a new habitat, and is time span the key to how they get a toehold on the system? Are there 'empty niches' that invaders take over? What is the measurement error associated with the scarce data that does exist? What is the specification error associated with the statistical biological analysis driven by pattern recognition? These questions suggest that useful generalizations are being searched for by researchers, and that species-ecosystem specifics still matter (van den Bosch et al., 1980; Carey, 1996; Grosholz, 1996; Rejmánek and Richardson, 1996; Williamson and Fitter, 1996). Representing biological drivers as a random variable is a reasonable placeholder while the field of invasion ecology attempts to address these open questions (see Kareiva, 1996). The framework can easily accommodate new information on cause and effect that would replace the simple random variable with reaction-diffusion models that capture the rate of spread (see Hastings, 1996).

- $F(\theta; \beta)$ is the cumulative distribution bounded over the support (a, b), which defines the mean and variance of the random variable, θ, which represents basic scientific uncertainty. Again this is a simplifying assumption that can be modified as new information is forthcoming.

- β represents exogenous collective investments in research to reduce the uncertainty about the likely impact of an invasive species. This research is a public good represented by a best-shot public good technology, $\beta = \max(\beta_1, \beta_2, ..., \beta_n)$, which implies that the most successful research effort to reduce uncertainty spreads throughout the entire scientific and policy community (Hirshleifer, 1983). In this case we are presuming that governments or universities are conducting the research for the common good. Private R&D investments in new information are likely to be protected by patent agreements that would keep this information private.

- $V_0[m - c(x, Q)]$ is the social value of a good state of nature that depends on net wealth, $w = m - c(x, Q)$, where m is endowed wealth and $c(x, Q)$ is the cost function for adaptation, x, and mitigation, Q, activities.

- $V_1[m - D(x; \theta) - c(x, Q)]$ is the social value of a bad state of nature. We could just as easily measure the value of pure ecological damages by reforming the value function so that the damage function is its own separate argument, $V_1[m - c(x, Q), D(x; \theta)]$. In this case, we would be trying to measure how a change in damages affects social welfare. We could move this damage function outside the welfare function, and make it part of some multicriteria analysis that does not try to put a value on each and every change (see Haimes, 1998).

- Assume $V_{0w} > 0$, $D_x < 0$, $F_\theta > 0$, $F_\beta < 0$, $c_i(x, Q) > 0$ ($i = x, Q$), where subscripts denote the relevant derivatives.

The necessary conditions for a manager's optimal levels of mitigation and adaptation reflect the standard result that an individual maximizes expected utility by equating the marginal cost of influencing probability or severity to the marginal wealth acquired. Economists naturally seek criteria and conduct analysis which permit a discrimination among risky and benign species in recognition of the existence of budget constraints. Such a model will allow economists to frame the invasive species debate in benefit–cost terms. Such calculations are bound to be uncomfortable and controversial, especially since the overwhelming fraction of costs from the risk of exotic invaders are likely to be in the nature of public goods. But it is doubtful whether universal species eradication regardless of cost is even possible, or if possible, whether it holds a moral trump card over all other priorities such as our children's health and education.

3   IMPLICATIONS FOR UNDESIRABLE EXOTIC INVADERS

Our framework suggests several implications on how to think about research into the risk reduction of exotic invaders. Here we summarize the results; the technical details can be found in cited references.

Implication 1   Recognize that the risk of undesirable invasive species is as much an economic question, as it is anything else. This implies that researchers must work to better integrate economics into risk assessment models and to integrate biology into risk management models.

Although this seems to state the obvious, recall the sanctioned view that risk assessment is best in the hands of the natural sciences and risk management is in the domain of the social sciences (NAS, 1983; Ruckelshaus, 1984; US Federal Register, 1984; Breyers, 1993). But as discussed earlier, people choose to mitigate and adapt to risk (Crocker and Shogren, 1999). Viewing environmental stress in isolation from human activities leads to a biased estimation of the actual risk. As such, risk assessment of invasive species should be considered as being influenced by both human activities that create risk *and* human reactions to that risk. This requires that we explore how and whether we can reform the traditional risk assessment–risk management framework as applied to invasive species risk studies, to a more integrated framework. This framework would assess invasive species risks as functions of both natural science parameters and adaptation decisions based on economic circumstances. Given the wealth, technology base, and other pertinent economic and social characteristics of individual nations, their relative marginal productivities of adaptation and mitigation influence choices they make to address invasive species risk. A detailed examination of the climate change literature on integrated modelling can improve our understanding of how to create such an integrated model for invasive species risk and policy (see, for example, Weyant and Hill, 1999).

Implication 2   Recognize that endogenous risk affects how we measure the benefits of risk reduction. First, unobservable utility terms can be removed from benefit estimation only under very restrictive assumptions about preferences. Second, increased risk does not necessarily require increased compensation to maintain a constant level of expected utility. Third, adaptation is not necessarily a lower bound on the benefits of risk reduction. Fourth, people might well pay a 'protection premium' to eliminate uncertainty about the effectiveness of risk reduction strategies. These four results challenge the standard view that those at greater risk and with greater wealth must value a given risk reduction more highly. Poor people may have fewer and more costly opportunities to mitigate and may thus value a risk reduction more highly than do the wealthy. Fifth, mitigation can create a threshold in a person's preferences in which he/she jumps from a high value to a low value for risk reduction. Ignoring these factors can lead to an excessive expenditure on risk reduction strategies (Shogren and Crocker, 1991, 1999; and Crocker and Shogren, 2000).

A better accounting of economic value helps policy makers refine resource allocation decisions across both market and non-market goods. Adaptation and mitigation complicate how one values the benefits of reduced environmental risk. The complexity arises because now one has to account for how people privately adapt to risk, how a collective mitigation policy is likely to affect this adaptation, and how adaptation will affect mitigation. The links between these two risk reduction strategies affect how a person values risk reduction from some government policy. The endogenous risk model reveals these links and creates a framework to better understand how people value alternative risk reduction options. Implication 2 implies that once one acknowledges that people adapt, standard environmental risk valuation techniques that assume the opposite are potentially biased.

The first four results in Implication 2 focus on the technology of risk reduction, and are summarized in Crocker and Shogren (1999). For invasive species, these results say that researchers need to capture the range of risk reduction options when assessing the benefits of alternative policies. The technology of risk reduction matters, and this needs to be accounted for. The fifth result shows how this technology affects the nature of revealed risk preferences. We now consider this result in more detail.

Mitigation efforts create a threshold in a person's preferences for risk reduction. The person has a discontinuity, a threshold in which he/she jumps from a high value to a low value for risk reduction (see Figure 4.1). Valuing risk reduction requires the nature of this discrete threshold to be addressed. For example, discreteness includes decisions to dam a river, to build a road through a forest, to construct a housing tract in a mountain meadow or a ridge top, and to introduce an exotic species into an ecosystem.

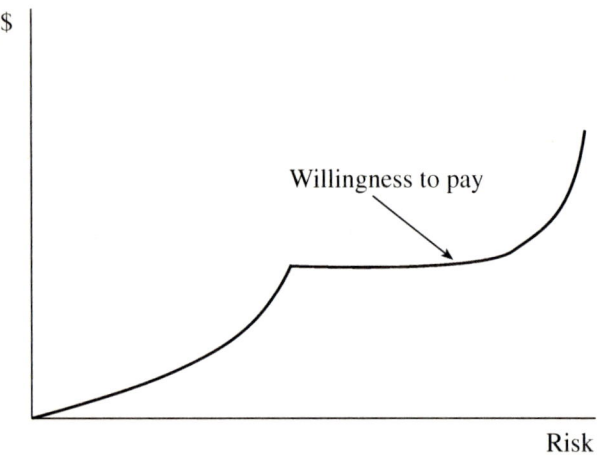

Figure 4.1   Willingness to pay with threshold

Why should policy makers care about a threshold in a value function for invasive species? The short answer is that policy makers who neglect this threshold can affect environmental outcomes by excessive provision of mitigation. In this case, this inefficiency arises from government failure not market failure. Policy makers failing to acknowledge the discrete value function can impose too much collective risk reduction.

To see this, suppose the manager influences risk through mitigation investments. Mitigation involves combinations of how the land is used and how much land is used. The manager's willingness to trade off risk for wealth given high mitigation exceeds in absolute magnitude his/her willingness given low mitigation. The comparative levels of expected utility depend on the relative magnitudes of the benefits and costs of mitigation. The expected utilities of high and of low mitigation are equal if the net benefits of high versus low mitigation equal their net opportunity costs. For a given level of wealth, if an owner perceives trivial, if any, real damages, then the difference in utility between states approaches zero, and the expected utility of low mitigation will most likely exceed the expected utility of high mitigation. Likewise, if the owner believes that his/her mitigation has a trivial impact on the likelihood of damages. Alternatively, if he/she perceives large potential damages, or that his/her mitigation has a significant impact on the likelihood of a good state of nature, the opposite holds.

But with a move to lower wealth and lower riskiness, the owner prefers low mitigation because the reduction in riskiness with the good state is not enough to compensate for the loss of wealth. By switching from high to low mitigation, the owner obtains a higher utility level, whereas if he/she had maintained high mitigation, then his/her utility level would be unchanged. Given this ability to switch mitigation efforts, the person's *ex-ante* willingness to pay for the collectively provided risk reduction has a discrete jump – a so-called 'non-convexity' – given the relative benefits and costs of mitigation. Assuming a constant wealth level, an owner chooses low over high mitigation when damage risks are small, and vice versa when damage risks are large.

Implication 3 First, a higher risk of invasive species directly increases adaptation. This adaptation is enhanced if the higher risk increases (decreases) the marginal productivity of mitigation, and if adaptation complements (substitutes for) the mitigation efforts. Otherwise, the incentive for additional adaptation is dampened. Second, if risk reduces the marginal productivity of mitigation, then a higher risk reduces mitigation. This direct effect is enhanced when mitigation and adaptation are substitutes – even less mitigation; the effect is dampened when the actions are complements – less reduction, or potential increase. Third, if risk sufficiently increases the marginal productivity of mitigation, then a higher risk increases mitigation. This direct effect is dampened when mitigation and adaptation are substitutes – less mitigation; the effect is enhanced when the actions are complements – more mitigation (Kane and Shogren, 2000).

We can use the endogenous risk framework to understand how additional risk about damages posed by exotic species affects the mix of mitigation and adaptation. First, consider how additional risk affects adaptation. More risk directly induces a manager to increase his/her optimal level of adaptation. This direct effect is then modified by how more risk affects mitigation, and then how indirect effect filters through to the adaptation choice.

Signing the indirect effect is complicated as it depends on how risk affects the incremental productivity of mitigation, and whether mitigation and adaptation are complements or substitutes. Complements exist when more mitigation leads to more adaptation; substitutes exist when more mitigation leads to less adaptation. As such, the indirect effect amplifies the direct effect if the marginal productivity of mitigation increases, and mitigation and adaptation are complements; or if marginal productivity decreases, and the actions are substitutes. Otherwise, the indirect effect dampens the direct effect. Which effect dominates is an empirical question.

Additional risk affects mitigation strategies in a similar fashion. The effect depends again on the sign and magnitude of the direct mitigation effect, and on the indirect effect that captures how risk affects adaptation, and whether the two strategies are complements or substitutes. The sign of the direct effect depends on how risk affects the marginal productivity of mitigation – less productivity, less mitigation; sufficiently more productivity, more mitigation. The indirect effect depends on whether mitigation and adaptation are complements or substitutes.

In addition, we must recognize that the effectiveness of mitigation and adaptation is likely to be uncertain. Treating mitigation and adaptation as risky inputs into the production of reduced invasive species risk makes sense. Risky inputs can cause even risk-neutral managers to invest less. Uncertainty about the underlying physical processes and random variability requires nations to decide whether to act now or wait for more information about the invasive species to judge the likely effectiveness of adaptation and mitigation. If we learn more about effectiveness, people have a clear incentive to increase their adaptation efforts because the incremental benefits exceed the costs. Mitigation is unclear, however, as it is unclear whether the benefits exceed the costs, because the productivity of mitigation might have been greater than expected.

In sum, adaptation affects mitigation, and vice versa. Understanding whether capturing these links matters in an empirical sense is an open question for invasive species. Other studies have shown that capturing them does matter. The gain of reducing the risk of lead poisoning in US children is doubled when one accounts for the parents' decisions to reduce exposures and body burdens (Agee and Crocker, 1996). The benefits from an average wetland acre are nine times greater once one accounts for the behavioural interactions of economies and ecosystems (Swallow, 1996).

4   CONCLUDING COMMENTS

Nations undertake numerous investment strategies to control the risk posed by invasive species to ecological and economic systems. Herein we use the economic theory of endogenous risk to frame alternative risk reduction actions, and how these actions affect the interaction of biology and economics, the value of reduced risk, and how people might react to more risk. The ramification of this perspective is that it can increase the precision of risk assessment, cause the benefits of risk reduction to be estimated more accurately, and temper the behaviour of those exposed to risk who spend excessively on mitigation. Failure to acknowledge the influence that economic behaviour has on invasive species risk will result in excessive economic expenditures at no gain in environmental quality. The key is to create incentives that reward those who attempt to unify risk assessment and management into an integrated system, and estimate individual preferences for alternative risk reduction strategies.

Further study is needed to extend the analysis and learn more about several issues. First, a dynamic treatment of the model is needed to reveal the direction and stability of different combinations of risk reduction strategies. Second, an evaluation should be made of how alternative policies might transform and transfer invasive species risk over time and space to create new risks for others. Third, we need to construct the likely damage functions that result from a specified range of risks to evaluate adaptation productivity. Fourth, an empirical investigation into how adaptation and mitigation activities are linked to better understand under what conditions they complement and substitute for each other would be useful. This would include exploring how each risk reduction strategy affects the other's incremental productivity. Finally, a comparison of the costs incurred by simultaneously investing in risk reduction strategies and by a sequential approach is needed.

REFERENCES

Agee, M. and T. Crocker (1996), 'Parental altruism and child lead exposure', *Journal of Human Resources*, **31**: 677–91.
Breyers, S. (1993), *Breaking the Vicious Circle: Toward Effective Risk Regulation*, Cambridge, MA: Harvard University Press.
Carey, J. (1996), 'The incipient Mediterranean fruit fly population in California: implications for invasion biology', *Ecology*, **77**: 1690–97.
Carlton, J. (1996), 'Biological invasions and cryptogenic species', *Ecology*, **77**: 1653–5.
Cohen, A. and J. Carlton (1998), 'Accelerating invasion rate in a highly invaded estuary', *Science*, **279**: 555–7.
Crocker, T. and J. Shogren (1999), 'Endogenous environmental risk', in J.C.J.M. van den Bergh (ed.), *Handbook of Environmental and Resource Economics*, Cheltenham: Edward Elgar: 215–22.
Crocker, T. and J. Shogren (2000), 'Ecosystems as lotteries', in H. Folmer, S. Gerking and A. Rose (eds), *Frontiers of Environmental Economics*, Cheltenham: Edward Elgar, forthcoming.
de Finetti, B. (1974), *Theory of Probability*, New York: John Wiley & Sons.
Drèze, J. (1987), *Essays on Economic Decisions under Uncertainty*, Cambridge: Cambridge University Press.
Dudgeon, D. (1992), 'Endangered ecosystems – a review of the conservation status of tropical Asian rivers', *Hydrobiologia*, **248**: 167–91.

Ehrlich, I. and G. Becker (1972), 'Market insurance, self-insurance, and self-protection', *Journal of Political Economy*, **80**: 623–48.

Elton, C. (1958), *The Ecology of Invasions by Animals and Plants*, London: Methuen.

Federal Interagency Committee for the Management of Noxious and Exotic Weeds (FICMNEW) (1998), *Invasive Plants: Changing the Landscape of America. Fact Book*, Washington, DC: FICMNEW.

Grosholz, E. (1996), 'Contrasting rates of spread for introduced species in terrestrial and marine systems', *Ecology*, **77**: 1680–86.

Haimes, Y. (1998), *Risk Modeling, Assessment, and Management*, New York: John Wiley & Sons.

Hastings, A. (1996), 'Models of spatial spread: is the theory complete?', *Ecology*, **77**: 1675–9.

Hirshleifer, J. (1983), 'From weakest-link to best-shot: the voluntary provision of public goods', *Public Choice*, **41**: 371–86.

Kane, S. and J. Shogren (2000), 'Linking adaptation and mitigation in climate change policy', *Climatic Change*, forthcoming.

Kareiva, P. (1996), 'Developing a prediction ecology for non-indigenous species and ecological invasions', *Ecology*, **77**: 1651–2.

MacIsaac, H. (1996), 'Potential abiotic and biotic impacts of zebra mussels on the inland waters of North America', *American Zoology*, **36**: 287–99.

Moyle, P. and T. Light (1996), 'Fish invasions in California: do abiotic factors determine success?', *Ecology*, **77**: 1666–70.

National Academy of Sciences (NAS) (1983), *Risk Assessment in the Federal Government Managing the Process*, Washington, DC: National Academy Press.

Rejmánek, M. and D. Richardson (1996), 'What attributes make some species more invasive?', *Ecology*, **77**: 1655–61.

Ruckelshaus, W. (1984), 'Risk in a free society', *Risk Analysis*, **4**: 157–62.

Savage, L. (1954), *The Foundation of Statistics*, New York: John Wiley & Sons.

Shogren, J. and T. Crocker (1991), 'Risk, self-protection, and *ex ante* economic value', *Journal of Environmental and Economic Management*, **20**: 1–15.

Shogren, J. and T. Crocker (1999), 'Risk and its consequences', *Journal of Environmental and Economic Management*, **37**: 44–51.

Shogren, J., J. Tschirhart, T. Anderson, A. Ando, S. Beissinger, D. Brookshire, G. Brown, Jr., D. Coursey, R. Innes, S. Meyer and S. Polasky (1999), 'Why economics matters for endangered species protection', *Conservation Biology*, **13**: 1257–67.

Soulé, M. (1990), 'The onslaught of alien species, and other challenges in the coming decade', *Conservation Biology*, **4**: 233–9.

Swallow, S. (1996), 'Resource capital theory and ecosystem economics: developing nonrenewable habitats with heterogeneous quality', *Southern Economic Journal*, **63**: 106–23.

United States Federal Register (1984), Parts II, III, V, and VI: Environmental Protection Agency, 24 September, Washington, DC.

Van den Bosch, F., J. Metz and O. Diekman (1990), 'The velocity of spatial population expansion', *Journal of Mathematical Biology*, **28**: 529–65.

Veblen, T., M. Mermoz, C. Martin and T. Kitzberger (1992), 'Ecological impacts of introduced animals in Nahuel Huapi National Park, Argentina', *Conservation Biology*, **6**: 71–83.

Viscusi, W.K. (1992), *Fatal Tradeoffs*, Oxford: Oxford University Press.

von Neumann, J. and O. Morgenstern (1944), *Theory of Games and Economic Behavior*, Princeton, NJ: Princeton University Press.

Weyant, J. and J. Hill (1999), 'Introduction and overview: the costs of the Kyoto Protocol – a multi-model evaluation', *Energy Journal*, May, vii–xliv.
Williamson, M. (1996), *Biological Invasions*, London: Chapman & Hall.
Williamson, M. and A. Fitter (1996), 'The varying success of invaders', *Ecology*, **77**: 1655–61.

5.   The economics of an invading species: a theoretical model and case study application

Duncan Knowler and Edward B. Barbier

---

1   INTRODUCTION

This chapter is concerned with the economics of an invading species, when there is interspecific competition between the invader and a resident species in the pre-existing, or 'host' ecosystem. Although it is possible for an invading species to yield economic benefits once it is established, our main concern is the more common occurrence where the invader becomes a 'pest', that is, with negative economic effects once it is established. In particular, we are interested in those negative impacts that arise from interspecific competition between the invader and an economically valuable resident species.

Although all potential invaders appear to have a small probability of becoming pests, the economic impacts of such pests are likely to be large, and will often involve some negative effect on one or more resident species. As Williamson (1996) notes, the 'tens' rule of thumb of biological invasions suggests that only 10 per cent of introduced, non-captive (that is, casual or feral) species will become established in a host environment, and that only 10 per cent of established invaders will become pests. However, the ultimate economic damage caused by invading pests can be extremely large. A recent estimate for the United States indicates that the cumulative losses from those harmful, non-indigenous species analysed amounts to almost $100 billion (OTA, 1993, quoted in Williamson, 1996). Moreover, this cost appears to be rising each year. Determining exactly how much of this damage is due to interspecific interaction between the invader and an economically valuable indigenous species is difficult; nevertheless, it is likely that many of the major economic impacts do take this form (Williamson, 1996; Drake et al., 1989). Although invaders appear to have a small probability of becoming pests, the economic impacts of such pests are likely to be large, and will often involve some negative effect on one or more resident species.

This chapter explores the economic consequences of one such invasion with significant impacts on a valuable resident species: the introduction of the ctenophore (comb-jelly) *Mnemiopsis leidyi* in the Black Sea and its effects on the commercial anchovy (*Engraulis encrasicolus*) fishery. However, in developing this case study we are also interested in the more general problem of determining the economic consequences of an invasion in situations where the impact of the established invader is to cause a perturbation, or structural change, in the population dynamics of a commercially harvested species, that is, a discontinuous shift in the latter's biological growth function. By taking into account these changes in the growth function in a standard bioeconomic model of a commercially harvested species, the economic impact of the invading species can be derived as the difference in the steady-state net returns before and after the invasion. We demonstrate this result both theoretically and through an empirical case study of the *Mnemiopsis leidyi* in the Black Sea.

The outline of the chapter is as follows. The next section develops our general theoretical approach to the economic impacts of an invasion. We discuss how this approach relates both to the more general model of interspecific interaction that allows for ecosystem effects and diffusion, as well as to the standard 'predator–prey' type model in the bioeconomics literature. We also show how these models are related to the special case of an invading species that causes a structural change in the biological growth of an economically valuable resident species. The latter model is then illustrated by the case study of the introduction of the *Mnemiopsis leidyi* in the Black Sea. We distinguish the pre- and post-*Mnemiopsis* effects on recruitment in the anchovy fishery, and derive the consequent impacts of these differing effects on equilibrium net returns in the fishery. The resulting loss in profits from the invasion appears to be dramatic, with rents in the anchovy fishery declining from US$17 million to US$0.3 million. We conclude the chapter by discussing the overall implications of this case study and our general modelling approach for the growing literature on the economics of biological invasions.

2 THEORETICAL MODEL

Any model of the economic consequences of the effects of an invader on the resident species must be based on two principles. First, the economic impacts of invasion will depend on the exact nature of the interspecific interaction, and second, the correct measure of these impacts should be based on a comparison of the *ex-post* and *ex-ante* invasion scenarios. In the following section, we demonstrate how these principles can guide us in constructing a simplified general model of the economics of invasion, in which the *ex-post* outcome is a significant structural change in the biological dynamics of the resident species affected by the invasion. Before developing this model in more detail, we first discuss how such an approach relates to more standard models of invasion, such as diffusion and predator–prey models.

Correctly modelling the key interspecific relationships is a critical part of analysing the economic impacts of invasive pests. An important initial consideration is determining whether the spread, or dispersal, of the invading species in turn affects the location and movement of the resident species in the pre-existing habitat, or whether the interspecific competition occurs solely in the same habitat area without diffusive movement of either species (Shigesada and Kawasaki, 1997; Williamson, 1996). In the former case, standard diffusion models can be used to model how resident species disperse with the spread of the invading species; in the latter, non-diffusion models of interspecific competition – including predator–prey models – are often used. In some complex examples, both species dispersal and some form of interspecific competition might occur as a result of an invasion, in which case both the diffusion and competition effects must be included in the same model.

Although the type of interspecific interaction that may result from an invasion can vary from case to case, and must be modelled appropriately, the same measure of the economic effects should always apply to every invasion. That is, these economic impacts should always be measured in terms of a comparison of the net economic benefits arising from the pre-invasion situation with the net economic benefits occurring in the post-invasion situation.[1] As the case we consider later is concerned with an invading species' impact on a commercially valuable resident species whose price is determined on international markets (for example, a 'traded' good), we can be more specific. The economic impact of an invasion is the difference between the profits, or net returns, derived from commercially exploiting the resident species before and after the invasion, that is:

$$\text{economic impact of invasion} = \pi_A - \pi_B \qquad (5.1)$$

where π refers to the economic profits from the commercially valuable species, and the subscripts A and B refer to the pre- and post-invasion situations, respectively.[2]

The rest of this section demonstrates how the above rule can be applied to various versions of the problem of a commercially harvested species that is affected by an invader, including special cases such as the Black Sea *Mnemiopsis* invasion. However, we start first with a more general bioeconomic model of invasion that contains both interspecific diffusion and competition effects.

Shigesada and Kawasaki (1997) show how the standard Fisher, or diffusion, model developed to determine the spread of an invasive species can be extended to include two-species interactions in the form of dispersal as well as competition or predation.[3] This approach can be used to construct a general bioeconomic model of interspecific interaction arising from an invasion. For instance, assume that an invading species spreads into a habitat area already occupied by a competing resident species, in which the following profit–maximizing bioeconomic model now holds:

$$\text{Max} \int_0^\infty \pi(h)e^{-rt}dt, \quad h = h(n_1, E), \quad h_n > 0, \quad h_E > 0 \qquad (5.2)$$

subject to:

$$\dot{n}_1 = \frac{\partial n_1(d,t)}{\partial t} = D_1 \frac{\partial^2 n_1}{\partial d^2} + F_1(n_1, n_2) - h(n_1, E),$$

$$F_1[n_1(d_0, 0)] = h[n_1(d_0, 0), E]$$

$$\dot{n}_2 = \frac{\partial n_2(d,t)}{\partial t} = D_2 \frac{\partial^2 n_2}{\partial d^2} + F_2(n_1, n_2), \quad n_2(0,0) = 0 \qquad (5.3)$$

where $n_1(d, t)$ is the population density of the commercially harvested resident species at any time t and any radial distance d from its original location in the habitat, and similarly, $n_2(d, t)$ is the population density of the invader that displaces the resident species. Profits, π, can be earned from harvests, h, of the resident species, and these harvests are a function of the species stock, n_1, and harvesting effort, E. It is assumed that the initial condition (that is, $t = 0$) is the pre-invasion state whereby the invasive species has not yet entered the habitat to displace the resident species, and so stocks of the former are effectively zero ($n_2 = 0$). The resident species is therefore at some initial location d_0, and its population is assumed stable (that is, natural growth is equal to harvest). Once invasion has occurred ($t > 0$), for both the resident and invasive species, the change in the population density at any location in its range is caused by the diffusion term (the first term on the right hand side of (5.3)) and the natural growth term (the second term). Due to interspecific competition, it is assumed that $\partial F_i / \partial n_j < 0$, that is, competition between species i and j has a negative impact on the growth of species i.[4] The coefficient D_i of the diffusion term is a measure of how quickly the organism disperses. Finally, as only the resident species is commercially exploited, the change in population density of this species must be net of any harvesting.

The above model can be solved for the long-run, or steady-state, level of profits from harvesting the resident species that occurs after the invader is successfully established and both populations are dispersed. Returning to (5.1), this is effectively π_B^*, the post-invasion level of profits (which is starred to indicate a steady-state value). Since these profits are dependent on exploiting the resident species only, they are directly affected by the degree of dispersion of this species in the long run. As Shigesada and Kawasaki (1997) demonstrate, depending on the dynamics of the interspecific competition underlying (5.3), two likely long-run dispersal outcomes are possible. First, the invading species not only succeeds in its invasion but ends up completely displacing the resident species from its habitat. Under this scenario, it is possible that $\pi_B^* \approx 0$, that is, in the long run the commercially valuable resident species can no longer be exploited and profits fall to zero.[5]

An alternative outcome is that the invader still manages to establish itself in the new habitat, but that competition with the resident species is relatively weak so that the two species coexist in the same habitat. Under this scenario, one would expect $0 < \pi_B^* < \pi_A^*$, that is, post-invasion profits from harvesting the resident species are not completely eliminated, although they are unlikely to reach pre-invasion levels. Thus, from (5.1), both outcomes depict a successful invasion with significant (that is, non-zero) economic costs, with the first scenario more likely to yield the greater cost.

Providing an actual estimate of the economic cost of the invasion also requires determining pre-invasion profits, π_A. It is possible to do this from the above model, given plausible assumptions concerning the initial conditions of the system. For example, in (5.3) the initial conditions of the model indicate that the pre-invasion situation is a steady state, in which the entire habitat area is occupied by the resident species (species 1), population density, $n_1(d_0, 0)$ is unchanging, and any natural growth is offset by harvesting. The invader species (species 2) has not entered the habitat, and so its population density is zero. These initial conditions imposed on the above model would essentially yield standard steady-state bioeconomic harvesting rules for a uniformly distributed species, from which π_A can easily be derived.

In certain cases of biological invasions, the resident and invasive species may compete while remaining in the same area without diffusive movement. This is clearly the situation with regard to the *Mnemiopsis* invasion of the Black Sea, where the closed system of this inland sea prevents the resident anchovy fishery from 'relocating' elsewhere. This type of invasion problem can be considered a 'special case' of the above general diffusion model with interspecific competition.

Essentially, the diffusion term of the model no longer applies, and only the interspecific competition component of the model is relevant. However, as we shall now demonstrate, how one chooses to model the interspecific interaction between the resident and invasive species is critical to analysing the economic costs of an invasion. There are essentially three possible cases: (i) by assuming that only the interspecific competition component of the above model is valid; (ii) by assuming that the interspecific relationship is best represented by a standard predator–prey (or host–parasite) model; or (iii) by modelling the impact of the invasion in terms of a structural shift in the biological growth function of the resident species.

It is fairly straightforward to show how the first case can be derived directly from the above general model. For example, if both species compete within the same habitat and cannot disperse, then neither the location of each species, d, within the habitat nor the rate of dispersal of organisms, D_i, matter in equation (5.3). As a consequence, the diffusion term on the right-hand side of the dynamic equations for both species can be dropped, and d no longer appears as an argument in the problem.[6] Otherwise, calculation of pre- and post-invasion profits follows the same procedure as in the general invasion model.

As noted above, the conventional predator–prey model can also be considered as a special case of the general invasion model in which there is also no diffusion occurring. However, the key assumption in this model is that, instead of each species impacting negatively on the natural growth of the other through competition over the habitat, one species benefits from 'preying' on the other. Nevertheless, it is possible to show how this special case of a predator–prey relationship can be derived from the general invasion model presented above.

For example, again in the absence of any dispersal, we can omit the diffusion term and radial distance, d, from equation (5.3). Also, with no diffusion, we can assume a fixed geographical boundary for the habitat area, k. This in turn allows us to transform the population density variable of each species (for example, biomass per m^2 or number of individuals per m^2) into an indicator of the size of the resource stock (for example, biomass or number of individuals), which is more commonly used in conventional bioeconomic models of interspecific competition (including predator–prey models). Thus, from equations (5.2) and (5.3), the profit-maximizing model of the post-invasion situation now becomes:

$$\text{Max} \int_0^\infty \pi(h)e^{-rt}dt, \; h = h(X_1, E), \; h_x > 0, \; h_E > 0 \qquad (5.4)$$

subject to:

$$\dot{X}_1 = \frac{\partial X_1(t)}{\partial t} = F_1(X_1, X_2) - h(X_1, E), \ F_1[X_1(0)] = h[X_1(0), E]$$

$$(5.5)$$

$$\dot{X}_2 = \frac{\partial X_2(t)}{\partial t} = F_2(X_1, X_2), \ X_2(0) = 0$$

where X_1 is some measure of the size of the population (for example, total biomass) of the commercially harvested resident species at any time t, and similarly, X_2 is the biomass of the invader into the host environment.[7] Note, however, we must also impose the condition on (5.5) that $\partial F_1/\partial n_2 < 0$ but $\partial F_2/\partial n_1 > 0$, that is, the invader (species 2) now preys on the resident species (species 1).

Equations (5.4) and (5.5) are therefore a basic formulation of the conventional predator–prey model that has been used extensively in the bioeconomic literature (for example, see Wilman, 1996; Ströbele and Wacker, 1995; Tu and Wilman, 1992; Clark, 1990; Wilen and Brown, 1986; Ragozin and Brown, 1985; Hannesson, 1983; and Bishop and Samples, 1980). However, it is important to recognize that in this literature the predator–prey model is generally *not* used to determine the economic costs of an invasion (that is, as specified in equation (5.1)). Instead, if a predator–prey model is applied to the pest invasion problem, the main aim is usually to analyse the economic impacts of the invading predator on the host prey, including the costs of pest control, *once the invader is already established*. That is, in such models, only the post-invasion profits, π_B, are of interest.[8]

One can of course derive the pre-invasion profits, π_A, from the initial conditions of the predator–prey model, just as we did above in the case of the general invasion model with diffusion. For example, a comparison of (5.3) and (5.5) shows that the initial conditions of the two models can be constructed similarly to indicate a pre-invasion state of equilibrium harvesting and profits. This in turn facilitates the use of equation (5.1) to determine the economic impacts of an invader that eventually ends up in a predator–prey relationship with a resident species.

However, a more fundamental question is whether a conventional predator–prey bioeconomic relationship, as depicted by equations (5.4) and (5.5) above, is always the correct depiction of the impact of an invasion, even if the end result is the introduction and establishment of a new predator in a host ecosystem that is 'closed' (that is, species cannot disperse). We would suggest that under certain conditions the conventional predator–prey approach may not be the correct way of modelling post-invasion impacts.

For example, the success of an invasion may be the result of changes in the underlying environmental conditions of the host ecosystem that: (i) allow the invader to establish itself, and (ii) continue to sustain its population in the system. Such conditions might include nutrient enrichment in a marine system or biodiversity loss. Moreover, the population dynamics of the resident species will have altered not only as a result of the initial system-wide change in environmental conditions but also due to the introduction of a new predator and any associated feedback effects (Perrings et al., 1992). In short, compared to the pre-invasion situation, the combination of a successful invasion by a competitor/predator and the ecosystem-wide changes stemming from the various ecological disturbances leads to a structural change in the population dynamics of the resident species. Under the above conditions, profit-maximizing behaviour is still determined by equation (5.4), but is now subject to the following pre- and post-invasion population dynamics:

Pre-invasion

$$\dot{X}_1 = \frac{\partial X_1(t)}{\partial t} = F_1(X_1) - h(X_1, E),$$

(5.6)

$$X_1(0) = X_{1_0}, \quad X_2(t) = 0.$$

Post-invasion

$$\dot{X}_1 = \frac{\partial X_1(t)}{\partial t} = G_1(X_1, X_2, \varepsilon) - h(X_1, E),$$

$$\dot{X}_2 = \frac{\partial X_2(t)}{\partial t} = G_2(X_1, X_2, \varepsilon),$$

(5.7)

$$X_1(0) = X_{1_0} \quad X_2(0) = X_{2_0}$$

Steady-state pre-invasion profits, π_A^*, can be determined by finding the long-run solution of the standard bioeconomic problem of optimally harvesting the resident species, using equations (5.4) and (5.6). As denoted by equation (5.7), in the post-invasion situation, the population dynamics of the resident species is now structurally altered by the combination of the establishment of the invader species, X_2, and changed environmental conditions (represented by some indicator ε). Since the invader preys on or competes with the resident species, we would expect $\partial G_1 / \partial X_2 < 0$. Consequently, steady-state post-invasion profits, π_B^*, can be derived through the long-run solution of equations (5.4) and (5.7), and economic impacts of the invasion can be calculated from (5.1).

Knowler (1999) indicates how the above model can be adapted to describe a special type of discrete time invasion problem, where the consequence of the invasion is a structural change in the population dynamics of the resident species that is commercially exploited. Moreover, this case assumes the seasonal availability of prey (X_1) determines the annual biomass of the invader (X_2), but that the invader's biomass in period $t + 1$ is independent of its level in period t. As a result, X_2 is independent of time (that is, autonomous) and it is no longer a state variable of the system and subject to an equation of motion. Instead, the annually-determined biomass of the invader is now a *constraint* on the system. With these modifications in mind, and recalling the shift to discrete time, we can restate expressions (5.6) and (5.7) as follows (note: individual species are numbered in discrete time using superscripts, that is, $X_1(t) \Rightarrow X_t^1$):

Pre-invasion

$$X_{t+1}^1 - X_t^1 = F_1(X_t^1) - h(X_t^1, E_t)$$

$$X_{t=0}^1 = X_0^1, \; X_t^2 = 0 \tag{5.8}$$

Post-invasion

$$X_{t+1}^1 - X_t^1 = G_1(X_t^1, X_t^2, \varepsilon) - h(X_t^1, E_t)$$

$$X_t^2 = G_2(X_t^1, \varepsilon) \tag{5.9}$$

$$X_{t=0}^1 = X_0^1, \; X_{t=0}^2 = X_0^2$$

Conveniently, we can make a substitution using $X_t^2 = G_2(X_t^1, \varepsilon)$ and restate expression (5.9) in X^1 alone as:

$$X_{t+1}^1 - X_t^1 = G_1[X_t^1, G_2(X_t^1, \varepsilon), \varepsilon] - h(X_t^1, E_t), \; X_{t=0}^1 = X_0^1. \tag{5.10}$$

In effect, we posit a structural change in the growth function governing the commercial species, as indicated by a comparison of (5.8) and (5.10). The problem can now be solved using the same approach discussed above, making the appropriate shift to discrete time in specifying the full system. The next section demonstrates how this model can be used to determine the economic impacts of the comb-jelly *Mnemiopsis leidyi* on the Black Sea anchovy fishery, by deriving the difference in the steady-state net returns before and after the invasion.

3 CASE STUDY: *MNEMIOPSIS LEIDYI* IN THE BLACK SEA

In this section, we describe the *Mnemiopsis* problem with regard to its impact on the commercial Black Sea anchovy fishery and then derive a model describing this phenomenon that is consistent with the previous section. We specify the anchovy recruitment function, estimating it empirically for the pre- and post-*Mnemiopsis* situations. Drawing on previous bioeconomic modelling of the Turkish anchovy fishery, we are then able to assess empirically the losses imposed by the entry of the comb-jelly into the Black Sea. An important attribute of the model is its assumption of optimal management of the anchovy fishery, which contrasts with the historic condition of de facto open access. In theoretical terms, the latter case does not allow for any sizeable long-run rents to be earned in the fishery, since the fishery is characterized by a price structure influenced by world anchovy prices and most fishing vessels are of a similar design and age (Dincer, 1992). Therefore, the entry of *Mnemiopsis* would have little economic cost in the sense of lost rents under the prevailing fisheries management regime.[9]

The Black Sea is one of the most polluted and mismanaged inland or semi-enclosed seas in the world (Caddy, 1990; UNEP, 1990; Zaitsev, 1992; Kideys, 1994). One of the most serious signs of environmental degradation is the gradual reduction in the value and importance of Black Sea fisheries, culminating in the collapse of the all-important anchovy fishery at the end of the last decade. Playing a major role in this unfortunate story has been the introduction of the comb-jelly *Mnemiopsis leidyi*, originating from the Chesapeake Bay area of the northeastern US coast (GESAMP, 1997). Initially, its entry into the Black Sea displayed the typical behaviour of an invading species: there was an explosion in its population over the period 1987–90, as the ecosystem conditions were favourable (for example, eutrophication) and natural enemies and other forms of natural control were non-existent. Other events possibly influencing the initial outbreak of *Mnemiopsis* include the high stock levels of zooplankton during the latter half of the 1980s, resulting from expanded catches of pelagic species that normally feed on zooplankton (GESAMP, 1994). Ultimately, the combination of high nutrient levels and high pelagic harvests, may have conspired to open a niche for *Mnemiopsis* (Caddy, personal communication). The initial outbreak phase was followed by a reduction in biomass, but then a further increase in its population occurred several years later (GESAMP, 1997).

The annual population dynamics of *Mnemiopsis* are not well understood. Figure 5.1 portrays the typical seasonal behaviour of the comb-jelly's biomass, with a winter die-off preceded by an expansion in its biomass over the summer, parallelling the increasing availability of prey (for example, an-

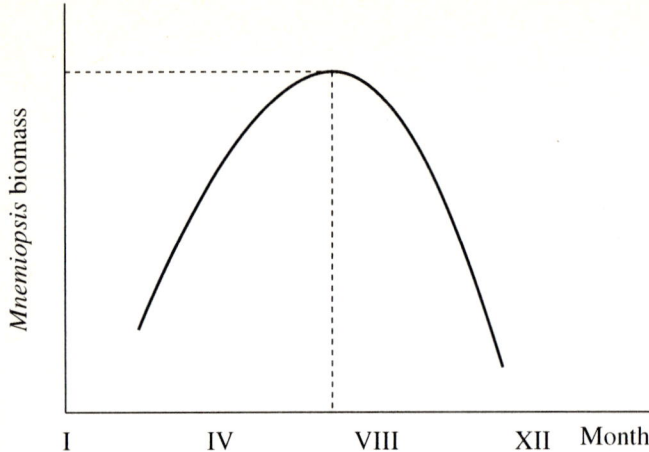

Source: Adapted from GESAMP (1997).

Figure 5.1   Stylized Mnemiopsis *seasonal population dynamics*

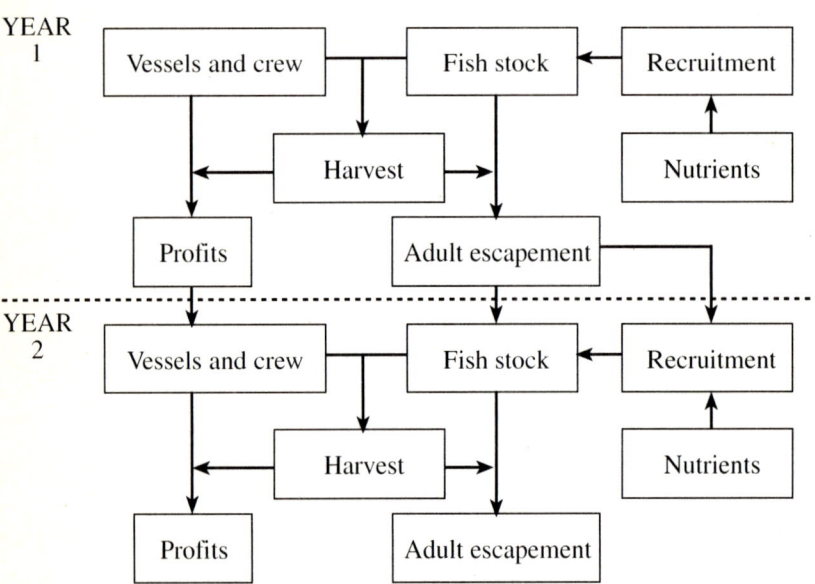

Source: Adapted from Knowler et al. (1997).

Figure 5.2   Structure of the Black Sea bioeconomic model

chovy larvae). Few individuals are thought to survive the winter, so that annual biomass is *not* typically determined by the prior year's biomass level, consistent with the model description at the end of the previous section (GESAMP, 1997).

To derive the economic costs of the introduction of *Mnemiopsis* into the Black Sea marine system we use a standard discrete time, dynamic bioeconomic model of an optimally managed fishery, as described by Conrad (1995) and illustrated in Figure 5.2. We model the invasion's impact on recruitment success as a reduction in the steady state or sustainable level of harvests and, ultimately, a loss of fishery profits.[10] Since anchovy is an internationally traded commodity, its domestic demand curve can be treated as perfectly elastic (that is, flat). Accordingly, the economic cost of the invasion can be represented by (5.1), where π_A^* and π_B^* refer to the annual economic profits or rents available from the anchovy fishery and the symbol * signifies that these rents are calculated at their equilibrium levels, with pre-*Mnemiopsis* conditions designated by the letter *A* and the situation after the entry of *Mnemiopsis* indicated with a *B*. We determine equilibrium profits in each case using a fairly standard profit-maximization formulation for the Turkish anchovy fishery, which is similar to expression (5.4) but formulated in discrete time. We also specify a growth function for the commercial species that is consistent with expression (5.10). Since this latter step is critical to the invasive aspect of the case study, we discuss it in some detail in the following paragraphs.

Previous research has shown that several influences have been important in determining anchovy stocks over the last few decades, in addition to the introduction of *Mnemiopsis*. The Black Sea has been characterized by nutrient enrichment and, consequently, has experienced both damaging effects on benthic species from cultural eutrophication and a boost in primary productivity as nutrient constraints have become relaxed. Apparently, the latter effect has benefited the anchovy stock while at the same time providing conditions which may have allowed *Mnemiopsis* to invade. The interannual effect of nutrient enrichment can be captured through the inclusion of phosphate concentrations as an additional explanatory variable in stock growth, for example. This approach allows us to incorporate an important feedback effect, since nutrients will influence the anchovy spawning biomass, which in turn affects the *Mnemiopsis* biomass.

It is easiest to formulate the problem in terms of anchovy adult biomass (*X*) and escapement (*S*), making use of the spawner-recruit approach suggested by Clark (1990).[11] As noted above, interannual stock growth may depend on influences other than spawning stock size (*S*), such as an environmental influence like nutrient enrichment (*P*), but may be prone to random perturbations such as biological invasions, with the latter structurally altering the stock growth relationship. Beginning with the growth functions in (5.8) and (5.10), we can express these in a single equation that recognizes two structural alternatives for the anchovy recruitment function (R), differing with respect to the presence or absence of the invader *Mnemiopsis*:

$$X_{t+1} - X_t = (\sigma - 1)X_t - \sigma h(X_t, E_t) + R^i[X_t - h(X_t, E_t), P_t] \quad (5.11)$$

where σ is the natural survival rate with $0 < \sigma < 1$, $h(X, E)$ is the catch function and $R^i(S, P)$ is a recruitment function that depends on escapement S and nutrient inputs P (phosphates). The notation i in the recruitment function refers to the environmental situation in place, either pre- or post-invasion, with $i = A$ or B, respectively.[12] Since escapement (S) represents the adult spawning population which survives the harvest season to then reproduce, the adult exploitable (harvested) and spawning stocks are not the same. However, they can be related in the following way, if we make the assumption that there is no natural growth or mortality during the harvesting season (Clark, 1990):

$$S_t = X_t - h_t. \quad (5.12)$$

Substituting (5.12) into (5.11) yields the following statement for adult biomass at time $t + 1$, which is a function of escapement, nutrient inputs and the structural form of the recruitment function in place at time t:

$$X_{t+1} = \sigma S_t + R^i(S_t, P_t). \quad (5.13)$$

The economic component of the model comprises the economic profits π generated by the harvest and is described by the following specification of expression (5.4):

$$\pi_t = p h(X_t, E_t) - c E_t \quad (5.14)$$

where p is the real ex-vessel, 'net' price for anchovy and is determined by a perfectly elastic demand curve, and c is the real unit cost of harvesting effort. Clark (1990) shows how expression (5.14) can be restated in terms of X and h, allowing E to be eliminated. Defining the inverse function $E_t = h^{-1}(X, h) = E(X, h)$, and substituting this latter function into (5.14), gives a new expression for profits,

$$\pi_t = p h_t - c E(X_t, h_t). \quad (5.15)$$

The cost function implied by (5.15) is linear in the parameter c. Using (5.12), the expression $h = X - S$ can be substituted into (5.15), eliminating the variable h. This substitution yields the following new statement for profits:

$$\pi_t = p(X_t - S_t) - c\, E(X_t, X_t - S_t)$$

$$= p(X_t - S_t) - C(X_t, S_t). \tag{5.16}$$

Assuming the general cost function $C(X, S)$ on the right-hand side of (5.16) is separable in X and S, the resulting profit function can be rewritten in the following way:[13]

$$\pi_t = \theta_1(X_t) - \theta_2(S_t)$$

$$\theta_i' > 0, \theta_i'' > 0,\ i = 1,\ 2. \tag{5.17}$$

If phosphate inputs are treated as a fixed parameter, that is, $P = \overline{P}$, the planner's problem under the assumption of optimal management can be expressed as:

$$\max \sum_{t=0}^{\infty} \rho^t \pi(X_t, S_t) = \sum_{t=0}^{\infty} \rho^t [\theta_1(X_t) - \theta_2(S_t)] \tag{5.18}$$

subject to

$$X_{t+1} = \sigma S_t + R^i(S_t, \overline{P}),\ \text{with}\ 0 \le S_t \le X_t,\ \text{and}\ S_0, X_0\ \text{given}.$$

In (5.18), ρ is the discount term, defined as $1/(1 + \delta)^t$, with δ denoting the appropriate social discount rate. Both p and c are assumed to be time invariant in real terms.

This type of discrete time optimization problem can be solved by using expression (5.18) to eliminate the variable X, which then reduces the problem to one of unconstrained optimization with a single choice variable. However, care is required to ensure consistency in the handling of stocks in different time periods, that is, X_{t+1} versus X_t. Using the change of summation index technique, Clark (1990) is able to show that by manipulation, the planner's problem can be simplified to the maximization of a value function $V(S)$ in the single variable S. As a result, the optimization problem can be rewritten as:

$$\max \sum_{t=0}^{\infty} \rho^t V(S_t) \tag{5.19}$$

subject to

$$0 \leq S_{t+1} \leq [\sigma S_t + R^i(S_t, \overline{P})], \text{ with } P = \overline{P} \text{ and } S_0 \text{ given}$$

where the value function $V(S)$ is defined as

$$V(S_t) = \rho \theta_1 [\sigma S_t + R^i(S_t, \overline{P})] - \theta_2(S_t). \tag{5.20}$$

The value function $V(S)$ involves the functions $\theta_1(X)$ and $\theta_2(S)$, which are familiar as the separable components of the profit function in (5.17), but the variable X has been substituted out. As indicated above, this is now a simple unconstrained optimization problem in a single choice variable but one having a unique solution for each of the two structural forms of the recruitment function.

The optimal solution to (5.19) can be characterized as a constant optimal escapement rule and is found by taking the first derivative of (5.20) and setting this equal to zero. This yields the following implicit statement which is satisfied by the desired optimal escapement value S^*,

$$V'(S^*) = \rho(\sigma + R^i_{S^*})\theta_1'[\sigma S^* + R^i(S^*, \overline{P})] - \theta_2'(S^*) = 0. \tag{5.21}$$

Expression (5.21) can be rearranged to give the following discrete time analogue to the well-known continuous time Golden Rule,

$$(\sigma + R^i_{S^*}) \frac{\theta_1'[\sigma S^* + R^i(S^*, \overline{P})]}{\theta_2'(S^*)} = 1 + \delta \tag{5.22}$$

where δ is the discount rate.[14] This implicit function gives distinct optimal escapement values for the pre- and post-invasion situations, and these values then are used to calculate the equilibrium profits required for expression (5.1). In the next step we parameterize the model, beginning with the anchovy recruitment function.

Given our spawner-recruit approach, we adopt the specification for the recruitment function introduced by Ricker (1975). The standard Ricker recruitment function can be expressed as:

$$R_t = S_t e^{\beta_0 + \beta_1 S_t} \tag{5.23}$$

where R is recruitment, S is the spawning stock, and β_0 and β_1 are density independent and density dependent mortality parameters, respectively, with $\beta_0 > 0$ and $\beta_1 < 0$. To capture the pre- and post-*Mnemiopsis* situations requires the estimation of separate anchovy recruitment functions for each period. Unfortunately, several problems arise in undertaking this task.

Most importantly, the data available for the anchovy recruitment estimation covers the period 1968–93 and this can be further divided into a pre-*Mnemiopsis* period, 1968–86, and a post-entry period, 1987–93. Thus, these two periods constitute the time-series data points available for estimating separate recruitment functions for the pre- and post-invasion situations. Comprising only seven years, the latter period is too short for the credible application of multiple regression techniques. Since we hypothesize that the entry of *Mnemiopsis* into the Black Sea system brought about a structural change in the anchovy recruitment relationship, this problem can be circumvented by using a dummy variable technique.[15] Pooling the data for the full period, we can insert a dummy variable to account for possible shifts in parameter values with the entry of *Mnemiopsis*.

A second concern is the influence of nutrient enrichment, already described above. We add phosphates (*P*) as a multiplicative explanatory variable to the Ricker recruitment function, which is consistent with the recommendations of Iles and Beverton (1998) for including an environmental variable in a recruitment function. Since the period of enrichment began abruptly in 1971, and may have had some lagged system effects, the full impact of enrichment is incorporated by including a second dummy variable for the years 1971–72 which allows for the marine ecosystem's adjustment to the new enriched regime.

The resulting recruitment relation to be estimated incorporates all of the above concerns and can be represented as:

$$\ln \frac{R_t}{S_t} = \phi_0 + \phi_1 S_t + \phi_2 D_1 + \phi_3 D_1 S_t + \phi_4 D_2 + \phi_5 \ln P_t + \xi_t \qquad (5.24)$$

where D_1 is a dummy variable with $D_1 = 0$ prior to 1987 and $D_1 = 1$ after this date, D_2 is a dummy variable with $D_2 = 0$ prior to 1971 and after 1972 and $D_2 = 1$ for the years 1971–72, and ξ_t is the regression error term. Estimating the anchovy recruitment curve required data for the anchovy spawning and recruitment biomass, which was obtained from Prodanov et al. (1995), and data on phosphate concentrations, which was available from Cociasu et al. (1997). All data covers the period 1968–93 and the regressions were run using the two stage least squares (2SLS) procedure from the econometric package LIMDEP 6.[16]

The initial attempts to include the *Mnemiopsis* dummy (*D₁*) on the intercept term and on the spawning biomass (*S*) created some difficulties. Although the overall fit of the equation improved when the dummy terms were included (as opposed to excluding them), the coefficients themselves were not significant, suggestive of a problem in statistically distinguishing between each of these effects. Table 5.1 shows the results of the initial estimation of a basic Ricker curve with no environmental considerations (Model 1) and the

Table 5.1   *2SLS estimation of the Black Sea anchovy stock-recruitment function, using the Ricker Specification, 1968–1993*

Variables	No *Mnemiopsis* Model 1	With *Mnemiopsis* Model 2	Model 3
Dependent variable	$\ln(R_t/X_t)$	$\ln(R_t/X_t)$	$\ln(R_t/X_t)$
Constant	−0.075		
	(−0.58)		
Parent stock (S_t)	−0.00034	−0.000614	−0.00056
	(−1.19)	(−6.13)	(−4.91)
		[−8.61]	[−5.77]
Intercept dummy, 1987–93 (D_1)			−0.15
			(−1.83)
			[−4.39]
Slope dummy, 1987–93 ($D_1 S_t$)		−0.00101	
		(−2.63)	
		[−2.10]	
Intercept dummy, 1971–72 (D_2)		−0.60	−0.58
		(−3.74)	(−3.00)
		[−4.70]	[−1.60]
Phosphates ($\ln P_t$)		0.117	0.079
		(3.03)	(2.14)
		[2.62]	[1.70]
Observations	26	26	26
Adj. R^2	0.02	0.70	0.56
F-statistic	1.47	20.22	11.60
	(1.24)	(3.22)	(3.22)
DW-statistic	1.09	2.18	1.92

Note: Figures in parentheses are standard *t*-statistics reported by the LIMDEP 6 program; the figures in square brackets are the *t*-statistics based on White's heteroskedasticity-corrected standard errors.

final estimation results when the D_1 intercept and slope terms were included separately, along with the other environmental influences discussed above (Models 2 and 3). Both these latter models provided a better fit without a constant term, so these were dropped in the estimation procedure.

The results appear better with only the slope dummy included (Model 2), although for both Models 2 and 3 all coefficients are of the expected sign and the *t*-statistics indicate highly significant coefficient estimates. The adjusted R^2 of 0.70 for Model 2 indicates that this estimated equation explains most (70 per cent) of the variation in recruitment over the period. Most importantly, the coefficient on the *Mnemiopsis* dummy variable (D_1) indicates that the entry and establishment of the comb-jelly had a statistically significant and highly negative impact on anchovy recruitment, which can be represented as a structural change or shift in the anchovy stock–recruitment relationship. The *t*-statistics derived from White's standard errors further support the statistical validity of this equation as they are consistent with the least squares *t*-statistics in showing all coefficients to be significant at acceptable levels. This indicates that the introduction of the dummy variables did not create a problem of heteroskedasticity.

To complete the empirical bioeconomic model, several additional economic and ecological parameters are required. For these parameters we draw primarily on a previous analysis of the Black Sea anchovy fishery (Knowler, 1999). Using data from a study of the Turkish Black Sea purse seine fishery (Dincer, 1992), we set the anchovy price (p) and unit vessel cost (c) at their 1989 real values, which are representative of the range of values experienced during the study period. These parameter values are US\$90 per tonne for fresh anchovy ex-vessel and net of the crew share, and US\$256 000 per annum per vessel, respectively. The catchability coefficient measures the efficiency of the fishing fleet and gear in catching fish and is defined as q; it was estimated at 0.0032.[17] Also required is the annual adult survival rate in biomass terms (σ), and this was set at 0.78, consistent with the virtual population analysis of the Black Sea anchovy in Prodanov et al. (1995). We also set the phosphate concentration at a fixed level, consistent with the average level prevailing at the time that *Mnemiopsis* first invaded. A level of 5.5 μM was selected for this purpose, based on the data of Cociasu et al. (1997). Finally, we set the social discount rate (δ) at 5 per cent.

These parameters and those derived from the estimated anchovy recruitment function can be inserted into expression (5.22), which gives separate estimates of the optimal anchovy escapement for each of the pre- and post-invasion situations. The optimal level of fishing effort and equilibrium profits associated with these variable values are then easily calculated, again distinguishing between the pre- and post-*Mnemiopsis* states. Making use of expression (5.1), we then determine the economic cost of the invasion of the Black Sea by *Mnemiopsis* in terms of its long-run impact on an optimally managed anchovy fishery.

Table 5.2 presents the results of the analysis and shows that the introduction of *Mnemiopsis* into the Black Sea system had a dramatic impact on the

Table 5.2 Long-run equilibrium values for the Black Sea anchovy fishery under optimal management and pre- and post-Mnemiopsis conditions (US$ 1989/90)

Ecological regime ('000 mt)	Escapement (S^*) ('000 mt)	Recruitment (R^*) ('000 mt)	Stock (X^*) ('000 mt)	Harvest (h^*) ('000 mt)	Effort (E^*) (vessels)	Profits (π^*) ('000 $)
A. pre-*Mnemiopsis* (1971–86)	1518	730	1914	396	72	17 080
B. post-*Mnemiopsis* (1987–93)	946	249	986	40	13	290
Difference due to invasion	–572	–481	–928	–356	–59	–16 790

anchovy fishery, when the basis for the evaluation is a comparison of the profit-maximizing levels of harvest and effort for each regime. For example, the steady-state level of harvest prior to *Mnemiopsis* is estimated at almost 400 000 tonnes per year, whereas with *Mnemiopsis* present the sustainable harvest declines by 90 per cent to 40 000 tonnes per year. In profit or rent terms this results in a decline from $US17 million to $US0.3 million per year, which is a deadweight loss to the Black Sea fishing nations (primarily Turkey in this case). In present-value terms, the loss would amount to hundreds of millions of US dollars over several decades. The introduction of the comb-jelly undoubtedly would have been devastating for local fishing communities dependent on the industrial purse seine fishery as well. As a measure of this impact, the equilibrium number of fishing vessels declines from 72 active vessels to only 13. Given that each vessel accommodates 20 to 30 crew, the direct impact would have been several thousand jobs plus associated effects on linked industries.

4   CONCLUSION

In this chapter we have developed a theoretical framework for assessing the economic costs of an invasion by an exotic species and applied this to a case study involving marine fisheries. The Black Sea anchovy case study demonstrates that the tools of bioeconomic analysis can be used to derive meaningful empirical estimates of the impacts of such invasions. It is worth noting again that the estimates presented here are contingent upon the optimal management of the fishery and that this has not been the case historically with this particular example. Additionally, the approach taken constitutes a comparison of the sustainable harvest and profits (rents) available from the fishery under such management and, as such, these ignore the adjustment path to a new equilibrium. With many invasive species situations, this adjustment period may be quite important. In the case of *Mnemiopsis* there was an initial population explosion followed by a period of reduced biomass, which may or may not herald ongoing fluctuations in the comb-jelly's influence on the commercial fishery in the future (GESAMP, 1997). In the end, both the theoretical models presented here and the empirical case study must be accepted as fairly simple representations of what are likely to be highly complex ecosystem events. However, modelling these interactions using a structural change approach rather than as a more narrowly defined predator–prey relationship is intuitively appealing.

NOTES

1. Economists will recognize that this is analogous to the standard 'cost–benefit' rule in project appraisal, in which the economic impacts of a project are determined by comparing the net economic benefits of the 'with project' and 'without project' scenarios.

2. The specification used here is the correct welfare measure under conditions of perfectly elastic demand, so that consumers' surplus is nil, and economic profits equal the producers' surplus (Freeman, 1993). We also assume that the sole social benefit attributable to the resident species is its commercial harvest value, and abstract from any ecosystem functions that the species may serve.

3. The development of the diffusion model of an invading species is generally attributed in the biological literature to Fisher (1937), as well as Skellam (1951). For further discussion, see Shigesada and Kawasaki (1997), Williamson (1996) and Drake et al. (1989). For an interesting use of the diffusion model in an economic model of an inshore/offshore fishery, see Clark (1990).

4. However, note that if interspecific competition in (5.3) takes the form of $\partial F_1/\partial n_2 < 0$ but $\partial F_2/\partial n_1 > 0$, then we have the special interspecific competition case of a *predator–prey relationship*.

5. In the above model there is more than one way in which this might occur. Strictly, the long-run solution of the model will simply show the resident species being displaced from its habitat, that is, it will relocate to a domain outside of its existing habitat. However, if the original habitat is unique, it is possible that the relocated species cannot survive, in which case population densities outside of the habitat fall below some minimum threshold level for survival. Alternatively, the species might survive in its new location, but the additional costs required to reach this new location and harvest the species are prohibitive. In the latter case, profits in equation (5.2) are also negatively related to the location, d, of the resident species, and fall to zero when d exceeds the domain of the existing habitat.

6. This type of interspecific competition, or Gause, model has been used on occasion in the bioeconomics literature (see Flaaten, 1991 and Clark, 1990). However, this literature does not generally distinguish the competing species as invader and resident species, nor does it use such models to calculate the economic impacts of an invasion along the lines suggested by equation (5.1).

7. Note that in transforming the n_i variables in (5.2) and (5.3) into the X_i variables we are assuming as a simplification that all functions are linear homogeneous of degree one.

8. However, such models have been used to examine post-invasion profits net of pest control costs (see Wilman, 1996).

9. Thus, the results presented later are predicated on the correction of the underlying property rights issue. Attempts are under way in the region to resolve this issue but have some way to go. See McConnell and Strand (1989) for a discussion of the theoretical aspects of this problem. It is also to be noted that sizeable welfare benefits could only accrue under the existing open access if prices were locally determined (downward-sloping demand curve) and fishing vessels were of differing efficiency levels.

10. We concentrate on the impact of *Mnemiopsis* on this measure of fishing activity but recognize that there will be an adjustment to the new equilibrium situation which may be quite important as well.

11. 'Escapement' refers to the biomass or numbers of adults that evade the harvest in a given year, enabling them to spawn.

12. We could equally show R^B as a function of the *Mnemiopsis* biomass too, that is, $R^B(S_t, P_t, Mn_t)$, where Mn refers to the aforementioned *Mnemiopsis* biomass. However, since we represent its influence on anchovy as a structural change, this influence is captured indirectly through changes in the function's parameters without introducing *Mnemiopsis* biomass directly into the equation. We achieve this result empirically by substituting out the *Mnemiopsis* term in the estimating procedure and replacing it with a dummy variable on spawning biomass.

13. A full description of the solution procedure, including the associated stability conditions, is provided in Knowler (1999).

14. If the function $V(S)$ is quasi-concave, in addition to the earlier requirement that the underlying profit function be separable in X and S, then the solution implied here is governed by a most rapid approach path or MRAP (Spence and Starrett, 1975). Providing that the initial condition is governed by $X_0 \geq S^*$, then the optimal steady-state harvest strategy (h^*) is given by $h^* = X^* - S^*$. If the initial condition is the reverse situation ($X_0 < S^*$), then the stock should be allowed to recover before commencing harvesting down to S^* in each subsequent time period.

15. Indeed, this approach is recommended even when each subperiod is of sufficient length (Gujarati, 1995).

16. The 2SLS procedure was used because of the possibility of simultaneous equation bias which might be anticipated because of the simultaneity implied by a predator–prey type of relationship. The possibility of additional ecosystem effects (for example, feedbacks) occurring only strengthens the case for using such an approach.

17. The estimate of q was obtained by estimating a harvest function of the form $h = X(1 - e^{-qE})$, which is often referred to as the discrete version of the Schaefer-Gordon harvest function (Clark, 1990). The final estimated equation was (with t-statistic in parentheses):

$$\ln[(X_t - h_t)/X_t] = -0.00319E_t$$
$$(-16.48)$$
$$\bar{R}^2 = 0.79, F = 47.10(1.12), DW = 1.56$$

where E is the level of fishing effort measured in vessels.

REFERENCES

Bishop, R.C. and K.C. Samples (1980), 'Sport and commercial fishing conflicts: a theoretical analysis', *Journal of Environmental Economics and Management*, **7**: 220–33.

Caddy, J. (1990), 'Contrast between recent fishery trends and evidence for nutrient enrichment in two large marine ecosystems: the Mediterranean and Black Seas', in K. Sherman, L.M. Alexander and B.D. Gold (eds), *Large Marine Ecosystems*, Washington, DC: AAAS Press: 137–47.

Clark, C.W. (1990), *Mathematical Bioeconomics*, 2nd edn, New York: John Wiley & Sons.

Cociasu, A., V. Diaconu, L. Popa, L. Buga, I. Nae, L. Dorogan and V. Malciu (1997), 'The nutrient stock of the Romanian shelf of the Black Sea during the last three decades', in E. Ozsoy and A. Mikaelyan (eds), *Sensitivity to Change: Black Sea, Baltic Sea and North Sea*, Dordrecht: Kluwer Academic Publishers: 49–64.

Conrad, J.M. (1995), 'Bioeconomic models of the fishery', in D. Bromley (ed.), *Handbook of Environmental Economics*, London: Blackwells: 405–32.

Dincer, A.C. (1992), 'A design study of Turkish Black Sea fishing vessels', MSc Thesis, Glasgow: Department of Naval Architecture and Ocean Engineering, University of Glasgow.

Drake, J.A., H.A. Mooney, F. di Castri, R.H. Groves, F.J. Kruger, M. Rejmánek and M. Williamson (eds) (1989), *Biological Invasions: A Global Perspective*, New York: John Wiley & Sons.

Fisher, R.A. (1937), 'The wave of advance of advantageous genes', *Annals of Eugenics*, **7**: 355–69.

Flaaten, O. (1991), 'Bioeconomics of sustainable harvest of competing species', *Journal of Environmental Economics and Management*, **20**: 163–80.

Freeman, A.M., III (1993), *The Measurement of Environmental and Resource Values*, Baltimore: Johns Hopkins University Press.

Group of Experts on the Scientific Aspects of Marine Environment Protection (GESAMP) (1994), 'Report of the first meeting of the GESAMP Working Group on opportunistic settlers and the problem of the Ctenophore *Mnemiopsis leidyi* in the Black Sea', Report of the Meeting, 10–14 January, Geneva.

Group of Experts on the Scientific Aspects of Marine Environment Protection (GESAMP) (1997), *Opportunistic Settlers and the Problem of the Ctenophore* Mnemiopsis leidyi *Invasion in the Black Sea*, Reports and Studies No. 58, London: International Maritime Organization (IMO)/United Nations Environment Programme (UNEP).

Gujarati, D.N. (1995), *Basic Econometrics*, 3rd edn, New York: McGraw-Hill International.

Hannesson, R. (1983), 'Optimal harvesting of ecologically interdependent fish species', *Journal of Environmental Economics and Management*, **10**: 329–45.

Iles, T.C. and R.J.H. Beverton (1998), 'Stock, recruitment and moderating processes in flatfish', *Journal of Sea Research*, **39**: 41–55.

Kideys, A.E. (1994), 'Recent dramatic changes in the Black Sea ecosystem: the reason for the sharp decline in Turkish anchovy fisheries', *Journal of Marine Systems*, **5**: 171–81.

Knowler, D. (1999), 'Valuing the commercial fishing benefits of joint environmental protection and fisheries management policies: a case study of the Black Sea', PhD Thesis, York: Environment Department, University of York.

Knowler, D., I. Strand and E. Barbier (1997), 'An economic analysis of Black Sea fisheries and environmental management', Final Report, Istanbul: Black Sea Environment Programme.

McConnell, K.E. and I. Strand (1989), 'Benefits from commercial fisheries when demand and supply depend on water quality', *Journal of Environmental Economics and Management*, **17**: 284–92.

OTA (1993), *Harmful Non-indigenous Species in the United States*, OTA-F-565 US Congress Office of Technology Assessment, Washington, DC: US Government Printing Office.

Perrings, C.A., C. Folke, and K.-G. Mäler (1992), 'The ecology and economics of biodiversity loss: the research agenda', *Ambio*, **21**(3): 201–11.

Prodanov, K., K. Mikhailov, G. Daskalov, K. Maxim, A. Chashchin, A. Arkhipov, V. Shlyakhov and E. Ozdamar (1995), *Environmental Management of Fish Resources in the Black Sea and Their Rational Exploitation*, Research Support Scheme of the Central European University No. 182 91/92, Soros Foundation.

Ragozin, D.L. and G. Brown Jr. (1985), 'Harvest policies and nonmarket valuation in a predator–prey system', *Journal of Environmental Economics and Management*, **12**: 155–68.

Ricker, W.E. (1975), 'Computation and interpretation of biological statistics of fish populations', Fisheries Resource Board of Canada Bulletin No. 191, Ottawa: Queen's Printer.

Shigesada, N. and K. Kawasaki (1997), *Biological Invasions: Theory and Practice*, Oxford: Oxford University Press.

Skellam, J.G. (1951) 'Random dispersal in theoretical populations', *Biometrika*, **38**: 196–218.

Spence, M. and D. Starrett (1975), 'Most rapid approach paths in accumulation problems', *International Economic Review*, **16**: 388–403.

Ströbele, W.J. and H. Wacker (1995), 'The economics of harvesting predator–prey systems', *Journal of Economics*, **61**(1): 65–81.

Tu, P.N.V. and E.A. Wilman (1992), 'A generalized predator–prey model: uncertainty and management', *Journal of Environmental Economics and Management*, **23**: 123–38.

UNEP (1990), *State of the Marine Environment in the Black Sea Region*, United Nations Environment Programme, Regional Seas Reports and Studies No. 124.

Wilen, J. and G. Brown Jr (1986), 'Optimal recovery paths for perturbations of trophic level bioeconomic systems', *Journal of Environmental Economics and Management*, **13**: 225–34.

Williamson, M. (1996), *Biological Invasions*, London: Chapman & Hall.

Wilman, E.A. (1996), 'Pests: sustained harvest versus eradication', *Journal of Environmental Management*, **46**: 139–47.

Zaitsev, Y.P. (1992), 'Recent changes in the trophic structure of the Black Sea', *Fisheries and Oceanography*, **1**(2): 180–89.

6. Weed invasions of Australian farming systems: from ecology to economics

Andrew R. Watkinson, Robert P. Freckleton and Peter M. Dowling*

1 INTRODUCTION

Many of the world's worst pest infestations result from the introduction of alien species. In the case of weeds of farming systems, examples include the invasion of *Bromus tectorum* into western North America (Mack, 1981), *Amarathus retroflexus* in Eastern Europe (Thomas and Annal, 1995) and the introduction of *Avena fatua* into Western Europe during the Iron Age. In Australia such invaders form a prominent component of the biota with approximately 11 per cent (1952 species) of the Australian flora being made up of alien species. In some states the proportion of the biota that is alien is considerably higher, with 21, 25 and 23 per cent of species in New South Wales, South Australia and Victoria, respectively, being introduced (Groves, 1997). These species can pose a considerable threat to both natural and managed ecosystems. In farming systems, in particular, introduced weeds are a major economic burden. In crops, the weeds *Chondrilla juncea*, *Heliotropium europaeum* and *Avena fatua* are estimated to cost A\$10m, A\$40m and A\$42m, respectively; in pastures *Echium plantagineum*, *Onopordum* spp. and *Vulpia* spp. are estimated to cost A\$30m, A\$20m and A\$30m, respectively (CSIRO, 1997). Where the economic state of farming may be somewhat precarious, particularly during droughts, profits are marginal and these losses are significant.

   In order to better manage such problems, a modelling approach has increasingly been adopted. Models have been developed, for example, to predict the population dynamics of *Nasella trichotoma* (Auld and Coote, 1981), *Avena fatua* (Pandey and Medd, 1991) and *Echium plantagineum* (Gregulis, 1999). A range of forms of analysis of such models exists that allows predictions of population dynamics and management at a variety of scales and levels. One approach to the analysis of weed population models is to use sensitivity analysis in order to target key areas of the life cycle where control is likely to be most effective (for example, Jordan et al., 1995). Alternatively, sensitivity analysis can tell us which parameters are most important in determining year-to-year fluctuations in population numbers and improve predictions of weed population sizes (Freckleton and Watkinson, 1998a, b). Furthermore, models can be used to predict the best strategies for control, allowing us, for example, to set threshold densities for spraying (Wallinga and van Oijen, 1997; Wallinga et al., 1999). Many of the population models that have been developed are based on simple difference equations, and this simplicity has allowed them to be combined with economic models (for example, Doyle et al., 1986; Cousens et al., 1986; Pandey and Medd, 1991; Jones and Medd, 1997). As we describe below, these models allow a full evaluation of the prospects for management both during the initial stages of weed invasion and after the weeds have become firmly established.

Apart from their use in management applications, ecological models can also be used to look at the underlying determinants of weed invasions. There are a range of ways in which models may contribute. Spatial models may be used to predict the rate at which plants spread throughout available habitat (Auld and Coote, 1980). Another approach is to employ sensitivity analysis in order to explore the key stages of the life cycle, determining population dynamics and the potential impact of the modification of life-history parameters on invasion. This approach is used commonly in the analysis of life histories, where sensitivity analysis of population models is used to identify key components of fitness (for example, de Kroon et al., 1986; Shea et al., 1993). Alternatively, comparative demography may be used to contrast the response of a suite of species to management (Lintell Smith et al., 1999); there are numerous possible applications for this type of analysis in the modelling of invasive weeds. These include exploring the life-history correlates of the success of invasions and subsequent population persistence, through identifying the model parameters that have the strongest influence on population change.

The aim of this chapter is to review the use of ecological models in predicting the abundance of invasive weeds of Australian farming systems. In particular, we concentrate on how models can be used strategically, to target key areas of the life cycle for control, and practically to feed into economic analysis of a range of management scenarios.

2 CASE STUDIES

We contrast two systems whose characteristics encompass the wider problems that face Australian agriculture. The first species (*Avena fatua*) is a weed in Europe, from where it was introduced. By contrast, the second species *Vulpia bromoides*, is not a weed where native. *A. fatua* is primarily a weed of cropping systems, whereas *V. bromoides* is a weed of pastures. In this section we outline the general biology and ecology of these species.

2.1   Wild Oats (*Avena fatua*) in Wheat

Avena fatua was introduced to Australia from Europe where, ironically, it was introduced with the spread of farming during the Iron Age. *Avena* spp. occur throughout the Australian grain-growing region, where they may occur on as many as two out of three farms (Medd, 1996a). The life cycle begins with germination of seed. Up to 60 per cent of seeds in the soil germinate in the autumn, although this may be staggered into a number of cohorts. Seeds may lie dormant in the soil for a number of years, so that a single outbreak may pose problems for a number of subsequent crops. *A. fatua* is extremely competitive, and greatly reduces yields through shading out the crop and removing nutrients. Plants produce as many as ~225 seeds each. These lack specialized dispersal mechansims, although seeds may be moved around through combining or soil cultivation.

Apart from the direct reduction in yields owing to competition between *A. fatua* and the crop, a number of other problems result from the presence of *A. fatua* (Medd, 1996b). It is possible, for example that the weed may act as reservoirs for disease such as take-all fungus (*Gaeumannomyces graminis*). Grain contamination with weed seed is also a problem when infestations are very high. Furthermore, in uncropped areas, or during the pasture or fallow phase of the rotation, high densities of *A. fatua* may generate a large fuel load and present a fire risk (Noble, 1991).

Control of the weed is mainly through herbicide application. *A. fatua* may be controlled within-season through applications of either pre- or post-emergence herbicides, the former generally being the more effective (Nietschke and Medd, 1996). When the rotation includes either a pasture or winter fallow phase there exists an opportunity to significantly reduce seed banks through depletion of the seed bank by weed emergence, and 'spray-topping' (with glyphosate or paraquat) prevents re-seeding. The development of resistance to class A herbicides may, however, necessitate modifications to current strategies (ibid.). A range of cultural control mechanisms also exist, for example through cultivation, crop stubble burning and improved sanitation leading to decreased immigration of weed seed into the crop (Nietschke, 1996).

2.2   Silvergrass (*Vulpia bromoides*) in Annual Pastures

Vulpia bromoides is one of a number of species of the genus *Vulpia* that have become a problem in annual pasture systems. The genus *Vulpia* is of Mediterranean origin and *Vulpia bromoides* occurs in pastures in Spain and Portugal at low levels, where it is not regarded as a problem (A. Sheppard, personal communication). *Vulpia* spp. were probably introduced to Australia during the end of the last century as a contaminant of seed or forage, and have spread widely throughout southern Australia. *Vulpia bromoides* appears to be the commoner of the species and may occur in as many as 75 per cent of pastures where *Vulpia* is present (data quoted in Dowling, 1996).

Like *A. fatua*, *V. bromoides* is a winter annual, producing seeds at the beginning of summer that carry over until autumn when they germinate. Very few seeds survive longer than a few months in the soil, however, so in contrast to *Avena*, *Vulpia* does not tend to produce a persistent seedbank. Following a period of slow growth during the autumn and winter, flowering occurs in spring. Although *V. bromoides* may provide some useful forage for livestock in the early stages of the growing season, heavy infestations present serious problems since the forage produced late in the season is of very low nutritional value, and because the seeds produced by the weed become tangled in the wool of sheep and may even cause physical injuries to livestock.

Long-term management of *Vulpia* is difficult in pastures that are dominated by annuals and where the perennial component is low. The problem of controlling *Vulpia* is compounded by the high seed production of the species which allows fast population recovery in the years following herbicide application, as well as high rates of compensatory growth of survivors following herbicidal control (Dowling et al., 1995). Results on the chemical control of *Vulpia* have been mixed (Bowran and Wallace, 1996). The most commonly used herbicide is simazine, which can potentially provide extremely high rates of plant kill (Leys et al., 1991). Cultural control may be effected through strategic grazing, fertilizer application or through cultivation. The overriding impression, however, is that control of *Vulpia* is problematic unless a high perennial component in the pasture may be maintained, which is generally difficult in the face of grazing or drought conditions (Dowling et al., 1996).

2.3 Key Questions

The key problems facing the study of the invasion of Australian agriculture by the species are as follows. In the case of *A. fatua* we need to understand the key parameters of the life cycle that determine population numbers, and to highlight areas of the life cycle at which controls may be effective. Furthermore, detailed economic predictions of the outcome of control are required. In the case of *Vulpia* the problems are to determine why the species is able to invade pasture systems: in particular, how does the composition of the pasture, and the occurrence of drought conditions affect the invasion and subsequent dynamics of this species? How does this affect approaches to management? Below we review how simple ecological approaches may be used to provide answers to such questions.

3   APPROACHES

The approach to modelling the two systems is composed of three elements: (i) an ecological demographic model, describing the changes in numbers of plants from year to year; (ii) some demographic measure of the impacts of management (or other conditions, such as drought) on the parameters of this model; (iii) combining (i) and (ii) to predict dynamics as management and environmental conditions are varied, including economic information when available. In this section we outline the formulation of the ecological models for the dynamics of the two systems.

3.1   Single Species Population Dynamics

The models for both weed species are based on difference equations that predict population size next year as a function of the population size this year. The model for *A. fatua* considers the dynamics of plants split into three cohorts, corresponding to three flushes of staggered seed germination and seedling emergence (Figure 6.1). In total, a proportion δ of the seed in the seed pool emerges, with proportions 0.3, 0.6 and 0.1, respectively, joining cohorts 1, 2 and 3. There is differential survival of seedlings following emergence, with the proportion surviving (γ) varying across the three cohorts. Later-emerging weeds will tend to be smaller than early-emerging weeds, hence there is differential reproduction (R seeds are produced per plant) across each of the $i = 1...3$ cohorts. A proportion κ of the seed produced survives ('new seed') and enters the seed pool. Of the non-germinating seed that remains in the seed pool, a proportion ψ survives per annum.

The overall dynamics of the species may be summarized in one simple equation that models the change in size of the seedbank (Pandey and Medd, 1991; Jones and Medd, 1997):

$$SB(t+1) = SB(t) - SR(t) - M(t) + N(t) \qquad (6.1)$$

The size of the seedbank (*SB*) at time $t + 1$ is a function of its size at time t as well as the seed lost through recruitment (*SR*) and mortality (*M*) and new seed added through reproduction at time t (*N*). Based on the life-cycle diagram in Figure 6.1, and equation (6.1) we can develop a model for predicting total population size as a function of population size in previous years through a series of simple equations that consider the reporduction of each of the

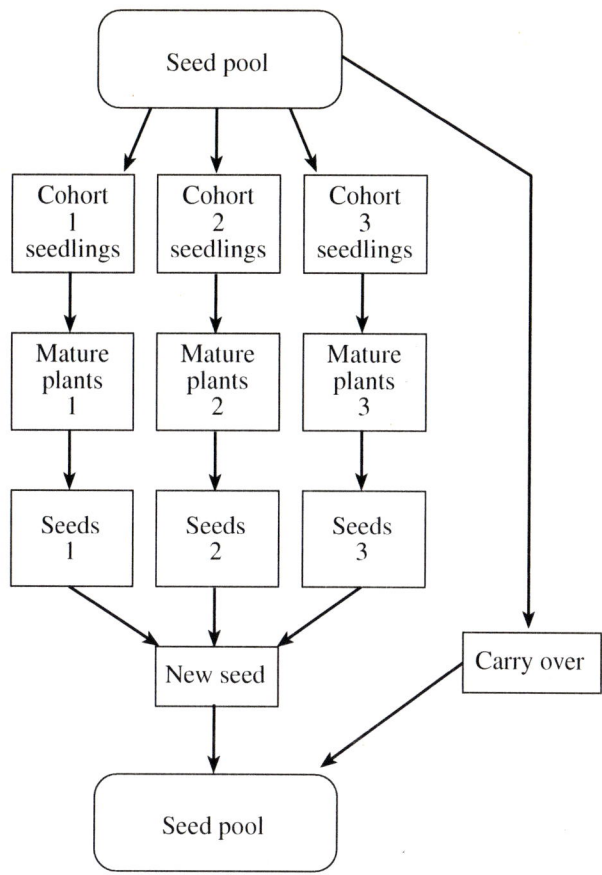

Figure 6.1   Schematic outline of the model for the population dynamics of
Avena fatua

three cohorts separately (based on Jones and Medd, 1997). Here S is the
density of seedlings, W is the density of adult plants (for the $i = 1...3$
cohorts), R is seed production by the whole population, C is the carry-over of
seed in the seedbank and other parameters are as defined above.

$S_{i=1...3}(t) = \delta_i SB(t)$: the density of seedlings emerging from the
  seedbank   (6.2a)

$W_{i=1...3}(t) = \gamma_i S_i(t)$: the survival of seedlings to adults plants   (6.2b)

$R_t = \sum_{i=1}^{3} s_{m,i} W_i(t)[1 + a_i W_i(t)]^{-1}$: the total seed output of the adult
  plants, as a function of density   (6.2c)

$N(t) = \kappa R(t)$: the number of viable seeds in the seed rain   (6.2d)

$C(t) = \psi(1-\delta)SB(t)$: the annual carry-over of seeds in the seed
bank   (6.2e)

$SB(t+1) = N(t) + C(t)$: the seedbank size determined by carry-
over and seed rain   (6.2f)

An important component of the model is the seed production submodel
(equation 6.2c). Since plants compete for a finite amount of resources, seed
production does not increase inexorably with plant density, but approaches an
asymptotic level. This is modelled through a classic hyperbolic yield-density
equation (Watkinson, 1980). The two parameters of this equation are s_m, the
maximal mean seed production of an individual plant, and a, a parameter that
scales the strength of the reduction in mean seed production per plant with

*Table 6.1   Summary of the parameters and state variables employed in the
              model for the population dynamics and management of* Avena

---

Parameters

δ	*proportion of seeds germinating
γ	*plant survivorship
s_m	*maximal mean seed production per plant
a	*intraspecific competition parameter
κ	seed rain survival
ψ	dormant seed survivorship
Y_m	maximal weed free wheat yield
σ	crop density
θ	marginal yield loss
ρ	maximal yield loss

State variables

$S(t)$	*seedling density
$W(t)$	*mature weed density
$R(t)$	*seed rain
$N(t)$	new seed recruited to seed bank
$C(t)$	seed bank carry-over
$L(t)$	land-use category

Note: * Indicates that separate values are adopted for each of the three cohorts.

Source: Jones and Medd (1997).

increasing density. Note that the parameters of equation (6.2c) are assumed to vary across the cohorts, and it is also assumed that seed production declines when seed kill control is applied. The model parameters and definitions are summarized in Table 6.1

Equations (6.2a–f) may be used to predict weed plant or seed densities at any point in the life cycle, from a given starting density and as a function of management. Alternatively, by combining equations (6.2a–f) we can predict the density of seeds as a single equation:

$$SB(t+1) = SB(t) \sum_{i=1}^{3} \phi_i [1 + \mu_i SB(t)]^{-1} + \psi(1-\delta)SB(t) \qquad (6.3)$$

where $\phi_i = \kappa_i s_{m,i} \delta_i \gamma_i$ and $\mu_i = a_i \delta_i \gamma_i$. To solve equation (6.3) to predict the equilibrium density of weeds, we set $SB(t+1) = SB(t)$. Owing to the presence of the non-linear competition function which is parameterized separately for each of the cohorts (equation (6.2c)) this solution is too large to comfortably fit on a single page.

The incorporation of management into the model takes four distinct forms (Jones and Medd, 1997). 'Plant kill' is the removal of plants with herbicides, while 'seed kill' is the mortality of seeds through spray-topping. These two control measures may then be combined. The other options for control are winter fallow and the introduction of a sorghum crop into the rotation. Costs associated with the various management options are listed in Table 6.2.

In order to be able to analyse the economics of controlling the weed, it is necessary to be able to predict the damage that the crop inflicts in economic terms. This is achieved through a yield model (Jones and Medd, 1997):

$$Y = Y_m \left[1 - W(\sigma\theta + W\rho^{-1})^{-1} \right] \qquad (6.4)$$

Here the value of the crop, Y, is related to its maximum potential value, Y_m and weed density, W, through a hyperbolic function where σ is the crop density, θ is the marginal yield loss as the weed density approaches zero and ρ is an estimate of the maximum yield loss of a weedy crop relative to a weed-free crop.

The density of weed seeds in the seedbank is one state variable used in the model for the dynamics of *Avena* populations subject to management. In this model, because land use is not constant, but may change from one year to the next, the second important state variable is the land use in a given year. This is a discrete variable which may take one of 14 values (see Table 1 in Jones and Medd, 1997). Owing to rotational constraints, there are rules governing which forms of land use may be juxtaposed. In broad terms, the options for management include winter fallow, cropping with sorghum, and cropping with winter wheat with plant and/or seed kill. It is assumed that land use prior

Table 6.2   *Costs and profit margins associated with the integrated*
                management of wild oats

Measurement	Value
Wheat grain price ($A/t)	133.00
Sorghum grain price ($A/t)	139.00
Weed-free wheat yield	
First year following fallow	3.5
Second year following fallow	2.8
Third year following fallow	2.1
Sorghum yield (t/ha)	3.75
Phytotoxic yield reduction (%)	
Plant kill	1.0
Seed kill	2.0
Wheat variable cost ($A/ha)	118.38
Sorghum variable cost ($A/ha)	154.04
Winter fallow variable cost ($A/ha)	31.08
Herbicide rate plant kill, tri-allate (L/ha)	2.0
Herbicide rate seed kill, flamprop-methyl (L/ha)	4.5
Herbicide rate, atrazine (L/ha)	3.6
Herbicide and application cost ($A/ha)	
Plant kill	25.40
Seed Kill	34.90

Source: Jones and Medd (1997).

to the analysis was continuous wheat resulting in a build-up of the population
of wild oats (initial seed bank density = 2000 m^{-2}).

3.2   Multispecies Pasture Model

The model we have analysed (Freckleton et al., 2000) is based on a field
experiment that looked at the population dynamics of *Vulpia bromoides* in a
simple annual pasture mix of *Lolium rigidum* (ryegrass) and *Trifolium
subterraneum* (subterranean clover). In this case the model for population
dynamics requires a difference equation for both the numbers of mature
plants and seeds in the seedbank of each of the three species, that is,

$$N_{i=1...3}(t+1) = \lambda_i N_i(t) \left[1 + \sum_{j=1}^{3} \alpha_{ij} N_j(t) \right]^{-1} + v_i S_i(t) \qquad (6.5a)$$

$$S_{i=1\ldots3}(t+1) = \lambda_i' N_i(t) \left[1 + \sum_{j=1}^{3} \alpha_{ij} N_j(t)\right]^{-1} + v_i' S_i(t) \qquad (6.5b)$$

There are three basic groups of parameters in this model: λ and λ' measure the per capita rate of change in numbers of mature plants and seeds, respectively, owing to seed production at the vegetative stage; v and v', respectively, measure the recruitment of plants from and persistence of seeds within the seed bank; and competition (for example resulting from shading or competition for water and other nutrients) between any pair of species i and j is measured by a parameter α_{ij}, which is the per capita reduction in population growth. Note that when i and j are different, α_{ij} refers to interspecific competition (that is, competition between species), but when they are the same the parameter measures intraspecific competition (that is, competition within the species). For the three species mixture there are, therefore, nine (that is, 3×3) competition coefficients.

This model may be parameterized in one of two ways. As in the case of *Avena*, we can break down the life cycle into its various components and combine a series of submodels to derive the overall dynamics of the system. Alternatively, one may fit the models defined by equations (6.5a) and (6.5b) directly to data on the counts of numbers of plants and seeds. We have combined these approaches, using counts of numbers of plants over five years, in conjunction with more detailed data on plant survival and seed germination when herbicides are applied and under drought conditions.

Equations (6.5a) and (6.5b) may be solved to yield the equilibrium density of species i as a function of the equilibrium densities of all three species, that is,

$$N_i^* = \hat{\lambda}_i N_i^* \left[1 + \sum_{j=1}^{3} \alpha_{ij} N_j^*\right]^{-1}$$

The new parameter is the net finite rate of population increase, $\hat{\lambda} = \lambda + v(1-v')^{-1}\lambda'$. This equation may be rearranged to yield:

$$N_i^* = \frac{\hat{\lambda}_i - 1}{\alpha_{ii}} - \sum_{i \neq j}^{3} \frac{\alpha_{ij}}{\alpha_{ii}} N_j^* \qquad (6.6)$$

An overall expression for the equilibrium density may then be obtained by substituting the other equilibrium densities into equation (6.6) and rearranging. This process may be repeated for each of the three species. When this is done, we can analyse the model in order to ask whether it is possible for all species to coexist (that is, are each of the N^* positive?) and if so, is the system stable?

While the equilibrium analysis deals with constant environmental conditions, in reality factors such as drought and herbicide applications impact considerably on population dynamics. Using field-derived estimates of the effects of droughts and herbicides on these species, we therefore explored a stochastic version of the model where the frequency of droughts and herbicide applications were varied.

4   IMPLEMENTATION

4.1   Strategic Modelling

The models described above may be used to ask some basic questions concerning the invasion of these species. While the equilibrium models are, in a sense, unrepresentative of the real world, they are nevertheless important. In the case of *A. fatua*, the equilibrium model allows us to explore the determinants of abundance and invasion under fixed management strategies, such as continuous winter wheat. For *V. bromoides*, we can use the basic model to define the underlying community structure, in order to set a baseline for understanding the long-term dynamics in a stochastic environment.

In the context of analysing the determinants of biological invasions, one thing we can do is to perform a sensitivity analysis of the models in order to determine to which parameters population size or growth is most variable. To do this we define the sensitivity of a model prediction (P, for example, population size or change in population size) to some parameter p as:

$$\sigma(p) = \partial \log P / \partial \log p \qquad (6.7)$$

Defined this way the sensitivity measures the relative effect of p on the model prediction. If $\sigma(p) = 1$ then the model prediction scales in exact proportion to changing the parameter value, whereas if $\sigma(p) > 1$ or $\sigma(p) < 1$ then model predictions scale, respectively, in greater than or less than proportion to changing the parameter. It is worth noting that this index does not tell us that a given parameter *is* important in determining invasion or persistence, as it does not include information on how that parameter *does* vary. It is nevertheless a useful indicator.

We can analyse model sensitivity under two conditions, first at equilibrium and second as the weed density becomes low (that is, tends to zero). This gives us important information on how the likely importance of different life-history variables or processes change, moving from the initial invasion to establishment. Figure 6.2 shows these sensitivity values for *A. fatua* (a) and for *V. bromoides* (b).

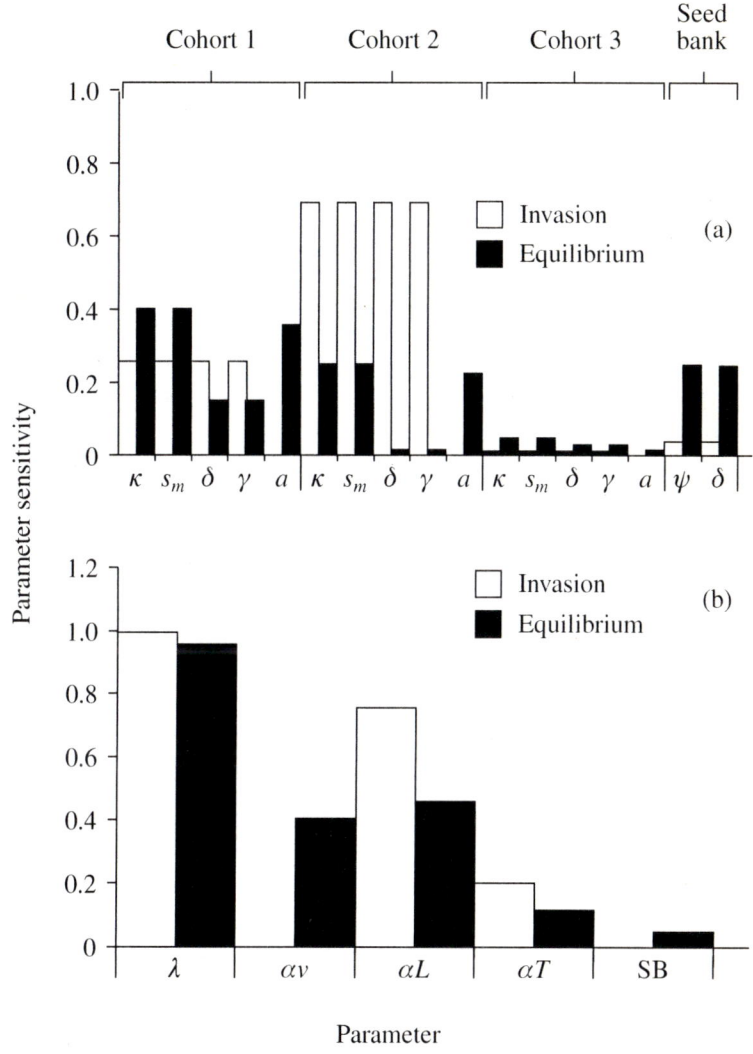

Note: Parameter definitions for *Avena* are listed in Table 6.1 and those for *Vulpia* are given in the text.

Figure 6.2   *Sensitivity analysis of the models for (a)* Avena fatua *and (b)*
              Vulpia bromoides

In the invasion phase of the population dynamics of *A. fatua*, the highest sensitivities are recorded for the seed production and survival parameters of cohort 2, as well as the plant survival parameter for cohort 2. These sensitivities are more than double those of the first cohort. The reason for this is that the mortality of cohort 1 plants is high, and hence these contribute less to population growth than the plants of the second cohort. On the other hand, at equilibrium, when plant densities are high, the highest sensitivities are recorded for the seed survival and production parameters of cohort 1, with these being higher than those of cohort 2. The reason for this is that, under conditions of zero net population growth, the larger maximal mean seed production per plant of cohort 1 contributes more to population growth than that of cohort 2. Importantly, while the sensitivities of plant survival (γ) and seed survival (κ), seed production (s_m) and germination (δ) parameters are the same during the invasion phase of population dynamics, at equilibrium they differ. At equilibrium, the sensitivities for plant survival and seed germination are much lower than those of the others. This is because these two parameters appear in the model (equation (6.3)) in an essentially compensatory way: both parameters affect μ and ϕ such that if ϕ, the maximal mean per capita rate of population change is altered, this is compensated for by a change in the per capita effects of competition, μ. The sensitivity of the model to the seedbank is effectively nil in the invasion phase of population dynamics, but increases at equilibrium.

In the multispecies model of the invasion of *V. bromoides*, the contribution of seed production (λ) and the competitive effect of the other annual grass, *Lolium* (α_{LV}), are the most sensitive parameters. The sensitivity of the population dynamics to intraspecific competition (α_{VV}) and to the seedbank parameters is much weaker. In this case, broadly the same is true at the projected three-species equilibrium. The main difference is that there is also a high sensitivity to intraspecific competition at the higher densities. The sensitivity of population growth to the seedbank parameters is still weak, however.

What this analysis allows us to do is to build up a picture of how key parameters affect the invasion and subsequent persistence of these invasive weeds. This can lead to some general strategic observations and recommendations on how to manage these species. In general terms the common factors for both species are the importance of population regeneration through seed production, seed survival and subsequent plant survival, compared with the secondary importance of the seed pool for both species. In practical terms the model highlights the areas of the life cycle towards which control may be best directed, and when. In the case of *A. fatua*, plant kill is highly sensitive in the initial stages of invasion, but less so at equilibrium. What the analysis highlights is the need for a flexible management approach for this species: while plant kill may be effective at very low densities, seed kill will be more effective at high densities. In the case of *Vulpia*, competition with *Lolium* is likely to be an important area at which control can be directed. In both cases, the lack of sensitivity of population dynamics to the seedbank, particularly as population sizes are reduced moving from the equilibrium back to the invasion phase of dynamics, means that reducing inputs of seed to the seed pool in the short term is of importance, as a build-up of seed in the longer term does not occur.

4.2   Management and Economics

The baseline dynamics of *Vulpia* in mixtures with *Lolium* and *Trifolium* are outlined in Figure 6.3a. The equilibrium mixture of the three species is

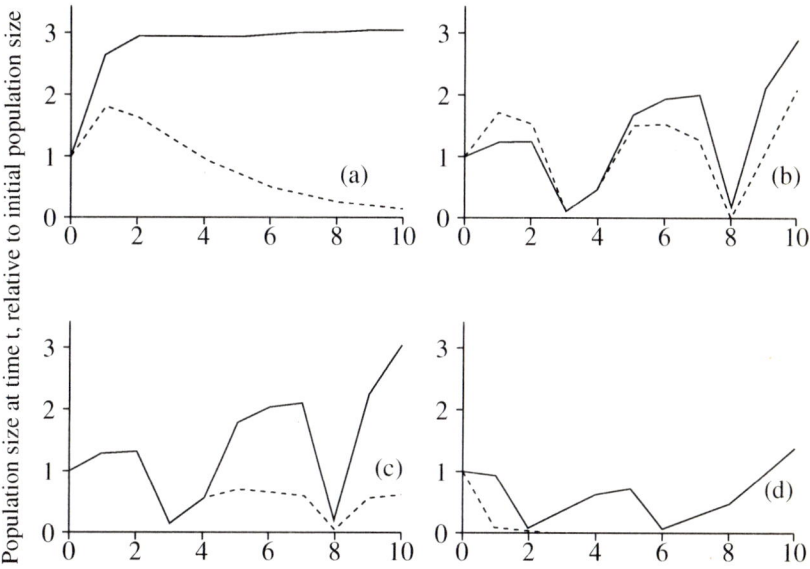

Notes:
(a) The effects of initial density on population establishment in a constant environment; (b) the effects of initial density on population establishment when periodic droughts occur. In (a) and (b) *Vulpia* invaded from a high density (solid line) or a low density (dashed line). (c) Effects of re-sowing pastures with *Lolium* following droughts on *Vulpia* population sizes (dashed line – pastures re-sown with *Lolium*; solid line – not re-sown). (d) Herbicidal control of *Vulpia* populations (solid line – herbicides applied periodically; dashed line – herbicides applied every year).

Figure 6.3   *Predicted population dynamics of* Vulpia bromoides *within annual pastures*

unstable with the consequence that a founder effect exists. Depending on the initial relative densities of *Vulpia* and *Lolium*, communities contain one or other of these species, but not both. As shown in Figure 6.3a, for example, *Vulpia* is able to invade only when its initial density is high enough. The *Trifolium* interacts only weakly with the two grasses, and hence its densities are affected only a little by the dynamics of the grasses. At first sight, therefore, it appears that the invasion of *Vulpia* into pastures dominated by *Trifolium* and *Lolium* may be difficult as it would need to exceed a critical density in order to invade. If the environment were constant, then this would be the case. In reality, however, the environment is not constant and perturbations of a range of forms occur. In particular, using data from 1993–94, when a severe drought occurred, we have shown that periodic severe droughts (long-term records show that severe droughts occur with a per annum frequency of 0.1–0.2) greatly facilitate the invasion of *Vulpia* (Freckleton et al., 2000). In Figure 6.3b, for example, where periodic droughts occur, *Vulpia* is able to invade from densities where it is eliminated under constant environmental conditions.

The strategic modelling of the determinants of invasion of *Vulpia* lead to some clear management recommendations. Given that the invasion of *Vulpia* is determined by an interaction between the probability of drought and the effects of competition with *Lolium*, one clear recommendation is that management of the pasture is essential following droughts. As illustrated in Figure 6.3c, one option is to re-sow the pasture with *Lolium*. Doing so prevents the invasion of *Vulpia* if *Lolium* is re-sown at a density higher than some critical density. This recommendation may be difficult or impossible to implement, however, as farms are likely to be under considerable economic pressure following droughts and the financial resources required for such actions may not be available. The second important recommendation is that herbicide application is likely to be ineffective, unless accompanied by some other management action. As shown in Figure 6.3d, *Vulpia* populations recover very quickly following the application of herbicides. One solution is to apply herbicides every year. Unfortunately as both species are affected by the herbicide, albeit *Vulpia* more so than *Lolium*, this eliminates not only *Vulpia*, but also *Lolium*.

The further information that is available on the economics of *Avena* means that some very detailed management prescriptions are possible. Jones and Medd (1997) employed this information in conjunction with the population model to predict the optimal cropping sequence. Formally this is achieved by determining the sequence of management decisions that maximizes the net present value of net returns for one hectare of land over a 15-year time horizon. This is achieved by using a recursive equation that is solved backwards:

$$V(t)[SB(t), L(t)] = \max_{k}\{\pi[SB(t), L(t)] + \beta V(t+1)[SB(t+1), L(t+1)]\} \quad (6.8)$$

$V(t)(\cdot)$ is the maximum present value of net returns from year t to the end of the planning horizon (that is, 15 years), $L(t)$ is the previous land use, k is the decision variable, $\pi(.)$ is the immediate return from the k th decision, and β is the discount factor. In their model, Jones and Medd explored three forms of land use (wheat, sorghum, fallow) together with two forms of herbicide control (conventional herbicidal control of plants and spray-topping).

In analysing this model, Jones and Medd (1997) looked at three control scenarios which were constrained in different ways. These were (i) no access to seed kill (spray-topping) or to sorghum; (ii) access to both seed kill and sorghum; (iii) access to seed kill tactic, but not sorghum. As shown in Table 6.3a, the optimal forms of control under any of the three scenarios require an integrated form of management that mixes several control options rather than just a single approach. In the case of scenarios (i) and (iii), the optimal approaches involve combining fallow years into the rotation, as well as varying the frequency of application of herbicides. When sorghum is available in scenario (ii), the optimal strategy also combines this into the rotation. The net present values for the three scenarios (Table 6.3b) highlight that an integrated approach, where a suite of rotational options is available, is compatible with high profitability and low rates of herbicide application.

5   DISCUSSION

The invasion of weeds into new areas involves a number of stages. These include the transport of the species, the initial establishment and then the subsequent spread and domination of the species. The analyses we have presented here deal with the latter aspects of invasion, namely how weeds invade systems, the determinants of their subsequent domination and options for management.

The degree to which population dynamics in Australia mirror patterns of dynamics in Europe varies between the two species. In the case of *Avena*, the broad characteristics of population dynamics would appear to be generally comparable between the two continents. Some of the details differ, however. For example, the finite rate of population increase (λ: the mean rate of increase of populations from low densities) for the populations in Australia is ~3.8 (with no herbicide application) for the model of Jones and Medd (1997). This compares with values for *Avena* growing in winter wheat in the UK quoted by Cousens and Mortimer (1995): 5 to 12.5 (when herbicide is applied; Cousens and Mortimer, 1995, p. 214); and 96.7 reduced to 13.2 when herbicides were applied (Mortimer, 1987). It would therefore appear that the

Table 6.3   *(a) Optimal decisions for three control scenarios and (b) Net*
              present values ($A) and cumulative herbicide applications (kg/ha)

(a)

Year	Scenario (i)[1]	Scenario (ii)[2]	Scenario (iii)[3]
1	Fallow	Fallow	Fallow
2	Wheat (plant kill)	Sorghum	Wheat (plant+seed kill)
3	Wheat (plant kill)	Fallow	Wheat (plant+seed kill)
4	Fallow	Sorghum	Fallow
5	Wheat (plant kill)	Fallow	Wheat (plant kill)
6	Wheat (plant kill)	Wheat (no control)	Wheat (plant kill)
7	Fallow	Wheat (no control)	Fallow
8	Wheat (plant kill)	Fallow	Wheat (no control)
9	Wheat (plant kill)	Wheat (no control)	Wheat (no control)
10	Fallow	Wheat (no control)	Fallow
11	Wheat (plant kill)	Fallow	Wheat (no control)
12	Wheat (plant kill)	Wheat (no control)	Wheat (no control)
13	Fallow	Wheat (no control)	Fallow
14	Wheat (plant kill)	Fallow	Wheat (no control)
15	Wheat (plant kill)	Sorghum	Wheat (no control)

(b)

	NPV	Herbicide
Scenario (i)	410	8.0
Scenario (ii)	1291	3.6
Scenario (iii)	1038	4.1

Notes:
1. No access to seed kill or sorghum.
2. Access to both seed kill and sorghum.
3. Access to seed kill but not sorghum.

Source: Jones and Medd (1997).

finite rate of population increase is considerably lower in Australia compared
with the UK. This may be a consequence of lower productivity leading to
lowered seed production under Australian conditions. In other ways the demography of the species in the two systems is comparable, however, with
levels of seed dormancy and patterns of emergence being similar.

The population dynamics of *Vulpia* spp. in Australian conditions are different in a number of respects from their counterparts in Europe. While detailed information on the dynamics of *V. bromoides* under European conditions is not available, the closely related *V. fasiculata* and *V. ciliata* have been studied extensively, the former being a weed in South Australia. In Europe, these species tend to be confined mainly to sand dunes or marginal heathland habitat (Watkinson, 1978; Watkinson et al., 1998). They do not occur extensively as they do in Australia. The finite rate of increase for *Vulpia* populations in Europe has been estimated as ~2–5 (Watkinson, 1990; Watkinson et al., 2000). This is much lower than the range of 50–250 recorded for populations of *V. bromoides* in Australia. Apart from determining the rate of population growth in terms of the density of plants, there are important implications of this high finite rate of increase of *V. bromoides* under Australian conditions for population (spatial) spread and hence invasion. The rate of population spread is proportional to the square root of the finite rate of population increase ($\sim \sqrt{\lambda}$; Fisher, 1937; Skellam, 1951). Since the finite rate of increase of populations under Australian conditions is at least 10–100 times larger than under UK conditions, we would expect populations to spread up to 10 times faster under Australian conditions, not accounting for differences between the dispersal functions in the two continents.

The success of these models we have reviewed lies in the ability to link mathematical models to field data. We can achieve this link in two ways: in the case of *Avena fatua* this was done by breaking the life cycle down into its various components and generating a submodel for each (Figure 6.1). Alternatively, the models for the other two species in the pastures containing *V. bromoides* were generated, in the main, by fitting equations (6.5a) and (6.5b) directly to census data. This regression-based approach to generating community models has been employed, for example, by Rees et al. (1996) and Law et al. (1997) and has the advantage that the data required are relatively easy to obtain: all that are required are counts of plants over time. Furthermore, while other methods such as plant removal experiments are unsuitable for estimating the strength of competition between species in the real world (Pacala and Levin, 1997), the modelling approach is robust (Freckleton and Watkinson, ms in review). There exists, therefore, a great potential for generating realistic models for comparatively complex communities such as annual and perennial pastures. The disadvantage of this more phenomenological approach is that we lose the details of population dynamics that may be important in modelling control. For some applications, such as *A. fatua*, the mechanistic approach may therefore be more desirable. Alternatively, one may combine approaches as we did in the case of *V. bromoides*, where some detailed data on plant survival and seed production to droughts and herbicides were used to include these effects.

The analyses we have presented are based on simple ecological models. More complex models for the dynamics of arable weeds have been developed (for example, Gonzalez-Andujar and Perry, 1995). These, however, are based on simple models of the sort presented above. While more complex models are useful in analysing the detailed ecology of invasive weeds, and can identify when factors such as spatial heterogeneity impact significantly on dynamics, they have the disadvantages that they are considerably more difficult to parameterize and, importantly, in a multidisciplinary context such as combining with economic and land-use models, they are highly intensive requiring a great deal more computational effort.

Additionally, the predictions of these simple models can be shown to be robust: in the case of *A. fatua*, sensitivity analysis shows that the predictions of the optimal control strategies are unaffected by varying model parameters within quite wide limits (Jones and Medd, 1997); the prediction that the *Vulpia* population will increase in response to droughts is mainly a function of the large finite rate of increase of this species compared with other species. In the future these models can be further developed to explore the potential for other management strategies such as biocontrol of wild oats or the effects of grazing and other pasture species on the dynamics of *Vulpia*.

NOTE

*   We should like to thank Randall Jones for his comments on a previous version of this chapter. This work was funded in part by Natural Environment Research Council (NERC) grant GR3/11458 to ARW. RPF and ARW would also like to acknowledge financial support of the Cooperative Research Centre (CRC) for Weed Management Systems in funding visits to Australia as well as NSW Agriculture for hospitality.

REFERENCES

Auld, B.A. and B.G. Coote (1980), 'A model of a spreading plant population', *Oikos*, **34**: 287–92.
Auld, B.A. and B.G. Coote (1981), 'Prediction of pasture invasion by *Nasella trichotoma* (Gramineae) in south east Australia', *Protection Ecology*, **3**: 271–7.
Bowran, D. and A. Wallace (1996), 'Chemical weed management of *Vulpia*', *Plant Protection Quarterly*, **11**: S211–S212.
Cousens, R., C.J. Doyle, B.J. Wilson and G.W. Cussans (1986), 'Modelling the economics of controlling *Avena fatua* in winter wheat', *Pesticide Science*, **17**: 1–12.
Cousens, R. and A.M. Mortimer (1995), *Dynamics of Weed Populations*, Cambridge: Cambridge University Press.
Commonwealth Scientific and Industrial Research Organization (CSIRO) (1997), URL: http://www.ento.csiro.au/research/rr95–97/weedm_tempweeds.html.

de Kroon, H., A. Plaisier, J. van Groenendael and H. Caswell (1986), 'Elasticity: the relative contribution of demographic parameters to population growth rate', *Ecology*, **67**: 1427–31.

Dowling, P.M. (1996), 'The ecology of *Vulpia*', *Plant Protection Quarterly*, **11**: S204–S206.

Dowling, P.M., D.R. Kemp, D.L. Michalk, T.A. Klein and G.D. Millar (1996), 'Perennial grass response to seasonal rests in naturalised pastures of central New South Wales', *Rangeland Journal*, **18**: 309–26.

Dowling, P.M., B. Verbeek, D. Lemerle and A.R. Leys (1995), 'Rapid regeneration of *Vulpia* (*Vulpia bromoides*) in pastures', in Proceedings of 15th Asian-Pacific Weed Society Conference, Tsukuba, Japan: 497–500.

Doyle, C.J., R. Cousens and S.R. Moss (1986), 'A model of the economics of controlling *Alpecurus myosuroides* Huds. in winter wheat', *Crop Protection*, **5**: 143–50.

Fisher, R.A. (1937), 'The wave of advance of advantageous genes', *Annals of Eugenics*, **7**: 255–369.

Freckleton, R.P. and A.R. Watkinson (1998a), 'How does temporal variability affect predictions of weed population numbers?', *Journal of Applied Ecology*, **35**: 340–44.

Freckleton, R.P. and A.R. Watkinson (1998b), 'Predicting the determinants of weed abundance: a model for the population dynamics of *Chenopodium album* in sugar beet', *Journal of Applied Ecology*, **35**: 904–20.

Freckleton, R.P. and A.R. Watkinson (MS), 'On detecting and measuring competition in spatially structured plant communities', *Ecology Letters*, in review.

Freckleton, R.P., A.R. Watkinson, P.M. Dowling and A.R. Leys (2000), 'Determinants of the abundance of invasive annual weeds: community structure and non-equilibrium dynamics', *Proceedings of the Royal Society*, series B, in press.

Gonzalez-Andujar, J.L. and J.N. Perry (1995), 'Models for the herbicidal control of the seed bank of *Avena sterilis*: the effects of spatial and temporal heterogeneity and of dispersal', *Journal of Applied Ecology*, **32**: 578–87.

Gregulis, K.A. (1999), 'The comparative population dynamics of *Echium plantagineum* L. between its native and invaded ranges', PhD Thesis, Australian National University, Canberra.

Groves, R.H. (1997), *Recent Incursions of Weeds to Australia, 1971–1995*, Canberra, Australia: CRC for Weed Management Systems.

Jones, R. and R. Medd (1997), 'Economic analysis of integrated management of wild oats involving fallow, herbicide and crop rotational options', *Australian Journal of Experimental Agriculture*, **37**: 683–91.

Jordan, N., D.A. Mortensen, D.M. Prenzlow and K.C. Cox (1995), 'Simulation analysis of crop rotation effects on weed seedbanks', *American Journal of Botany*, **82**: 390–98.

Law, R., T. Herben and U. Dieckmann (1997), 'Non-manipulative estimates of competition coefficients in a montane grassland community', *Journal of Ecology*, **85**: 505–17.

Leys, A.R., B. Plater and W.J. Lill (1991), 'Response of *Vulpia* (*Vulpia bromoides* (L.) S.F. Gray and *Vulpia myuros* (L.) C.C. Gmelin) and subterranean clover to rate and time of application of simazine', *Australian Journal of Experimental Agriculture*, **31**: 785–91.

Lintell Smith, G., R.P. Freckleton, L.G. Firbank and A.R. Watkinson (1999), 'The population dynamics of *Anisantha sterilis* in winter wheat: comparative demography, and the role of management', *Journal of Applied Ecology*, **36**: 455–71.

Mack, R.N. (1981), 'Invasion of *Bromus tectorum* L. into western North America: an ecological chronicle', *Agroecosystems*, **7**: 145–65.

Medd, R.W. (1996a), 'Ecology of wild oats', *Plant Protection Quarterly*, **11**: S185–S187.

Medd, R.W. (1996b), 'Wild oats – what is the problem?', *Plant Protection Quarterly*, **11**: S183–S184.

Mortimer, A.M. (1987), 'The population ecology of weeds – implications for integrated weed management forecasting and conservation', 1987 British Crop Protection Conference – Weeds, Farnham: British Crop Protection Council: 935–44.

Nietschke, B.S. (1996), 'Cultural weed management of wild oats', *Plant Protection Quarterly*, **11**: S187–S189.

Nietschke, B.S. and R.W. Medd (1996), 'Chemical weed management of wild oats', *Plant Protection Quarterly*, **11**: S190–S192.

Noble, J.C. (1991), 'Behaviour of a very fast grassland wildfire on the riverine plain of southeastern Australia', *International Journal of Wildland Fire*, 1: 189–96.

Pacala, S.W. and S.A. Levin (1997), 'Biologically generated spatial pattern and the coexistence of competing species', in D. Tilman and P. Kareiva (eds), *Spatial Ecology: The Role of Space in Population Dynamics and Interspecific Interactions*, Princeton: Princeton University Press: 204–32.

Pandey, S. and R.W. Medd (1991), 'A stochastic dynamic programming framework for weed control decision making: an application to *Avena fatua* L.', *Agricultural Economics*, **6**: 115–28.

Rees, M., P.J. Grubb and D. Kelly (1996), 'Quantifying the impact of competition and spatial heterogeneity on the structure and dynamics of a four species guild of winter annuals', *American Naturalist*, **147**: 1–32.

Shea, K., M. Rees and S.N. Wood (1993), 'Trade-offs, elasticities and the comparative method', *Journal of Ecology*, **82**: 951–7.

Skellam, J.G. (1951), 'Random dispersal in theoretical populations', *Biometrika*, **38**: 196–218.

Thomas, T. and G. Annal (1995), 'Sugar beet production in the Ukraine', *British Sugar Beet Review*, **63**: 27–31.

Wallinga, J., J. Grasman, R.M.W. Groeneveld, M.J. Kropff and L.A.P. Lotz (1999), 'Prediction of weed density: the increase of error with prediction interval, and the use of long-term prediction for weed management', *Journal of Applied Ecology*, **36**: 307–16.

Wallinga, J. and M. van Oijen (1997), 'Level of threshold weed density does not affect the long-term frequency of weed control', *Crop Protection*, **16**: 273–8.

Watkinson, A.R. (1978), 'Biological flora of the British Isles, *Vulpia fasciculata* (Forskål) Samp.', *Journal of Ecology*, **66**: 1033–49.

Watkinson, A.R. (1980), 'Density-dependence in single-species populations of plants', *Journal of Theoretical Biology*, **83**: 345–57.

Watkinson, A.R. (1990), 'The population dynamics of *Vulpia fasciculata*: a nine year study', *Journal of Ecology*, **78**: 196–209.

Watkinson, A.R., R.P. Freckleton and L. Forrester (2000), 'Population dynamics of *Vulpia ciliata*: regional, metapopulation and local dynamics', *Journal of Ecology*, in press.

Watkinson, A.R., K.K. Newsham and L. Forrester (1998), '*Vulpia ciliata* Dumort. ssp. *ambigua* (Le Gall) Stace and Auquier (*Vulpia ambigua* (Le Gall) More, *Festuca ambigua* Le Gall)', *Journal of Ecology*, **86**: 690–705.

PART II

Case Studies

7. An introduced disease in an invasive host: the ecology and economics of rabbit calicivirus disease (RCD) in rabbits in Australia

Piran C.L. White and Geraldine Newton-Cross*

1 INTRODUCTION

The European rabbit (*Oryctolagus cuniculus*) is the most destructive of Australia's vertebrate pests (Vertebrate Biocontrol CRC, 1997). Wild rabbits have a substantial negative impact on agricultural production and nature conservation in Australia, and their impact is most pronounced in pastoral agriculture (Williams et al.,1995). The European rabbit is native to the Iberian peninsular. Rabbits have never been regarded as a pest in mainland Spain, but are valued for their ability to use poor grazing and are used for both meat and fur. Domestic rabbits were first imported to Australia in 1788 but failed to spread. Wild rabbits were first introduced in Victoria in 1859, primarily to be shot for game. However, rates of spread and population increase were far greater than expected, and in the absence of competitors and predators, rabbits rapidly colonized the country, spreading at a rate of between 20 and 100 km per year (Anderson and Nowak, 1997). This rapid spread occurred mainly through natural reproduction and dispersal, but it was helped by further releases as well.

By 1880, rabbits had reached pest proportions in South Australia. This explosion in the rabbit population coincided with the large increase in sheep farming in Australia, with numbers of sheep increasing from less than 1 million in 1830 to more than 100 million in 1890 (Goodall, 1974). It is believed that the abundance of sheep in Australia contributed to the successful colonization of rabbits, due to the close cropping of grass swards by sheep which provided ideal grazing conditions for the rabbits (Lever, 1994).

2   THE IMPACT OF RABBITS IN AUSTRALIA

Rabbits are perceived as pests in Australia because they affect primary production significantly, act as a sylvatic reservoir of disease, cause degradation
of natural ecosystems and threaten rare or endangered native animals and
plants (Cowan and Tyndale-Biscoe, 1997). Economic damage including the
cost of control and production losses is approximately A$600 million per
year (Wilson, 1995). Additional environmental damage is as yet unquantified,
but is often irreparable (CSIRO, 1997a).

Rabbits are well-suited to achieving pest status due to their high breeding
potential (ibid.). One female can produce a litter of 4–6 young every four
weeks under ideal conditions. Thus, in a typical breeding season, one female
can produce 4–5 litters, giving a theoretical tenfold population increase over six
months. Problems of control are greatest in the arid interior of Australia due to
the high density of rabbits there. Many areas contain 100 warrens per km^2, with
an average of 15 rabbits per warren. This equates to 1500 rabbits per km^2
which represents a very high level of unmanaged grazing pressure (ibid.).

Before the release of myxomatosis, there were estimated to be up to one
billion rabbits in Australia (Short, 1985). The resultant overgrazing of pasture
proved economically and socially catastrophic for farmers, many of whom
abandoned their holdings and moved to the towns, with a consequent deterioration in the country's economy (Twyford, 1991). However, few studies have
quantified the economic impact of rabbits on agriculture, particularly at a
national scale. Most economic production losses are a result of grazing
competition between rabbits and agricultural stock. Henzell (1989) calculated that A$17.4 million was lost annually in livestock production in South
Australia's arid zone due to this interspecific competition. In Granite Creek,
northeast Victoria, a similar study estimated that competition between sheep
and rabbits resulted in production losses of A$7 million per year (CSIRO,
1997a).

The presence of rabbits in Australia has had significant effects on entire
ecosystems, especially in semi-arid and subalpine zones (Wilson et al., 1992).
Rabbit grazing reduces vegetation cover which reduces the food supply for
domestic stock and endemic grazing marsupials (Lever, 1994). A study by
Douglas (1972) in the Mallee region showed that consumption by rabbits of
palatable ephemeral plants and grasses had forced livestock to browse on
scrub. Losses of these palatable plants will lead to the invasion of woody
weed species, and consequently reduce the carrying capacity of the land
(CSIRO, 1997a). Overgrazing threatens the survival of native birds, mammals and insects that rely on plants for food and shelter (ibid.). It also inhibits
the regeneration and seeding of grasses, thus reducing the food available for
granivorous birds (Myers and Poole, 1963). In some cases, river courses have

been altered as a result of bank erosion due to excessive rabbit grazing and deposition of sediment eroded during warren construction (Vertebrate Biocontrol CRC, 1997).

Rabbits can cause significant damage to young trees and shrubs. Where trees are planted in afforestation programmes, even relatively low densities of rabbits can destroy up to 90 per cent of seedlings (CSIRO, 1997a). Many species of arid-zone trees and shrubs are at risk of extinction unless rabbit numbers are permanently lowered from pre-RCD levels, since rabbits prevent these native plants from regenerating (Lange and Graham, 1983; Cooke, 1991; Williams et al., 1995). For example, rabbits have been identified as the most significant herbivore of purple wood wattle (*Acacia carnei*) in Kinchega National Park, New South Wales (Auld, 1993). However, a recent study by Tiver and Andrew (1997) suggested that the level of herbivory due to rabbits, goats and kangaroos was in fact much less than that due to sheep.

Native fauna are affected by rabbits, both directly through competition for grazing pasture and indirectly through the effects of rabbits on the abundance of predators. High rabbit populations support high densities of introduced predators, in particular red foxes and feral cats, and these predators may also have a significant impact on other fauna. Wild rabbits have been implicated in the severe range contraction and decline of many species of endemic marsupials in Australia including the eastern or brown-hare wallaby (*Lagorchestes leporides*), the mainland form of the eastern bettong (*Bettongia gaimardi gaimardi*), the bridled nail-tail wallaby (*Onychogalea fraenata*), bilbies (*Macrotis lagotis* and *Macrotis leucura*) and common wombats (*Vombatus ursinus*) (Lever, 1994; CSIRO, 1997a).

3   THE IMPACT OF MYXOMATOSIS ON RABBITS IN AUSTRALIA

Prior to the introduction of myxomatosis, the main methods of rabbit control were trapping, poisoning with 1080, shooting, netting, digging and gassing. Drought was the only significant natural factor controlling the growth of rabbit populations. Myxomatosis was first assessed as a potential biological control agent on Wardang Island, South Australia, in the 1930s. Initially the results suggested that the disease would not persist. However, in December 1950, an epidemic started at one of the test sites and by 1953 the disease had spread across a wide area of Australia (Anderson and Nowak, 1997). Initially, myxomatosis killed more than 99 per cent of the rabbits, and within three years of its escape, 80–90 per cent of Australia's rabbits had been eradicated. This led to a consequent rise in the annual wool-clip of 40 million kg, equivalent to A$60 million (Frith, 1979).

Although myxomatosis was extremely effective at reducing rabbit numbers in the short term, genetic resistance soon developed in the rabbit population (Fenner and Ratcliffe, 1965). The subsequent coevolution of immunity in the rabbit population and an associated reduction in the virulence of the myxoma virus has now led to an equilibrium at an intermediate state where 30–50 per cent of the rabbits survive (Fenner and Ross, 1994). Myxomatosis is not equally effective in all parts of Australia, and is least effective in arid areas. Mosquitoes, which are the main vector for the disease, occur at lower densities in such areas, so the vector-based transmission process breaks down. In some arid regions, Spanish fleas have been introduced in an attempt to establish suitable vectors for the disease, but this has met with little success.

4   THE USE OF RCD AS A NEW BIOLOGICAL CONTROL AGENT FOR RABBITS IN AUSTRALIA

RCD, also known as rabbit haemorrhagic disease, was first recorded in China in 1984. It spread rapidly throughout Asia and Europe (Kovaliski, 1998), reaching the UK in 1992 (Duff et al., 1994), and now affects European rabbits in 40 countries on four continents. In Italy, 64 million farmed rabbits were killed within only a few months of its introduction (MAF Rabbit Biocontrol Advisory Group, 1996) and the disease passed quickly into the wild rabbit population, causing high mortality. These characteristics prompted scientists to consider RCD as a potential biological control agent for wild rabbits in Australia.

RCD was taken into quarantine in June 1991 at the CSIRO Australian Animal Health Laboratory in Geelong for a three-year programme of testing. The tests showed that RCD was entirely species specific to the European rabbit. It did not produce disease in any Australian native or domesticated animals, nor in hares, American cottontail rabbits, or any other species tested (Table 7.1). Following laboratory testing, RCD was released in quarantine facilities on Wardang Island in order to further evaluate its potential as a biological control agent (Cooke, 1996). However, despite strict quarantine regulations, the virus was discovered on the mainland in October 1995 (Mutze et al., 1998). The disease spread rapidly through South Australia and the neighbouring states at a rate of up to 18 km per day (Cooke, 1996; Kovaliski, 1998). The impact of the disease has been especially dramatic in arid areas, and in parts of Western Australia, Northern Territory and South Australia, rabbit populations fell by 95 per cent within a few weeks (Mutze et al., 1998). Within two months of RCD escaping, five million rabbits had been killed by the disease (Anderson, 1995a).

Table 7.1   Categories of non-target species tested by CSIRO for response to RCD

Category	Species
Domestic species	Horse, cow, sheep, deer, goat, pig, dog, cat, chicken
Feral species	Fox, hare, ferret, rat, mouse
Australian native mammals	Bush rat (*Rattus fuscipes*), Spinifex hopping mouse (*Notomys alexis*), plains rat (*Pseudomys australis*), fat-tailed dunnart (*Sminthopsis crassicaudata*), northern brown bandicoot (*Isoodon macrourus*), brush-tailed bettong (*Bettongia penicillata*), Tammar wallaby (*Macropus eugenii*), brushtail possum (*Trichosurus vulpecula*)
Birds	Long-billed corella (*Cacatua tenuirostris*), feral pigeon (*Columba livia*), silver gull (*Larus novaehollandiae*), brown falcon (*Falco berigora*)
Reptiles	Common bluetongued lizard (*Tiliqua scincoides*)

Note: The tests consisted of four individuals of each species being directly inoculated with 1000 × rabbit LD50 of RCD. Animals were considered to be unaffected if they showed no evidence of productive infection or disease.

Source: CSIRO (1997a).

RCD can be transmitted between rabbits directly through contact of susceptible individuals with infected individuals or their faeces, or indirectly via vectors. The relative importance of direct versus indirect transmission in the field is not yet established. However, the rapid rate of spread of the disease in Australia suggests that vectors such as mosquitoes, the European rabbit flea, the Spanish rabbit flea and the Australian bush fly are important (Robinson, 1997). Field evidence confirms that flies are a major source for oral or conjunctival transmission of the virus between rabbits (Asgari et al., 1998). Seasonal patterns of prevalence also provide circumstantial evidence that flying insects play a significant role. For example, RCD occurs at a higher prevalence in spring and autumn, coinciding with moderate temperatures which improve virus survival and factors affecting insect activity. The same temperature-related trends have been observed for the disease in Spain (Villafuerte et al., 1995).

RCD is not equally effective in all regions of Australia, and even within regions there may be considerable variation (Saunders et al., 1998). The reasons for this are not known, but it is likely that climatic differences play a role. In contrast with myxomatosis, some evidence suggests that the impact of RCD is greater in drier areas (< 300 mm rainfall per year). In these areas, rabbit populations may be reduced by up to 95 per cent (Mutze et al., 1998), whereas in wetter areas, populations are generally reduced by less than 65 per cent. However, these figures may be biased by the higher rabbit breeding rate in wetter areas, which means that increased numbers of rabbits entering the observable population compensate for the loss of older individuals from the population due to the disease (CSIRO, 1997a). In addition to climate, it is possible that other factors such as habitat and landscape may also be important in determining rates of transmission, since these may be linked with the direct transmission pathways or the ecology of the vector organisms (for example, White et al., 1993).

5 COSTS AND BENEFITS OF BIOLOGICAL CONTROL USING RCD

Following the introduction of RCD, a monitoring programme has been established to record its impact on the rabbit population throughout Australia. However, no quantified analysis of the ecological and economic costs and benefits has been attempted. This section of the chapter will therefore review what is known of the costs and benefits of the introduction of RCD. Both direct and indirect costs and benefits of the introduction will be considered, including the implications for the native flora and fauna. A summary of the costs and benefits of using RCD to control rabbit numbers in Australia is provided in Table 7.2, and the principal impacts are discussed further below.

5.1 The Impact of RCD on Ecosystems

Following the national release of RCD, field evidence has shown that the virus is persisting and regularly becoming epidemic, maintaining rabbit populations at 10–20 per cent of their original levels (Cooke, 1998). This is in line with predictions from modelling studies (Barlow and Kean, 1998). As a result of RCD-induced rabbit declines, the vegetation in many areas of Australia has generally benefited from reduced grazing pressure, with increases in vegetation cover and changes in species diversity. Native grasses, some arid-zone acacias and other highly palatable perennial plants have been regenerating well where rabbits have declined (CSIRO, 1997a).

Reduced rabbit numbers will generally have beneficial consequences in two main respects. First, greater vegetation cover will reduce soil erosion and loss of top soil, which not only has immediate benefits to the nutrient quality of soil, but will also result in less sediment being washed into water courses. Second, an increase in pasture biomass will result from reduced competition between domestic animals, herbivorous marsupials and rabbits (Pech and Hood, 1998). Decreases in rabbit abundance due to RCD will therefore be beneficial for other herbivores which normally compete with rabbits for food and potentially allow these other herbivores to increase in number.

Some animal species are likely to suffer adverse effects due to changes in the availability of rabbits as prey. There are two main areas of concern. First, the abundance of certain native raptors, which have become dependent on rabbits as their primary food, may decline (Newsome et al., 1997). Second, there may be increased predation on native wildlife by exotic carnivores, in particular red foxes and feral cats, seeking a source of alternative prey (ibid.). This would exacerbate the already substantial loss of vertebrate species in Australia (Woinarski and Braithwaite, 1990).

Too little time has elapsed since the release of RCD to fully predict the long-term ecological implications for predator–prey relations in Australia. However, the most likely impacts are summarized in Table 7.3. Previous examples of population crashes in rabbit populations (induced by drought or myxomatosis) have shown that predation pressure on native mammals from foxes, feral cats, dingoes and raptors greatly intensifies. The implications of such 'prey-switching' following RCD introductions is of major concern. Pech and Hood (1998) modelled the impact of reduced rabbit numbers on fox populations in both single-prey (rabbits alone) and two-prey (rabbits plus alternative prey) situations. They predicted that declines in fox density would follow the reduction in rabbit numbers due to RCD, but that the presence of alternative prey would reduce the impact of decreases in rabbit abundance on the fox population.

Empirical work has shown that fox abundance is correlated with the availability of rabbits over the preceding rabbit breeding season (Catling, 1988; Pech et al., 1992). A time delay would therefore be expected in the response of fox populations to rabbit declines. This will give rise to a short-term period of excess predator numbers when they will be most likely to have an adverse impact on alternative prey. Williams et al. (1995) have estimated that it would take between six months and two years for predator numbers to stabilize following RCD. Since exotic predators tend to be generalists, they will have a greater potential impact on alternative prey than a specialist predator. The risk to the native fauna posed by these species will therefore be particularly severe. Data already show that brushtail possums, which are native to Australia, have started to suffer more heavy predation since RCD was released (CSIRO, 1997a). However, in the long term, once predator numbers reach a new, lower, equilibrium level, some researchers argue that the net effect of RCD for native mammals is likely to be beneficial (Pech and Hood, 1998).

Raptors provide an example of a more specialist predator, and in Australia, four raptor species depend almost entirely on rabbits for prey, namely

Table 7.2   *Summary of the market and non-market costs and benefits of using RCD as a biological control agent against rabbits in Australia*

	Nature of costs	Value of costs	Nature of benefits	Value of benefits
Market values				
Public sector including government environmental agencies	National release of RCD: 20 inoculated rabbits at 280 sites	Unknown	RCD persisting in the field producing reduction in rabbit control costs	Unknown (depends on continued virulence of RCD)
	Continuing monitoring and surveillance programme for RCD	A$2.5m per year[1]	Increased lifespan of dams, previously reduced due to siltation following soil erosion due to rabbit grazing and warren building[2]	Unknown
	Monitoring and increased protection for vulnerable species such as raptors	Unknown		
Agriculture	Possible increased losses of cattle[3] and lambs[4] due to decreased availability of prey for predators	Unknown	Reduced crop losses due to rabbit grazing	National crop losses prior to RCD estimated at A$6.5m[5]
			Reduced need for rabbit control, e.g. use of 1080 poison reduced by up to 2/3.[6] However, some control such as warren-ripping still required	Extent of reduced costs depend on continued virulence of RCD
				National control costs prior to RCD were A$20m[7]
				Fox control in NSW costs A$1.12 per ha[8]
			Reduced rabbit populations result in increased stocking capacity of land	Potential benefits: wool A$300m, sheep meat A$70m, cattle A$150m, crops A$80m
				Total value to agricultural sector A$600m

124

	Reduction in losses to other pest species such as red kangaroos and wallabies due to prey switching by dingoes		Kangaroos and wallabies cost pastoral industry A$100–200m per year in lost productivity. Costs of land degradation are a further A$50m per year[9] Crop loss due to marsupials A$40m per year[10] Unknown
	Reduced reservoir of parasites such as liver fluke and diseases including toxoplasmosis, brucellosis and leptospirosis[11]		
Commercial rabbit industry	RCD could reduce size and value of harvests. In worst case scenario, industry could collapse Vaccination of all farmed rabbits	Up to current value of industry, A$5.2–5.8m[12] Unknown	
Forestry	Reduced rabbit damage		A$300m estimated as annual cost to replace tree seedlings damaged by rabbits[1] Damage from browsing equivalent to $800 per ha at clear-felling[13] Rabbit control in forestry plantations costs A$7 per ha per year in NSW forests[11] and up $80 per ha per year in private forests[14]

Table 7.2 *continued*

	Nature of costs	Value of costs	Nature of benefits	Value of benefits
Pet owners	Vaccination of pet rabbits against RCD	Unknown	Reduced marsupial damage due to increased predation on marsupials	Marsupials cause A$10m per year damage to forestry[10]
Non-market values				
Not divided by sector	Threats to native fauna from increasing predation pressures	Unknown	Improved ecosystem services including reduced soil erosion	Unknown
	Threat of rabbit calicivirus jumping to other species	Unknown, depending on species affected	Increases in populations of some native fauna and increased regeneration of native flora[14,15]	Unknown
			Reduction in the use of 1080 chemical poison, reducing risks to non-target wildlife[5]	Unknown
			Reduction in use of more traditional control techniques, thereby reducing animal distress and suffering	Unknown

Sources: 1. G. Eggleston, personal communication; 2. Wilson (1995); 3. Newsome (1990); 4. Anderson (1995b); 5. Henzell (1989); 6. Cooke (1998); 7. Anon (1988); 8. Gibson and Young (1987); 9. Saunders et al. (1997); 10. Cowan and Tyndale-Biscoe (1997); 11. Williams et al. (1995); 12. Ramsay (1991); 13. Griffith and Dolman (1985); 14. CSIRO (1997a); 15. Pech and Hood (1998).

Table 7.3 Possible impact of RCD-induced rabbit declines on major rabbit predators in Australia

Predator	Distribution	Importance of rabbits in diet	Possible impact of decline in rabbit numbers
Red fox	Common throughout southern Australia, central arid zones and urban areas	Rabbits are primary prey for foxes, accounting for almost 100% of the diet when abundant	Foxes are relatively adaptable at changing their diets in response to lower rabbit numbers Predation could increase on vulnerable native prey species
Dingo	Largest mammalian predator in Australia, widespread throughout the country	Dingoes prey almost exclusively on rabbits when they are abundant[1]	Dingoes commonly increase their predation on the red kangaroo when rabbit populations decline; may be beneficial as red kangaroo is a pest[2] Some concern over dingoes taking increased numbers of cattle[3] Dingoes rarely take vulnerable species
Feral cat	Common and widespread, occupies all environments across the continent[4,5]	Prey mostly on young rabbits where present, but can survive on insects, reptiles, birds and native mammals Will prey on rare and endangered species if present	If RCD affects an area during the rabbit breeding season, cats likely to concentrate on the young rabbits (5–8 weeks) which are able to survive the disease; this will reduce the number of immune survivors in the rabbit population Cat populations will decline at least 3–4 months after a 'crash' in rabbit numbers, so any impact of feral cats on native species will be most severe immediately following RCD. Susceptible native species are small mammals, birds, and to a lesser extent, reptiles Species living at low densities in limited areas or fragmented habitats particularly susceptible to predation by cats[5]
Raptors	Widespread, some species uncommon	Where rabbits are found, they are the major prey for 13 species of raptor, but only four species depend almost entirely on them – wedge-tailed eagle, little eagle, black kite, swamp harrier	It is likely that many native raptor species are being supported at elevated densities over extended areas due to rabbits Raptors likely to decline following rabbit declines Some species may show changes in behaviour and diet, turning to increased carrion, young lambs and small marsupials[6]

Sources: 1. Corbett (1995); 2. Cowan and Tyndale-Biscoe (1997); 3. Corbett and Newsome (1987); 4. Wilson et al. (1992); 5. Dickman (1996); 6. Anderson (1995b).

127

the wedge-tailed eagle, little eagle, black kite and swamp harrier. Field data collected by Birds Australia have revealed that the overall abundance of birds of prey has declined in areas affected by RCD (Nowak, 1998). However, RCD could also benefit raptors, at least in the short term, through an increase in carrion. The number of roadside sightings of wedge-tailed eagles has doubled during the summers since the release of RCD (ibid.), and this change in behaviour could be the response of the eagles to scarcity of their normal food. Carrion is also known to be a substantial component of the diet of foxes (Catling, 1988). In Spain, red kites benefited after the introduction of RCD, since they gained access to dead and dying adult rabbits which would be an otherwise unavailable prey (Vinuela and Veiga, 1992). However, during the initial, 1995 epizootic in the Flinders Ranges area of South Australia, most rabbits infected with RCD died in warrens rather than on the surface (Kovaliski, 1998; Pech and Hood, 1998), thus proving relatively inaccessible to predators.

The economic value of these various potential ecological impacts is unknown and most represent non-market costs and benefits. The value of changes in the abundance of particular rare or endangered species could be addressed using hypothetical markets to generate willingness to pay values (White et al., 1997). However, some of the impacts represent changes in the nature of ecological functions and these could be addressed indirectly using real market prices. For example, one beneficial consequence of increased vegetation cover is a reduction in soil erosion. This could be quantified in economic terms by examining the savings accruing to the water and irrigation industries as a result of reduced purification costs and increased life expectancies of dams and irrigation channels (Wilson, 1995). However, the delivery of such environmental benefits is dependent on other interactions. First, that exotic carnivores keep grazing pressures low, which means accepting the threat of loss of native fauna (potentially a significant non-market cost) unless protection programmes for specific species, particularly raptors, are established at additional costs to conservation agencies. Second, that farmers do not increase their stocking densities of cattle and sheep in response to a reduction in rabbit numbers. If this did occur, it is likely that the environmental benefits of releasing RCD would be rapidly curtailed.

5.2   The Impact of RCD on Industry and Commerce

The national release of RCD in Australia to control rabbits is likely to have significant economic implications for industry and commerce. RCD could have a direct impact on both commercial rabbit farmers and private pet owners, and under the worst case scenario the industry could collapse. The cost to the industry of vaccinating rabbits against RCD is unknown, but the cost of not vaccinating could be as high as the current value of the industry itself, which is estimated at A$5.2–5.8 million (Ramsay, 1991).

RCD is likely to have major economic impacts on agriculture as a result of rabbit population declines. Wheeler and Nicholas (1987) estimated that rabbits living in scrub alongside the boundary of a crop took one-third of the crop within 50 metres of the boundary, and Henzell (1989) estimated annual crop losses to rabbits in South Australia to be about A$6.5 million. The introduction of RCD will have reduced these losses substantially in areas where it has been effective. Rabbits also act as hosts for some parasites of livestock including liver fluke (Dunn, 1969), and may also serve as reservoirs for infectious diseases including toxoplasmosis, distemper, brucellosis and leptospirosis (Williams et al., 1995). The effect of RCD would therefore be to reduce the risk of transmission of these infections to livestock. However, by far the most significant benefits of RCD would result from a predicted increase in pasture biomass and nutritional quality of vegetation following reduced competition from rabbits. For example, on one grazing property in South Australia, stock numbers were able to increase by 40 per cent following intensive rabbit control (ibid.).

A preliminary assessment of the economic impact of rabbit declines on agricultural production in Australia was undertaken by Wilson (1995), who assessed the average density of rabbits at the rural 'statistical local area' level and then applied previously calculated production increases following the removal of rabbits to different agricultural sectors. Wilson predicted that the national savings would be A$300 million to the wool industry, A$70 million to sheep meat producers, A$150 million to the cattle industry and A$80 million to arable crop production. These figures represent improvements in gross production revenue of 12, 12, 4 and 1 per cent, respectively, but do not include any savings in current expenditure on rabbit control. On the basis of these figures, the overall saving to agriculture was estimated to be A$600 million, which equates to a 3 per cent improvement in gross production revenue.

The actual increase in pasture biomass following rabbit declines will be dependent upon the dynamics of predator–prey relations that emerge after RCD has affected an area (Pech and Hood, 1998). For a maximum increase in pasture biomass, numbers of exotic carnivores must remain high enough to maintain low densities of other herbivorous animals (including native species). If predator numbers remain high in the absence of rabbits, this may have additional beneficial effects for agriculture. For example, the proportion of red kangaroos and wallabies in the diet of foxes increases when rabbit numbers are low (Newsome, 1990). Nationally, kangaroos and wallabies have been estimated to cost the Australian pastoral industry between A$100 and 200 million per year in lost productivity, with the costs of land degradation being an additional A$50 million per year (Gibson and Young, 1987). Crop losses due to marsupials amount to A$40 million annually, with another A$10 million lost in forestry. All of these losses may be ameliorated under conditions of high predator densities, although the extent of such amelioration is unknown. Conversely, under conditions of shortages in their normal prey, predators may switch to economically important species as a source of alternative food, which will place additional costs on farmers. For example, in central Australia there is some evidence to suggest that the proportion of cattle in the diet of dingoes has increased in response to rabbit population declines (Newsome, 1990).

Another potential impact of RCD is on the costs of rabbit control. Before the arrival of RCD, rabbit control costs were estimated at A$20 million per year (Anon., 1988). RCD significantly reduces rabbit populations in a short period. However, young rabbits are immune to the virus for the first five weeks of their life (Fuller et al., 1993; Lenghaus et al., 1995). Therefore, RCD will never wipe out a rabbit population completely, and the high fecundity of rabbits means that the populations will start to recover rapidly, albeit to very reduced levels. RCD then persists in the rabbit populations in an endemic state, occasionally becoming epidemic. As a result, rabbit populations undergo fluctuations in density, although they remain at comparatively low numbers. Nevertheless, the survival of the rabbit population means that continued control is required, normally in the form of mechanical methods such as warren-ripping. Such an integrated approach to rabbit control, involving both RCD and traditional mechanical methods, is the most effective way of maintaining rabbit populations at very low numbers. There are also animal welfare benefits from a reduced emphasis on techniques such as gassing and warren-ripping which cause distress and suffering to the rabbits. Therefore, RCD does not eliminate control costs, but it does considerably reduce them. RCD also facilitates a reduction in the dependence on chemical poisons such as 1080, which themselves carry high environmental costs, in particular posing risks to non-target species (Cooke, 1998).

6   WIDER CONSIDERATIONS AND CONCLUSIONS

The use of a fatal disease to control wildlife populations is not a novel approach, as the example of myxomatosis shows. However, it does have moral implications in terms of whether it is morally 'right' or 'wrong' to control wildlife populations in this way. Questions of morality are very difficult to judge directly. However, public preferences can be used to indicate general consensus of opinion, which gives some indication of overall public feelings on the morality of specific courses of action. Studies of public preference are rare in the area of wildlife management, but there are recent examples for possum control in New Zealand (Anon., 1995) and rabies prevention in the UK (Cox et al., 1999). A survey of 1537 members of the general public in Australia prior to the introduction of RCD showed that 96 per cent of respondents thought rabbit control was important (CSIRO, 1997c). The most acceptable method to control rabbits would be an infertility virus (84 per cent), but a significant majority (68 per cent) of respondents believed that RCD should be used to control rabbits.

Consultation with animal welfare groups has formed a key part of the RCD programme in Australia, and the proponents of RCD have adopted the cause of animal welfare to promote its use. One such argument is that without control, rabbit populations follow a boom and bust cycle related to climatic variability, so that most young rabbits are destined for a violent death through predation or suffering the effects of starvation (CSIRO, 1997b). The moral argument therefore hinges on judgements about the extent of pain and suffering that rabbits suffer naturally compared with that inflicted by control, and whether the suffering of a few individuals due to additional disease is preferable to the collective suffering of the population (Williams and Munro, 1994). Some pressure groups in Australia that oppose the use of RCD, such as the Defence Coalition against Rabbit Calicivirus Disease, are concerned about the prospect of losing a species completely, albeit an invasive one. However, this appears to be a minority viewpoint, and scientific evidence shows that this will not happen due to RCD alone because of the resistance of young rabbits.

Notwithstanding the moral uncertainties over the use of RCD as a biological control agent, several other factors need to be considered when assessing its long-term economic significance. For example, it remains unknown how long the effectiveness of RCD will last, or whether attenuation may occur through the coevolution of genetic resistance in rabbits and virulence of the virus. This process became highly significant after the introduction of the myxoma virus to Australia in the 1950s (Fenner and Ross, 1994). If such changes in virulence and resistance were to occur with RCD, it would have profound implications for any economic analysis since the costs and benefits of particular impacts would change over time. However, no reduction in virulence of RCD has yet been recorded in Europe, Mexico or China. In fact, in Australia, some researchers believe that RCD is acting synergistically with myxomatosis, increasing the overall effectiveness of rabbit control (Mutze, 1998).

The long-term specificity of RCD is another major concern. Detrimental impacts on animal species other than rabbits could potentially result from the RCD virus itself. Although laboratory tests conducted between 1991 and 1993 concluded that RCD is specific to the European rabbit (CSIRO, 1997a), research in America has shown that some caliciviruses can jump host species (Anderson, 1996). However, no field evidence exists to suggest that this has yet occurred anywhere. The implications of such an occurrence would depend on which other species became susceptible. However, if it included domestic agricultural animals, native fauna, important predators or even humans, the economic consequences could be extremely significant.

Although this chapter is concerned with the impact of RCD in Australia, RCD has also been introduced as a rabbit management technique in New Zealand during the last two years. In July 1997, based on the experiences in Australia, the New Zealand Ministry of Agriculture and Forestry initially decided not to introduce RCD to the country (MAF, 1997). Landholders in New Zealand are legally obliged to control rabbits on their land, but changes in government policy over the last few years have meant that they, rather than the government, are now responsible for the costs of this control. This has increased the pressure from farmers for more cost-effective rabbit control measures, and as a result of this, RCD was introduced illegally in August 1997. After further illegal releases, the government changed the legislation to make the possession and use of RCD legal in September 1997 (ibid.). Since that time, the disease has spread over most of the North and South Islands of New Zealand. Initially, RCD reduced rabbit populations by an average of 21 per cent in the North Island and 78 per cent in the South Island, but it has not been successful in controlling rabbit numbers in all areas (Parkes et al., 1999). Research programmes to monitor the effects of RCD in New Zealand are ongoing, but, as is the case for Australia, the lack of empirical data means that much uncertainty remains about the long-term implications of RCD for wildlife in New Zealand.

In the future, other alternatives to traditional mechanical control may become available to manage rabbit populations. The most significant of these is probably fertility control. There is currently an extensive research programme concerned with the development of immunocontraception for the rabbit in Australia, based around the myxoma virus (Tyndale-Biscoe, 1995). If an effective immunocontraceptive is developed and released, this would have a significant impact on the future management of rabbits in Australia. However, as with RCD, the effects of such an immunocontraceptive would not be restricted to the rabbits alone, but may also indirectly affect many other species. The fundamental problem of immunocontraception is irreversibility (Tyndale-Biscoe, 1994), so any plan to release a rabbit immunocontraceptive would need to be considered very carefully in the light of all the other factors involved, including RCD.

The management of wildlife pests requires the effective allocation of resources between different control options. However, very little work has been done to evaluate the costs and benefits of pest species. The focus of control

efforts for wildlife pests is increasingly shifting towards integrated management strategies, employing the use of more than one technique in combination.
For cost-effective management, a thorough understanding of the economic
investment and return on various control options, both alone and in combination, is required, as well as an understanding of any wider ecological
implications.

On the basis of the evidence presented in this chapter, and summarized in
Table 7.2, the potential benefits of RCD considerably outweigh the potential
costs. In terms of market values, the immediate economic benefits of RCD to
sectors such as agriculture and forestry are substantial. For non-market
values, the picture is not quite so clear. Although the non-market benefits of
RCD do still seem to exceed the costs, accurate quantification of the benefits
and costs is not straightforward and would require the use of non-market
valuation techniques. The final caveat is that we have only been able to assess
the evidence based on current scientific understanding. Much uncertainty
surrounds the exact nature of the costs and benefits associated with the
ecosystem effects of RCD via grazing competition and predator–prey interactions. However, the key unknown risk factor is undoubtedly the possibility of
RCD jumping species, and if this were to occur, this could substantially
increases the long-term costs associated with the introduction of RCD.

NOTE

*   We are grateful to The Royal Society and The Worshipful Company of Farmers for helping
    to fund this work. We would also like to thank Glen Saunders and John Parkes for useful
    discussions.

REFERENCES

Anderson, I. (1995a), 'Killer rabbit virus on the loose', *New Scientist*, **148**, 21
    October: 4.
Anderson, I. (1995b), 'Runaway rabbit virus kills millions', *New Scientist*, **148**, 9
    December: 4.
Anderson, I. (1996), 'Australia's rabbits face all-out viral attack', *New Scientist*, **151**,
    7 September: 6.
Anderson, I. and R. Nowak (1997), 'Australia's giant lab', *New Scientist*, **153**, 22
    February: 34–7.
Anon. (1988), 'The economic impact of pasture weeds, pests and diseases on the
    Australian wool industry', Report prepared by Sloane, Cook and King Pty Ltd for
    the Australian Wool Corporation, Australia.
Anon. (1995), 'Public perceptions of management of possums', URL: http://
    www.maf.govt.nz/articles-man/posat/posat001.htm.
Asgari, S., J.R.E. Hardy, R.G. Sinclair and B.D. Cooke (1998), 'Field evidence for

the mechanical transmission of rabbit haemorrhagic disease virus (RHDV) by flies (Diptera: Calliphoridae) among wild rabbits in Australia', *Virus Research*, **54**: 123–32.

Auld, T.D. (1993), 'The impact of grazing on regeneration of the shrub Acacia carnei in arid Australia', *Biological Conservation*, **65**: 165–76.

Barlow, N.D. and J.M. Kean (1998), 'Simple models for the impact of rabbit calicivirus disease (RCD) on Australasian rabbits', *Ecological Modelling*, **109**: 225–41.

Catling, P.C. (1988), 'Similarities and contrasts in the diets of foxes and cats relative to fluctuating prey populations and drought', *Australian Wildlife Research*, **15**: 147–54.

Commonwealth Scientific and Industrial Research Organization (CSIRO) (1997a), 'Home page index of/communication/rabbits', URL: http://www.csiro.au/communication/rabbits/.

Commonwealth Scientific and Industrial Research Organization (CSIRO) (1997b), 'Animal welfare and rabbit calicivirus: reducing suffering through effective rabbit control', URL: http://www.csiro.au/communication/rabbits/qa9.htm.

Commonwealth Scientific and Industrial Research Organization (CSIRO) (1997c), 'Sorry bugs – rabbit popularity plummets', URL: http://www.csiro.au/communication/mediarel/mr95077.htm.

Cooke, B.D. (1991), 'Rabbits – indefensible on any grounds', *Search*, **22**: 193–4.

Cooke, B.D. (1996), 'Analysis of spread of rabbit calicivirus from Wardang Island through mainland Australia (Project CS236)', Meat Research Corporation, Australia.

Cooke, B.D. (1998), 'RCD – a useful biological control', URL: http://www.science.org.au/nova/001/cooke.htm.

Corbett, L.K. (1995), *The Dingo in Australia and Asia*, Sydney: University of New South Wales Press.

Corbett, L.K. and A.E. Newsome (1987), 'The feeding ecology of the dingo. III. Dietary relationships with widely fluctuating prey populations in arid Australia: an hypothesis of alternation of predation', *Oecologia*, **74**: 215–27.

Cowan, P.E. and C.H. Tyndale-Biscoe (1997), 'Australian and New Zealand mammal species considered to be pests or problems', *Reproduction, Fertility and Development*, **9**: 27–36.

Cox, M., E.B. Barbier, P.C.L. White, G.A. Newton-Cross, L. Kinsella and H.J. Kennedy (1999), 'Public preferences regarding rabies-prevention policies in the UK', *Preventive Veterinary Medicine*, **41**: 257–70.

Dickman, C.R. (1996), *Overview of the impact of feral cats on Australian native fauna*, Canberra: Australian Nature Conservation Agency.

Douglas, G.W. (1972), 'Ecological problems caused by introduced animals and plants', *Victoria's Resources*, **14**: 2–6.

Duff, J.P., D. Chasey, R. Munro and M. Wooldridge (1994), 'European brown hare syndrome in England', *Veterinary Record*, **134**: 669–73.

Dunn, A.M. (1969), 'The wild ruminant as a reservoir host of helminth infections', *Symposia of the Zoological Society of London*, **24**: 221–48.

Fenner, F. and F.N. Ratcliffe (1965), *Myxomatosis*, Cambridge: Cambridge University Press.

Fenner, F. and J. Ross (1994), 'Myxomatosis', in H.V. Thompson and C.M. King (eds), *The European Rabbit, the History and Biology of a Successful Colonizer*, Oxford: Oxford University Press: 205–39.

Frith, H.J. (1979), *Wildlife Conservation*, Sydney: Angus & Robertson.

Fuller, H.E., D. Chasey, M.H. Lucas and J.C. Gibbens (1993), 'Rabbit haemorrhagic disease in the United Kingdom', *Veterinary Record*, **133**: 611–13.

Gibson, L.M. and M.D. Young (1987), 'Kangaroos: counting the cost. The economic effects of kangaroos and kangaroo culling on agricultural production. Project report No. 4', Canberra: Commonwealth Scientific and Industrial Research Organization Division of Wildlife and Rangelands Research.

Goodall, A. (1974), 'Sheep', *The Australian Encyclopaedia*, **5**: 311–16, Sydney: The Grolier Society of Australia.

Griffith, A. and K. Dolman (1985), 'Economics of wild animal control/management in production forests', Report to New Zealand Forest Service (unpublished).

Henzell, R. (1989), *Proclaimed Animal Research in South Australia – Cost-Benefits, Future Directions and Related Issues*, Adelaide: Animal and Plant Control Commission.

Kovaliski, J. (1998), 'Monitoring the spread of rabbit haemorrhagic disease virus as a new biological control agent for control of wild European rabbits in Australia', *Journal of Wildlife Diseases*, **34**: 421–8.

Lange, R.T. and C.R. Graham (1983), 'Rabbits *Oryctolagus cuniculus* and the failure of regeneration in Australian arid zone Acacia', *Australian Journal of Ecology*, **8**: 377–82.

Lenghaus, C., B.J. Collins, N. Ratnamohan and C. Morissey (1995), 'Investigation of a new rabbit calicivirus for biological control of wild rabbits in Australia', Proceedings of the 10th Australian Vertebrate Pest Control Conference: 378–80.

Lever, C. (1994*), Naturalized Animals: The Ecology of Successfully Introduced Species*, London: T & A D Poyser.

Ministry of Agriculture and Forestry (MAF) (1997), 'RCD media releases', URL: http://maf.govt.nz/MAFnet/index.htm.

Ministry of Agriculture and Forestry (MAF) Rabbit Biocontrol Advisory Group (1996), 'A hundred years of rabbit impacts, and future control options', URL: http://www.maf.govt.nz/MAFnet/articles-man/rbag/rbag0010.htm#E10E84.

Mutze, G. (1998), 'Latest research on rabbit control – an anti-rabbit research foundation', URL: http://www.csiro.au/communication/rabbits/14sep98.htm.

Mutze, G., B. Cooke and P. Alexander (1998), 'The initial impact of rabbit haemorrhagic disease on European rabbit populations in South Australia', *Journal of Wildlife Diseases*, **34**: 221–7.

Myers, K. and W.E. Poole (1963), 'A study of the biology of the wild rabbit, Oryctolagus cuniculus, in confined populations. IV. The effects of rabbit grazing on sown pastures', *Journal of Ecology*, **51**: 435–57.

Newsome, A.E. (1990), 'The control of vertebrate pests by vertebrate predators', *Trends in Ecology and Evolution*, **5**: 187–91.

Newsome, A.E., R.P. Pech, R. Smyth, P. Banks and C. Dickman (1997), *Potential Impacts on the Australian Native Fauna of Rabbit Calicivirus Disease*, Canberra: Environment Australia.

Nowak, R. (1998), 'Starvation diet – raptors are paying the price as Australia wins the war against rabbits', *New Scientist*, **160**, 31 October: 18.

Parkes, J.P., G.L. Norbury and R.P Heyward (1999), 'Has rabbit haemorrhagic disease worked in New Zealand?', Landcare Research, Lincoln, New Zealand, mimeo.

Pech, R.P. and G.M. Hood (1998), 'Foxes, rabbits, alternative prey and rabbit calicivirus disease: consequences of a new biological control agent for an outbreaking species in Australia', *Journal of Applied Ecology*, **35**: 434–53.

Pech, R.P., A.R.E. Sinclair, A.E. Newsome and P.C. Catling (1992), 'Limits to preda-

tor regulation of rabbits in Australia: evidence from predator-removal experiments',
Oecologia, **89**: 102–12.

Ramsay, B.J. (1991), 'Commercial use of wild rabbits in Australia', Bureau of Rural
Resources Working Paper, Canberra: Australian Government Publishing Service.

Robinson, T. (1997), 'Rabbit haemorrhagic disease virus: possible arthropod vectors', URL: http://users.wantree.com.au/~rabbit/arthvec.htm.

Saunders, G., D. Choquenot, J. McIlroy and R. Packwood (1998), 'Initial effects of
rabbit haemorrhagic disease on free-living rabbit (*Oryctolagus cuniculus*)
populations in central-western New South Wales', Unpublished Technical Note,
New South Wales Agriculture: Vertebrate Pest Research Unit.

Saunders, G., C. Greentree and L. McLeod (1997), 'Fox predation: impact and
management on agricultural land and associated remnant habitats. Final report to
the Bureau of Resource Sciences, Department of Primary Industries and Energy',
New South Wales Agriculture: Vertebrate Pest Research Unit.

Short, J. (1985), 'The functional response of kangaroos, sheep and rabbits in an arid
grazing system', *Journal of Applied Ecology*, **22**: 435–47.

Tiver, F. and M.H. Andrew (1997), 'Relative effects of herbivory by sheep, rabbits,
goats and kangaroos on recruitment and regeneration of shrubs and trees in eastern
South Australia', *Journal of Applied Ecology*, **34**: 903–14.

Twyford, G. (1991), *Australia's Introduced Animals and Plants*, Balgowlah: Reed
Books.

Tyndale-Biscoe, C.H. (1994), 'Fertility control in wildlife', *Reproduction Fertility
and Development*, **3**: 339–43.

Tyndale-Biscoe, C.H. (1995), 'Vermin and viruses: risks and benefits of viral-vectored
immunosterilisation', *Search*, **26**: 239–44.

Vertebrate Biocontrol CRC (1997), *Controlling Australia's major pests*, Lyneham,
Australian Capital Territory: Vertebrate Biocontrol Cooperative Research Centre.

Villafuerte, R., C. Calvete, J.C. Blanco and J Lucientes (1995), 'Incidence of viral
haemorrhagic disease in wild rabbit populations in Spain', *Mammalia*, **59**: 176–9.

Vinuela, J. and J.P. Veiga (1992), 'Importance of rabbits in the diet and reproductive
success of Black Kites in southwestern Spain', *Ornis Scandinavica*, **23**: 132–8.

Wheeler, S.H. and D.A. Nicholas (1987), 'Quantitative effects of rabbits on crop and
pasture and the economics of control', Working Papers of the 8th Australian
Vertebrate Pest Control Conference, Coolangatta: 28–32.

White, P.C.L., J.A. Brown and S. Harris (1993), 'Badgers (*Meles meles*), cattle and
bovine tuberculosis (*Mycobacterium bovis*): an hypothesis to explain the influence
of habitat on the risk of disease transmission in southeast England', *Proceedings of
the Royal Society of London* B, **253**: 277–84.

White, P.C.L., K.W. Gregory, P.J. Lindley and G. Richards (1997), 'Economic values
of threatened mammals in Britain: a case study of the otter *Lutra lutra* and the
water vole *Arvicola terrestris*', *Biological Conservation*, **82**: 345–54.

Williams, R. and R. Munro (1994), 'Possible costs and benefits of RHD', in R.K.
Munro and R.T. Williams (eds), *Rabbit Haemorrhagic Disease: Issues in Assessment for Biological Control*, Canberra: Bureau of Resource Sciences: 79–90.

Williams, K., I. Parer, B. Coman, J. Burley and M. Braysher (1995), *Managing
Vertebrate Pests: Rabbits*, Canberra: Australian Government Publishing Services,
Bureau of Resource Sciences and Commonwealth Scientific and Industrial Re-
search Organization Division of Wildlife and Ecology.

Wilson, G.R. (1995), 'The economic impact of rabbits on agricultural production in

Australia – a preliminary assessment', ACIL Economics and Policy Pty Ltd, Internal Report to International Wool Secretariat, Melbourne, Australia.

Wilson, G.R., N. Dexter, P.H. O'Brien and M. Bomford (1992), *Pest Animals in Australia: A Survey of Introduced Wild Animals*, Sydney: Kangaroo Press and Bureau of Rural Resources.

Woinarski, J.C.Z. and R.W. Braithwaite (1990), 'Conservation foci for Australian birds and mammals', *Search*, **21**: 65–8.

8. Invasive species in tropical rain forests: the importance of existence values

Jon C. Lovett*

1 INTRODUCTION

Tropical rain forests are often considered to be one of the most biologically diverse terrestrial ecosystems on Earth. This diversity is the basis for many of the arguments in favour of rain forest conservation. When rain forests are heavily disturbed or converted to agriculture, they are replaced by less diverse secondary forests or cropping regimes. The shift from a highly diverse state of nature to a less diverse one is perceived to be associated with a loss of economic value. The perceived loss of value to a species rich rain forest is greatest when a primary, primeval *Urwald* (*Ur* = primitive, *wald* = forest) type of forest is replaced by secondary forest or other vegetation that is the product of anthropic activities. This is not to say that all *Urwald* is naturally in a static state, as many forests are exposed to disturbance due to storms, earthquakes, climatic fluctuations, herbivore infestation (both large and small herbivores) and other phenomena. Similarly, rain forests are not entirely composed of species that have evolved *in situ* and contain many plant species which have arrived naturally by long-distance dispersal, a process which is taking place all the time. Changes in economic values resulting from a transition from an *Urwald* state to an invaded and/or disturbed state are usually associated with human intervention precipitating the change, rather than other forms of disturbance. The change in state can have an important effect on land use. For example, a tropical rain forest may be replaced by tea estates if it is considered to be secondary rather than *Urwald*, as has happened in Tanzania. Or the justification for an oil pipeline being routed through rain forest might be because it is not considered *Urwald*, as has happened in Bolivia.

Concern about the impact of invasive plant species in tropical rain forests often relates to loss of diversity, as formerly species rich forests can be dominated by one or a few invasive species (for a review of invasive woody plants, see Binggeli, 1996). The characteristics of plant species that invade tropical forests can be assessed from a few examples (Cronk and Fuller, 1995). *Clidemia hirta*, originally from South America, has been introduced and naturalized in many areas in the tropics, and is invasive in Hawaii, Fiji and Singapore. *Myrica faya*, originally from the Azores, is invasive in Hawaii. *Pittosporum undulatum*, originally from Australia, is invasive in a number of tropical oceanic islands and South Africa. *Psidium cattleianum* originally from South America, is invasive on tropical oceanic islands. *Maesopsis eminii*, originally from West and Central Africa, is invasive in eastern Africa. These plants have relatively broad environmental tolerances, grow in both shade and light, have prolific seed production, a rapid growth rate, are dispersed by birds, and can form dense thickets which prevent regeneration of native tree species.

Are invasive species the key problem, or is it disturbance of ecosystems that should be prevented? The places where plants invade are often disturbed, or if undisturbed then the invader has built up a population in adjacent disturbed areas. Undisturbed tropical rain forest does not appear to suffer greatly from colonization by invasive plants (Whitmore, 1991), an observation in accord with ecological theory which predicts that fewer resources would be available to potential invasive species in diverse communities (Tilman, 1999). Oceanic islands are particularly susceptible to invasion, and it is interesting to note that isolated continental habitat islands, such as the rain forests of eastern tropical Africa, also suffer from invasive plants. Natural disturbance can favour invasive plants. For example, the hurricane that passed over Jamaica in 1988 caused disturbance in the forest that favoured the establishment of *Pittosporum undulatum* as one of a cohort of species classified as a usurper, though it is interesting to note that *Pittosporum* plants were also uprooted by the high winds (Bellingham et al., 1995).

Why should we be concerned over the loss of diversity in tropical rain forests? A strong argument for the maintenance of highly diverse ecosystems is the empirical evidence that plant diversity is positively correlated with stability, resilience and productivity (reviewed in Tilman, 1997, 1999), and theoretical models correlating stability with diversity (McCann et al., 1998). Clearly the maintenance of these key functional attributes of ecosystems will be of economic importance, but only if the empirical and modelling studies are applicable to the rain forests susceptible to invasion. In addition to values associated with functional attributes of diversity, an economic argument often advanced is that more diverse forests have higher option values. For example, it is often suggested that they contain a greater potential diversity of chemical compounds that could be used as pharmaceuticals or for plant breeding (reviewed in Myers, 1997). Moreover, species rich forests can contain many plants that are locally valued for non-timber forest products (Grimes et al., 1994; Melnyk and Bell, 1996; Peters et al., 1989).

Biological diversity is not distributed evenly throughout tropical forests. Most of the planet's terrestrial species diversity is located in a small proportion on the land area with the top 24 biodiversity hotspots covering 2 per cent of the land surface with 46 per cent of all vascular plant diversity endemic to them. Seventeen of the top 24 biodiversity hotspots contain tropical rain forest and nine are exclusively tropical rain forest (Mittermeier et al., 1998). While these biodiversity rich areas may have important functional, option and direct use values, they also have an additional existence value. Biodiversity hotspots are estimated to have attracted $300 million in management-orientated funding since 1989 (Myers, personal communication) and are a particular focus of conservation attention, particularly on the grounds that more species can be preserved per amount of money expended than in other less diverse areas.

This chapter deals specifically with the case of *Maesopsis eminii*, an invasive tree species in submontane rain forests of the East Usambara mountains of eastern Tanzania. The East Usambara are part of the Eastern Arc biodiversity hotspot, which is one of the top 24 global hotspots (Mittermeier et al., 1998; Myers, 1990) and is an area well known for its high degree of endemism in a range of biological groups (Rodgers and Homewood, 1982). The high diversity and endemism in this biodiversity hotspot has been attributed to an exceptionally long period of environmental stability (Lovett and Friis, 1996). This unusual climatic and geological history has made the forests continental habitat islands, in that they are islands of rain forest surrounded by a sea of semi-arid woodland. The forests contain many useful plants for medicine, timber, building poles, ropes and twine, fuelwood, household utensils, food, dyes, fibre for weaving, sources of honey and for ornament (Ruffo, 1989; Ruffo et al., 1989). They have been subject to extensive disturbance by mechanical logging (Hamilton and Mwasha, 1989), leading to the invasion of disturbed areas by *Maesopsis eminii*. Concern has been expressed about *Maesopsis* as an invasive, with *Maesopsis* colonizing gaps and it is thought that the tree will eventually dominate the canopy (Binggeli, 1989; Sheil, 1994). Invasion is also correlated with changes in soil, with *Maesopsis* nearly always associated with loss of organic soil horizons (Macfadyen, 1989). Although there may be functional changes associated with *Maesopsis* invasion, I shall attempt to demonstrate here that the main economic concern is that of loss of existence value due to a change in the floristic composition of the forests, with a loss of endemic species resulting from disturbance. Ecologically, there should be no particular reason why *Maesopsis* on its own should have a negative impact on the forests. In the next section the phytogeography of *Maesopsis* is discussed, and the concluding section discusses the nature and importance of existence values.

2 DISTRIBUTION AND ECOLOGY OF *MAESOPSIS EMINII*

By reference to the historical phytogeography of Africa, this section discusses the possibility that *Maesopsis eminii* could occur naturally in the Eastern Arc forests. The reason why it does not occur naturally is then placed in the context of the unusual ecological conditions that have led to the Eastern Arc being designated as a biodiversity hotspot, which has also resulted in particular management policies for the area.

One of the phytogeographic puzzles of tropical Africa is the similarities and differences between the moist forests of the Guineo-Congolian region (in the sense of White, 1983, as are the other phytochoria cited here), and those of the coast and ancient crystalline mountains of eastern Tanzania and southeast Kenya (referred to here as eastern forests). The similarities are marked, with about half of the eastern forest species also occurring in the Guineo-Congolian region (Lovett, 1993a). The differences are that at least a quarter of the eastern forest flora is endemic at species level (Lovett, 1988) and many widespread Guineo-Congolian species, for example, *Maesopsis eminii* and *Klaindoxa gabonensis* (Ixonanthaceae), Guineo-Congolian genera, for example, *Antrocaryon* (Anacardiaceae) and *Anthonotha* (Leguminosae: Caesalpinoideae), and Guineo-Congolian families, for example, Scytopetalaceae, are not found in the eastern forests. Among the eastern forest endemic species there are a number of species belonging to genera which are otherwise Guineo-Congolian. Examples include *Octoknema* (Olacaceae) with one species in eastern Tanzania and five Guineo-Congolian species, *Uvariopsis* (Annonaceae) with one species in eastern Tanzania and 12 Guineo-Congolian species, *Allanblackia* (Clusiaceae) with two species in eastern Tanzania and eight Guineo-Congolian species, and *Omphalocarpum* with one species in eastern Tanzania and about six Guineo-Congolian species (Lovett, 1988; Harvey and Lovett, 1999).

Under current climatic conditions the Guineo-Congolian and eastern moist forests are separated by an arid corridor which runs from the horn of Africa to the Kalahari desert (Balinsky, 1962 cited in Werger, 1978). The arid corridor is represented phytogeographically in the north by the Somalia–Masai region, and in the south by dry Zambezian woodland. The easterly-most extension of the Guineo-Conglian region is at Lake Victoria, about 500 km from the eastern forest type, with the isolated forested volcanic peaks of Kilimanjaro and Meru in between. The high level of endemism of the eastern forests indicates that they have been isolated for some time from the western forests, yet similarities between the Guineo-Congolian and eastern forests at species and generic levels suggests that either they were once part of the same pan-African forest, or species can readily disperse between them (Lovett,

1993b). For example, in the last two million years the climate of tropical Africa has fluctuated considerably in response to changes in the Earth's precession cycle (Pokras and Mix, 1987) with cool arid periods corresponding to glacial maxima alternating with warmer wetter conditions (reviewed by Hamilton, 1982, 1988). Not everywhere in Africa was dry during glacial maxima, as climate models suggest that the eastern forests were wetter than expected during the last glacial maximum (Hostetler and Mix, 1999). It is possible that the tropical African forest species could disperse from west to east during one of the warm wet phases of the Quaternary, and survive the dry phases in those areas which remained wet (Faden, 1974; Morton, 1972). The distribution patterns of some moist forest species, particularly those with large poorly dispersed seeds such as *Allanblackia*, are likely to be relicts from a former ancient pan-African forest which is thought to have existed from the late Cretaceous (75 Myr BP) to the middle Miocene (25 Myr BP) (Axelrod and Raven, 1978). But other taxa, such as *Maesopsis eminii*, are readily dispersed and their present-day distribution pattern could represent dispersal during wetter phases of Quaternary climate fluctuations.

Maesopsis eminii is the only species in a taxonomically isolated genus of the Rhamnaceae (Johnston, 1972; Figure 8.1) which is restricted in natural

Source: Drawn by Jilly Lovett and reproduced with permission from Schulman et al. (1998).

Figure 8.1   Flowering branch of Maesopsis eminii

distribution to the Guineo-Congolian region. Two subspecies are recognized, a smaller subspecies *berchemioides* distributed from the west Congo to Liberia (Halle, 1962); and a taller subspecies *eminii* from central Africa. It is the taller typical subspecies that is grown in plantation in many tropical areas. It is fast growing, easy to propagate, and yields good timber which is reasonably resistant to fungi and insects (Fenton et al., 1977; Webb et al., 1980). Because of its qualities as a plantation timber tree it was introduced into the East Usambara mountains of Tanzania in 1923 (Brenan and Greenway, 1949) where it is readily dispersed by hornbills and has become naturalized in disturbed forest.

In its natural distribution *Maesopsis* has spread to the extreme limits of the Guineo-Congolian region (Figure 8.2). It is naturally distributed over the range of latitudes 8° 10' N to 11° 30' S and longitudes 11° 20' W to 34° 52' E extending some 5000 km westwards from Kenya to Sierra Leone. It occurs over a wide range of altitudes, generally below 500 m in western Africa, and up to 1500 m in east central Africa. *Maesopsis* apparently occurs under a wide range of mean annual rainfall (670–3200 mm), but the main area of distribution receives an annual rainfall of 1000–1800 mm; those records

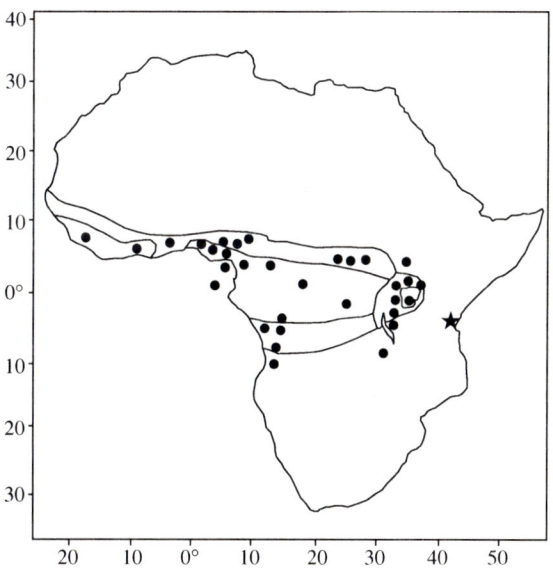

Sources: Plotted by reference to herbarium material deposited in Kew, Oxford, the British Museum of Natural History, and specimens cited in the literature.

Figure 8.2   Distribution of Maesopsis

where the rainfall is abnormally low are in areas where the moisture is received from sources other than rain. Over its distribution in western Africa, monthly mean values of daily temperature maxima are 26–34° C with a corresponding minima from 19–26° C. In the east African localities, monthly mean values of daily temperature maxima are 25–32° C with a corresponding minima from 15–20° C. It grows on a wide variety of soils; basement complex, Quaternary and recent alluvials, lacustrine and coastal deposits. There are some remarkable outlying populations, as far south as the dembos forests of southern Angola (White and Werger, 1978) at 11° 30' S and northeast to the Imatong Mountains (Smith, 1949). In both of these extreme distributions the occurrence of *Maesopsis* is related to unusual sources of water. In the dembos forests it is from mist, and in the foothills of the Imatongs it is a subsoil water supply, so that there is more moisture available than the rainfall suggests. Despite having outliers to the south and north, the species is not currently part of the natural eastern African moist forest flora, although it grows well when introduced and can invade the existing native forests.

Dispersal of *Maesopsis* during pluvial periods need not necessarily have been via continuous forests, but could have been via 'stepping stones' or islands of moist forest that are no longer extant. If the climate was wet enough to create stepping stones then gallery forests along rivers draining the central Tanzanian plateau would have offered an additional means of dispersal for *Maesopsis*. Rather than being limited by dispersal, it seems more likely that *Maesopsis* is not present in the eastern forests for ecological reasons.

Ecologically, *Maesopsis* is a typical secondary forest or pioneer species (Eggeling and Harris, 1939; Dale and Greenway, 1961; Langdale-Brown et al., 1964) and is associated with other secondary species such as *Albizia* spp. (Leguminosae: Mimosoideae), *Alchornea cordifolia* (Euphorbiaceae), *Antiaris toxicaria* (Moraceae), *Harungana madagascariensis* (Clusiaceae), *Musanga cecropioides* (Moraceae), *Myrianthus arboreus* (Moraceae), and *Piptadeniastrum africanum* (Leguminosae: Mimosoideae). In colonizing *Maesopsis* forest the species represents 50–80 per cent of trees 41 cm diameter at breast height and over (Eggeling, 1947), and is also the canopy dominant. This is in marked contrast to its low density in high forest where it rarely contributes more than 2 per cent of the tree density (Taylor, 1960; Anon., 1960). The fact that a successful, readily dispersed, and widely spread pioneer species in tropical Africa such as *Maesopsis* is naturally absent from the eastern African forests suggests that the unusual ecology of the eastern forests make them an unsuitable habitat in the absence of excessive disturbance.

A remarkably long period of geological and climatic stability in the Eastern Arc has led to the accumulation of species and the morphological differentiation of a high proportion of them to form narrow-range endemics which are adapted to environmental stability (Lovett and Friis, 1996). When the Eastern Arc forests are disturbed, both species richness and presence of endemic plants decreases (Lovett, 1999). In the East Usambara mountain forests, which have been heavily disturbed by logging, a new habitat was created by the logging activities suitable for colonization by *Maesopsis*. Disturbance causes the shift from a state of nature of species and endemic rich Eastern Arc *Urwald*, to one which has fewer species and endemics and which is susceptible to invasive by *Maesopsis*. If the disturbed state occurred naturally, then it seems likely that *Maesopsis* would be a normal component of the eastern forest ecosystem as there is no particular reason why it should have failed to disperse from western to eastern Africa during past periods of climate change. It is thus disturbance, rather than *Maesopsis per se* that alters the value of the forest.

The national and international importance of the high biodiversity of the Eastern Arc forests is reflected in Tanzanian forest policy. The Eastern Arc was named as the key component of the ecosystems and genetic resources section of the Tanzania Forestry Action Plan (Bensted-Smith and Msangi, 1989). Following an international outcry, logging in the East Usambara mountains, which was supported by the Finnish donor organization FINNIDA during the mid- to late 1980s, was replaced by a FINNIDA-supported forest conservation programme. A number of other donor organizations, such as the Danish DANIDA and German GTZ also followed the recommendations of the Tanzania Forestry Action Plan by including conservation of the Eastern Arc forests in their project plans. The Tanzanian Forest Ordinance was modified in 1998 to explicitly include biodiversity conservation as a management objective. These policies are in place because of the high value placed on the existence of Eastern Arc *Urwald*, and it is these values which are lost when the forests are disturbed and invaded by *Maesopsis*. The next section will discuss existence values and their general importance in relation to loss of economic values resulting from invasive species.

3   EXISTENCE VALUES

In a standard cost–benefit approach to land-use decision making, the preferred land-use option will be the one which gives the most economic returns. For example, an *Urwald* forest might be replaced by cash crop agriculture because the agricultural option gives higher financial returns due to the *Urwald* values not being captured in normal markets. The difficulty of including environmental values in cost–benefit decisions has led to the development of a variety of techniques to monetize non-market values in an attempt to avoid market failure.

In the case of the East Usambara forests being invaded by *Maesopsis*, there are some direct use values that might be important to consider. A high species diversity could lead to increased productivity, sustainability and resilience. However, the high species diversity of the Eastern Arc forests results from environmental stability over evolutionary time-scales, so the native flora are adapted to low disturbance regimes. This does not make the forests particularly productive and they are rather unstable. Large perturbations result in major changes in the floristic composition of the forest. The particular nature of the forest thus conforms with the high diversity leads to instability model (May, 1973), rather than diversity-promoting community persistence and stability (McCann et al., 1998). Indeed, promoting disturbance and introducing a disturbance-tolerant timber species such as *Maesopsis* will increase resilience and both biological and economic productivity.

Use values associated with minor forest products are probably overstated. Food and household utensils from the forest have a market and can be substituted by alternatives. In developing countries the trend is away from the collection of non-timber forest products for food and household goods, and towards their substitution by manufactured goods. High local use values of non-timber forest products as a means of justifying the protection of natural forests *'are sustainable as long as underdevelopment, economic stagnation, unemployment and low wages persist'* (Bruenig, 1996, p. 153). The value of retaining traditional uses of the forests probably has more to do with the value placed on retaining cultural diversity than with an economic return from a forest management option.

The economic interest in the Tanzanian *Urwald*, and hence the conservation-orientated policies and concern about invasion by *Maesopsis*, is existence value of the endemic species the forests contain. The issue of existence value and how it can be incorporated into policy decisions, for example through a cost–benefit rule, is the subject of some controversy (Boardman et al., 1996; McConnell, 1997; Sagoff, 1998).

The concept of existence value has been recognized for some time: *'When the existence of a grand scenic wonder or a unique and fragile ecosystem is involved, its preservation and continued availability are a significant part of the real income of many individuals'* (Krutilla, 1967, p. 779). Assuming that existence values are real, then a market for them should exist, or if the market is missing, then once created the values could be traded and an optimal equilibrium level of scenic wonders and fragile ecosystems reached. Krutilla (1967) identified several impediments to the creation of a market based on existence values. One was the problem of uncertainty about the characteristics of an ecosystem and the risk that it may not be valuable. This has been overcome to some extent by improved biogeographical knowledge, and we can say with some certainty now where global biodiversity hotspots are situated, and indeed conservation organizations do purchase tracts of land with high biodiversity values. Another impediment was the public good nature of large areas containing threatened species, leading to the potential for free-riding and market failure. Representing existence values in cost–benefit decisions requires the use of techniques such as contingent valuation to elicit responses to a hypothetical market. Respondents may have many motives for giving particular values in their replies (McConnell, 1997). Although this might give an interesting insight into public preferences and motivations, the values obtained may not be comparable to other costs and benefits. The pervasive use of values in decision making, and the difficulty in representing existence values may be responsible for the development and probable overstatement of option values, such as for pharmaceuticals, local use values, or functional goods and services, as conservationists seek a tangible reason for forest conservation that can be presented to policy makers.

An alternative to the representation of existence values in decision making is to separate consumer preferences from citizen preferences (Sagoff, 1998). Consumer preferences are amenable to incorporation in market-based models, whereas citizen preferences are those an individual chooses for the good of society as a whole. Citizens' preferences for public goods such as species-rich old-growth natural forests, which should be conserved for ethical reasons and the good of society as a whole, are perhaps best treated in decision making by deliberation and consensus-formation rather than in a cost–benefit approach (ibid.). There is nothing inappropriate in presenting an argument for conservation based on a zero tolerance of society to human-induced extinction of the other species on the Earth. It is not necessary to induce spurious economic arguments, such as the effects of invasive species, when in reality the invasive species are simply a symptom of disturbance caused by a particular management regime.

4 SUMMARY

Natural vegetation is very often composed of species that have arrived by long-distance dispersal rather than evolving *in situ*. In the case of *Maesopsis eminii*, it is quite likely that it could have reached the eastern Tanzanian forests naturally during previous periods of wetter climate when species were more readily able to disperse from the large Guineo-Congolian forests to the smaller habitat islands of forest in eastern Africa. The reason why *Maesopsis* does not naturally occur in the eastern forests today is probably because of competitive exclusion, not because of an inability to have reached the area. Recent logging in the East Usambara forests has created a habitat for *Maesopsis*, which it was able to invade because of its presence in nearby plantations. The concern arising from *Maesopsis* invasion is not to do with any particular financial loss, but rather with a change in state of nature from a species and endemic rich *Urwald* forest, to a derived forest ecosystem that has been notably altered by human intervention. The loss of value with this change in state of nature is existence value. Loss of existence value is not a trival matter and concern for the continued existence of the endemic species of the Eastern Arc forests has motivated national and international policy changes. It is not an easy value to quantify, and is probably better represented in decision making as a social preference rather than a monetized value. The difficulty of placing a monetary amount on declines in existence value associated with invasive species should not deter policy makers from recognizing its importance. Rather it can be used to bound decision making and determine socially appropriate courses of action.

NOTE

*   The phytogeographical notes on *Maesopsis* were derived from an unpublished MS circulated in 1986. I am grateful to comments on this chapter from Dr John Hall.

REFERENCES

Anon. (1960), *Working Plan for the Bugoma Forest, Period 1960–1970*, Entebbe: Uganda Forest Department.

Axelrod, D.I. and P.H. Raven (1978), 'Late Cretaceous and Tertiary vegetation history of Africa', in M.J.A. Werger (ed.), *Biogeography and Ecology of Southern Africa*, The Hague: Junk: 77–130.

Balinsky, B.I. (1962), 'Patterns of animal distribution of the African continent', *Annals of the Cape Provincial Museum*, **2**: 299–310.

Bellingham, P.J., E.V.J. Tanner and J.R. Healey (1995), 'Damage and disturbance of Jamaican montane tree species after disturbance by a hurricane', *Ecology*, **76**: 2562–80.

Bensted-Smith, R. and T.H. Msangi (1989), *Report on the Conservation of Ecosystems and Genetic Resources*, United Republic of Tanzania: Tanzania Forestry Action Plan.

Binggeli, P. (1989), 'The ecology of *Maesopsis* invasion and dynamics of the evergreen forest of the East Usambaras, and their implications for forest conservation and forestry practises', in A.C. Hamilton and R. Bensted-Smith (eds), *Forest Conservation in the East Usambara Mountains Tanzania*, Cambridge and Gland: IUCN: 269–300.

Binggeli, P. (1996), 'A taxonomic, biogeographical and ecological overview of invasive woody plants', *Journal of Vegetation Science*, **7**: 121–4.

Boardman, A.E., D.H. Greenburg, A.R. Vining and D.L. Weimer (1996), *Cost–Benefit Analysis: Concepts and Practice*, Englewood Cliffs, NJ: Prentice Hall.

Brenan, J.P.M. and P.J. Greenway (1949), *Check List of the Forest Trees and Shrubs* of the British Empire, No. 5: Tanganyika Territory, Part II, Oxford: Imperial Forestry Institute.

Bruenig, E.F. (1996), *Conservation and Management of Tropical Rainforests. An Integrated Approach to Sustainability*, Wallingford: CAB International.

Cronk, Q.B. and J.L. Fuller (1995), *Plant Invaders*, London: Chapman & Hall.

Dale, I.R. and P.J. Greenway (1961), *Kenya Trees and Shrubs*, Nairobi: Buchanan's Kenya Estates Ltd.

Eggeling, W.J. (1947), 'Observations on the ecology of the Budongo rain forests, Uganda', *Journal of Ecology*, **34**: 20–87.

Eggeling, W.J. and C.M. Harris (1939), *Forest Trees and Timbers of the British Empire, (IV): Fifteen Ugandan Timbers*, Oxford: Clarendon Press.

Faden, R.B. (1974), 'East African coastal–West African rain forest disjunctions', in E.M. Lind and M.E.S. Morrison (eds), *East African Vegetation*, London: Longman: 202–3.

Fenton, R., R.T. Roper and G.R. Watt (1977), *Lowland Tropical Hardwoods. An Annotated Bibliography of Selected Species with Plantation Potential*, Wellington: Ministry of Foreign Affairs.

Grimes, A., S. Loomis, P. Jahnige, M. Burnham, K. Onthank, R. Alarcon, W. Palacios Cuenca, C. Ceron Martinez, D. Neill, M. Balick, B. Bennett and R. Mendelsohn (1994), 'Valuing the rain forest: the economic value of nontimber forest products in Ecuador', *Ambio*, **23**: 405–10.

Halle, N. (1962), 'Rhamnaceae', *Flora du Gabon*, **4**: 51.

Hamilton, A.C. (1982), *Environmental History of East Africa. A Study of the Quaternary*, London: Academic Press.

Hamilton, A.C. (1988), 'Guenon evolution and forest history', in A. Gautier-Hion, G. Bourlière, J.-P. Gautier and J. Kingdon (eds), *A Primate Radiation: Evolutionary Biology of the African Guenons*, Cambridge: Cambridge University Press: pp. 13–34.

Hamilton, A.C. and I.V. Mwasha (1989), 'History of resource utilization and management after independence', in A.C. Hamilton and R. Bensted-Smith (eds), *Forest Conservation in the East Usambara Mountains Tanzania*, Cambridge and Gland: IUCN: 45–56.

Harvey, Y.B. and J.C. Lovett (1999), 'A new species of *Omphalocarpum* (Sapotaceae) from Tanzania', *Kew Bulletin*, **54**: 197–202.

Hostetler, S.W. and A.C. Mix (1999), 'Reassessment of ice-age cooling of the tropical ocean and atmosphere', *Nature*, **399**: 673–6.

Johnston, M.C. (1972), 'Rhamnaceae', in R.M. Polhill (ed.), *Flora of Tropical East Africa*, Rotterdam: Balkema.

Krutilla, J.V. (1967), 'Conservation reconsidered', *American Economic Review*, **57**: 777–86.

Langdale-Brown, I., H.A. Osmaston and J.G. Wilson (1964), *The Vegetation of Uganda*, Entebbe: Government Printer.

Lovett, J.C. (1988), 'Endemism and affinities of the Tanzanian montane forest flora', *Monographs in Systematic Botany of the Missouri Botanical Garden*, **25**: 591–8.

Lovett, J.C. (1993a), 'Eastern Arc moist forest flora', in J.C. Lovett and S.K. Wasser (eds), *Biogeography and Ecology of the Rainforests of Eastern Africa*, Cambridge: Cambridge University Press: 33–55.

Lovett, J.C. (1993b), 'Climatic history and forest distribution in eastern Africa', in J.C. Lovett and S.K. Wasser (eds), *Biogeography and Ecology of the Rainforests of Eastern Africa*, Cambridge: Cambridge University Press: 23–9.

Lovett, J.C. (1999), 'Tanzanian forest tree plot diversity and elevation', *Journal of Tropical Ecology*, **15**: 689–94.

Lovett, J.C., D.M. Bridson and D.W. Thomas (1988), 'A preliminary list of the moist forest angiosperm flora of the Mwanihana Forest Reserve, Tanzania', *Annals of the Missouri Botanical Garden*, **75**: 874–88.

Lovett, J.C. and I. Friis (1996), 'Some patterns of endemism in the tropical north east and eastern African woody flora', in L.J.G. van der Maesen, X.M. van der Burgt and J.M. van Medenbach de Rooy (eds), *The Biodiversity of African Plants. Proceedings XIVth AETFAT Congress 22–27 August 1994, Wageningen, The Netherlands*, Dordrecht: Kluwer Academic Publishers: 582–601.

Macfadyen, A. (1989), 'A brief study of the relationships between *Maesopsis* and some soil properties in the East Usambaras', in A.C. Hamilton and R. Bensted-Smith (eds), *Forest Conservation in the East Usambara Mountains Tanzania*, Cambridge and Gland: IUCN: 333–43.

May, R. (1973), *Stability and Complexity in Model Ecosystems*, Princeton: Princeton University Press.

McCann, K, A. Hastings and G.R. Huxel (1998), 'Weak trophic interactions and the balance of nature', *Nature*, **395**: 794–8.

McConnell, K.E. (1997), 'Does altruism undermine existence value?', *Journal of Environmental Economics and Management*, **32**: 22–37.

Melnyk, M. and N. Bell (1996), 'The direct-use values of tropical moist forest foods: the Huottuja (Piaroa) Amerindians of Venezuela', *Ambio*, **25**: 468–72.

Mittermeier, R.A., N. Myers, J.B. Thomsen, G.A.B. da Fonseca (1998), 'Biodiversity hotspots and major wilderness areas: approaches to setting conservation priorities', *Conservation Biology*, **12**: 516–20.

Morton, J.K. (1972), 'Phytogeography of the West African mountains', in D.H. Valentine (ed.), *Taxonomy, Phytogeography, and Evolution*, London: Academic Press: 221–36.

Myers, N. (1990), 'The biodiversity challenge: expanded hot-spots analysis', *The Environmentalist*, **10**: 243–56.

Myers, N. (1997), 'Biodiversity's genetic library', in G.C. Daily (ed.), *Nature's Services: Societal Dependence on Natural Ecosystems*, Washington, DC: Island Press: 255–73.

Peters, C.M., A.H. Gentry and R. Mendelsohn (1989), 'Valuation of a tropical forest in Peruvian Amazonia', *Nature*, **339**: 655–6.

Pokras, E.M. and A.C. Mix (1987), 'Earth's precession cycle and Quaternary climatic change in tropical Africa', *Nature*, **326**: 486–7.

Rodgers, W.A. and K.M. Homewood (1982), 'Species richness and endemism in the Usambara mountain forests, Tanzania', *Biological Journal of the Linnean Society*, **18**: 192–242.

Ruffo, C.K. (1989), 'Some useful plants of the East Usambara mountains', in A.C. Hamilton and R. Bensted-Smith (eds), *Forest Conservation in the East Usambara Mountains Tanzania*, Cambridge and Gland: IUCN: 185–93.

Ruffo, C.K., I.V. Mwasha and C. Mmari (1989), 'The use of medicinal plants in the East Usambaras', in A.C. Hamilton and R. Bensted-Smith (eds), *Forest Conservation in the East Usambara Mountains Tanzania*, Cambridge and Gland: IUCN: 194–206.

Sagoff, M. (1998), 'Aggregation and deliberation in valuing environmental public goods: a look beyond contingent pricing', *Ecological Economics*, **24**: 213–30.

Schulman, L., L. Junikka, A. Mndolwa and I. Rajabu (1998), *Trees of Amani Nature Reserve, NE Tanzania*, Tanzania: Ministry of Natural Resources and Tourism.

Sheil, D. (1994), 'Naturalized and invasive plant species in the evergreen forests of the East Usambara Mountains, Tanzania', *African Journal of Ecology*, **32**: 66–71.

Smith, J. (1949), *Distribution of Tree Species in the Sudan in Relation to Rainfall and Soil Texture*, Bulletin No. 4, Sudan: Ministry of Agriculture.

Taylor, C.J. (1960), *Synecology and Silviculture in Ghana*, London: Thomas Nelson.

Tilman, D. (1997), 'Biodiversity and ecosystem functioning', in G.C. Daily (ed.), *Nature's Services: Societal Dependence on Natural Ecosystems*, Washington, DC: Island Press: 93–112.

Tilman, D. (1999), 'The ecological consequences of changes in biodiversity: a search for general principles', *Ecology*, **80**: 1455–74.

Webb, D.E., P.J. Wood and J. Smith (1980), *A Guide to Species Selection for Tropical and Sub-tropical Plantations*, Tropical Forestry Papers No. 15, Oxford: Commonwealth Forestry Institute.

Werger, M.J.A. (1978), 'The Karoo-Namib region', in M.J.A. Werger (ed.), *Biogeography and Ecology of Southern Africa*, The Hague: Junk: 231–99.

White, F. (1983), *The Vegetation of Africa*, Paris: UNESCO.

White, F. and M.J.A. Werger (1978), 'The Guineo-Congolian transition to southern Africa', in M.J.A. Werger (ed.), *Biogeography and Ecology of Southern Africa*, The Hague: Junk: 599–620.

Whitmore, T.C. (1991), 'Invasive woody plants in perhumid tropical climates', in P.S. Ramakrishnan (ed.), *Ecology of Biological Invasion in the Tropics*, New Delhi: International Scientific Publications: 35–40.

9. Economic consequences of alien infestation of the Cape Floral Kingdom's Fynbos vegetation

Jane Turpie and Barry Heydenrych*

1 INTRODUCTION

Fynbos (meaning 'fine bush') is the name of the dominant vegetation of the Cape Floral Kingdom on the southwestern part (6 per cent) of South Africa. The Cape Floral Kingdom is the smallest of the world's six floral kingdoms, and is also the richest (Cowling and Richardson, 1995). It has been described as 'the worlds hottest hotspot' (Myers, 1990) in terms of its biodiversity, having 8700 species of which 68 per cent are endemic to the kingdom (Low and Rebelo, 1996).

Although much of this heath-like Fynbos vegetation remains today, thanks to its occupation of relatively sandy, infertile soils, it is becoming increasingly threatened by the rapid invasion of alien trees and shrubs, far more so than other South African biomes. While this process of degradation has been continuing for more than a century, it is only relatively recently that people have begun to realize the magnitude of the ecological and economic consequences that this may have. Serious control programmes have thus been initiated, but ecologists would argue that even more funding needs to be spent on the problem. However, with South Africa's pressing socioeconomic needs, funding is hard to come by and every cent spent needs to be strongly justified.

This chapter reviews existing published and unpublished information on the ecology and economic consequences of alien infestation of Fynbos vegetation, and attempts to fill some of the gaps by analysis of existing data. We restrict our analysis to the Western Cape province, which contains most of South Africa's Fynbos vegetation. Finally, we review the costs of control action and examine the economic incentives for control under different circumstances.

2   FYNBOS

Within the Cape Floral Kingdom, which also includes small areas of Succulent Karoo, Nama Karoo, Thicket and Forest, the Fynbos biome comprises two main vegetation types: Fynbos and Renosterveld (Low and Rebelo, 1996). Fynbos and Renosterveld are ecologically very distinct. Most Fynbos occurs on sandy, nutrient-poor soils. Renosterveld, which occurs on relatively rich soils, has mostly been lost by conversion into ploughed lands for cereal cropping (ibid.), with only 3 per cent of West Coast Renosterveld remaining (McDowell and Moll, 1992; Hilton-Taylor and Le Roux, 1989).

Fynbos is characterized by the presence of restios, or Cape reeds (Restionaceae). Other dominant families such as the Protea family (Proteaceae) and the heath or Erica family (Ericaceae) are also typically present. Fynbos vegetation has undergone considerable speciation (for example, it contains more than 625 species of *Erica*), and is responsible for most of the diversity of the Cape Floral Kingdom, having 7000 species and seven endemic families.

Fynbos is dependent on fire to stimulate regrowth, and its biomass in any one place is directly related to post-fire age. In unmanaged Fynbos, fires occur with a frequency of 4–45 years, with different fire intervals favouring different groups of species, depending on their reproductive mode. In managed areas, a fire cycle of 12–15 years is the accepted norm. The optimal fire frequency is determined by the type of Fynbos vegetation, micro-climatic conditions and other factors.

Due to various factors, including the low soil nutrient status, summer drought in the region, the low water-holding capacity and the fact that it needs regular fires, Fynbos is low growing and typically treeless. It also exhibits a high degree of sclerophylly (leaf hardness), making it generally unpalatable to mammalian herbivores. Nevertheless, Fynbos supports many endemic amphibians, birds and small mammals.

Fynbos can be divided into six types (Figure 9.1 maps five types: Grassy Fynos is largely absent from the Western Cape), largely determined by soil type, although one of these – Strandveld or Dune Fynbos/Thicket mosaic – is sometimes classified as belonging to the Thicket biome rather than the Fynbos biome (Low and Rebelo, 1996). The total original area of each of the above vegetation types in South Africa and in the Western Cape is given in Table 9.1.

The dominant type of Fynbos, Mountain Fynbos, is merely the Fynbos that occurs on the mountains of the Fynbos biome, although it does extend to low altitudes in places (Figure 9.1). It is not rigorously defined in floristic or structural terms, although it does have a strong proteoid component, which makes it particularly attractive. Grassy Fynbos replaces Mountain Fynbos in

Table 9.1   Total original area of each vegetation type in South Africa, and the total original area within the Western Cape

Fynbos type	Total original area (ha)	Original area (ha) in Western Cape*
Mountain	2 746 190	2 417 800
Grassy	594 000	20 600
Laterite	61 620	61 600
Limestone	214 820	214 800
Sand Plain	521 490	520 800
Strandveld	366 630	301 900
Total	4 504 750	3 537 500

Note: * To nearest 100 ha.

Source: Low and Rebelo (1996).

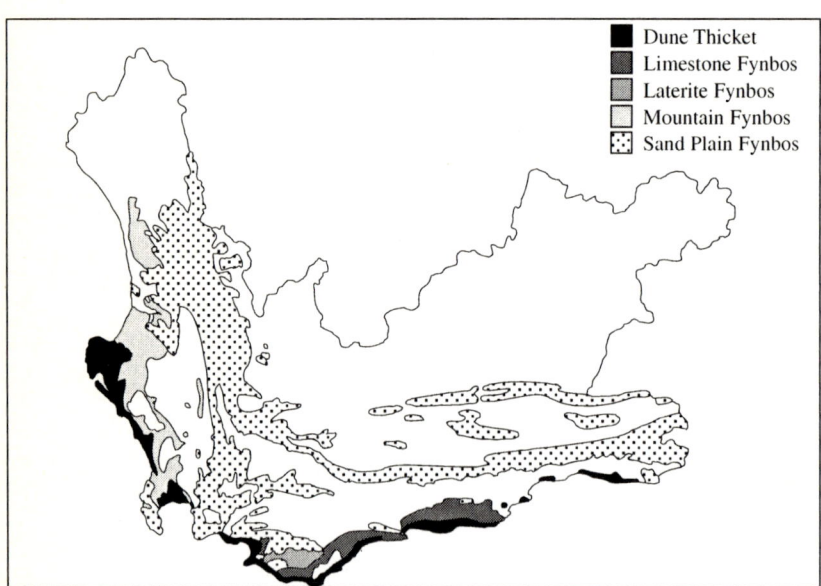

Source: Low and Rebelo (1996).

Figure 9.1   Vegetation types in the Western Cape (as used in this study)

areas where summer rainfall increases and grasses replace the restioid component. Laterite Fynbos is a very restricted vegetation type, occurring on the lowland Elim Flats of the Agulhas Plain. It is a dwarf shrubland, which is not particularly attractive but has a high degree of endemism. Limestone Fynbos comprises 'Limestone Fynbos proper' occurring on limestone outcrops, and Neutral Sand Fynbos which occurs on the deeper sands associated with these outcrops, and endemism occurs within these subtypes. Sand Plain Fynbos occurs on the acidic, well drained sandy soils of the west coast region, and also has a relatively high degree of endemism. Strandveld occurs on dune sands, and is characterized by a mosaic of Dune Fynbos and Thicket vegetation of subtropical affinity. In the absence of fire the Dune Fynbos component (characterized by the presence of members of the Restionaceae) gives rise to taller, broad-leafed Thicket vegetation. Strandveld does not contain proteas.

3   INVASION OF FYNBOS BY ALIEN PLANTS

Fast-growing alien plants, in the absence of their native pests and pathogens to keep them in check, have successfully invaded large areas of Fynbos. Although Fynbos ecosystems are also threatened by other processes, such as increasing conversion of areas to monoculture of indigenous species (Malan, 1996), inappropriate burning regimes and overharvesting, the invasion of alien vegetation is thought to constitute by far the greatest threat to its diversity, integrity and ecological functioning (Richardson et al., 1992).

It is estimated that alien plants have invaded nearly a tenth of South Africa's total surface area of about 120 million ha. Across most of the country, invasion is concentrated along river courses. In the Fynbos-dominated Western Cape, however, large-scale invasion of landscapes has also occurred, with some 28.8 per cent of the province's 12.9 million ha having been invaded to some degree by aliens (Versfeld et al., 1998). This accounts for more than a third of the country's invaded area in a province of about one-tenth of South Africa's total area. The degree of invasion of Fynbos is high compared with other South African biomes, and indeed, when compared with other Mediterranean climate regions of the world (Richardson et al., 1992).

Fynbos invaders essentially fill an open ecological niche. Although the Fynbos area is bioclimatically suited to tree growth, indigenous trees are relatively uncommon and largely restricted to rivers and ravines. These trees are of Afromontane origin and do not have the capacity to survive in low-nutrient, fire-prone environments (for example, they lack mycorrhizal associates and have fleshy fruits; ibid.). Fire excludes trees that take longer than about eight years to mature. The fact that pre-adapted trees do invade Fynbos shows that the soils can support a higher biomass than they do under

Fynbos, supporting the notion that the invasives are exploiting a vacant niche. This niche vacancy also exists in other low biomass vegetation types, but it is thought that the Fynbos vegetation's particularly high susceptibility to invasion is facilitated by the lack of vigorous indigenous plants in the immediate post-fire phase (ibid., 1992).

A large number of alien plant species have invaded South Africa, although 15 species account for 90 per cent of the problem (van Wilgen et al., 1998). However, fewer than 20 species (mostly trees and shrubs) have actually invaded natural (unmodified) Fynbos (Richardson et al., 1992). Within the Fynbos area, invasives are dominated by *Pinus*, *Hakea* and *Acacia* species. Pines were introduced from the Mediterranean region for timber plantations in the 1680s. The Cluster Pine *P. pinaster* has been widely planted throughout the biome and has invaded all types of Fynbos. The *Hakea*s and acacias were introduced from Australia during the 1800s (ibid.). Despite only having been planted on a limited scale as a hedge plant, *Hakea* has spread very rapidly throughout mountain Fynbos areas. The Long-leafed Wattle *A. longifolia* is also partial to mountain Fynbos. Thus, *Hakea*, *P. pinaster* and *A. longifolia* are the main invaders of mountains and foothills, with Black Wattle *A. mearnsii* being the primary invader in riparian habitats in mountain Fynbos. Rooikrans *A. cyclops* and Port Jackson Willow *A. saligna* are the most prolific invaders on coastal lowlands (Versveld et al., 1998), where they were introduced to stabilize dunefields.

The most successful Fynbos invaders often have high seed crops with frequent intervals, a low mean age of first reproduction and generous dispersal distances (Rejmánek and Richardson, 1996 in Dean, 1998). They also tend to produce large, high-quality seeds that permit rapid growth and high survivorship after fire (Dean, 1986). Because the climate in the Fynbos biome is well suited for seed hardening, this allows seed dormancy, and as a result, considerable seed banks build up in invaded areas. Acacia seeds are effectively dispersed by birds, ants and water, and the Cape's high-velocity summer winds promote seed dispersal of *Hakea*s and pines (Richardson et al., 1992). While the plants seldom survive fires, late summer fires stimulate germination of pines, *Hakea*s and acacias just before the onset of winter rains (ibid.). Introduced mychorrhizal symbionts have also facilitated invasions by enabling species to cope with nutrient poor conditions (ibid.).

Whereas populations of some alien species rapidly build up and then decline, but remain present, the more successful invaders tend to increase slowly to large numbers. Two processes are recognized during invasion by alien vegetation: expansion into new areas and densification of alien plants in invaded areas. In serotinous invaders (*Pinus* and *Hakea*): satellite foci establish when the seeds are dispersed by wind over several kilometres. In bird-dispersed acacias (for example, *A. cyclops*), new foci are established well away from existing stands. The foci then grow and coalesce to form dense stands (ibid.). These processes are usually facilitated by disturbance events, and in the Fynbos, expansion and densification is typically initiated by fires (ibid.). In general, disturbed or modified areas are more easily invaded than natural areas. Despite a relatively good understanding of the ecology of invasions, it has proved difficult to model these processes with much accuracy, partly because rare long-distance dispersal events are biologically important in determining alien spread (Higgins, 1998).

We used a Geographic Information System (GIS), to estimate the current status of Fynbos vegetation in the Western Cape with respect to its invasion by alien vegetation. First, the latest coverage of areas from which native vegetation cover has been removed (based on Moll and Bossi, 1984), was superimposed on Low and Rebelo's (1996) vegetation types to identify the remaining area of each vegetation type (Table 9.2). Then a GIS map coverage of the level of alien infestation (in five categories) of the Western Cape (Versveld et al., 1998) was superimposed on the remaining Fynbos area to estimate the degree of infestation of each Fynbos vegetation type. The current status of each vegetation type is summarized in Table 9.2.

4 ECOLOGICAL–ECONOMIC IMPACTS OF THE INVASION OF FYNBOS

Invasive alien trees and shrubs have had several effects on Fynbos ecosystems, mainly through reducing biodiversity and increasing biomass and their resultant effects. Most effects are negative, notably the loss of productive areas of Fynbos, the loss of water, soil, scenic beauty and biodiversity. However, there are some positive aspects as well, such as the provision of firewood in a formerly almost treeless environment.

Fynbos ecosystems provide several types of economic value, and without the quantification of these values, the full economic losses incurred by alien infestations cannot be quantified. Many of the economic values of Fynbos are only qualitatively recognized, however, and until recently, very few, if any, attempts have been made to quantify them.

In this section we collate existing published and unpublished information on goods, services and values that are lost or gained due to the invasion of Fynbos by alien vegetation. We categorize the types of value yielded by Fynbos following the conventional breakdown of total economic value of natural resources into use, indirect, option and non-use values (Munasinghe, 1994). We acknowledge, however, that option and non-use values are difficult to separate and their quantification is especially controversial.

Table 9.2   Original area of Fynbos in the Western Cape divided into areas of decreasing quality

Fynbos type	No infestation	Remaining Fynbos (ha)				Transformed Fynbos (ha)
		Occasional infestation	Scattered infestation	Medium infestation	Dense infestation	
Mountain	890 738	1 052 519	177 724	76 799	74 952	145 068
	(36.8)	(43.5)	(7.4)	(3.2)	(3.1)	(6)
Grassy	2 094	0	0	0	17 682	824
	(10.2)	(0)	(0)	(0)	(85.8)	(4)
Laterite	144	1 423	319	21 634	4 209	33 891
	(0.2)	(2.3)	(0.5)	(35.1)	(6.8)	(55)
Limestone	32 839	3 880	77 925	44 991	44 426	10 740
	(15.3)	(1.8)	(36.3)	(20.9)	(20.7)	(5)
Sand Plain	28 868	22 300	70 276	33 822	974	364 560
	(5.5)	(4.3)	(13.5)	(6.5)	(0.2)	(70)
Strandveld	40 438	64 967	26 809	44 460	19 561	105 665
	(13.4)	(21.5)	(8.9)	(14.7)	(6.5)	(35)
Total	995 121	1 145 089	353 053	221 706	161 804	660 748

Note: Areas range from pristine or uninvaded Fynbos to densely infested Fynbos and finally, the area that has been lost by habitat transformation. The degree of infestation by alien vegetation is described using standard CSIR Forestek (1994) categories: occasional (< 5 per cent alien cover), scattered (5–25 per cent cover), medium (25–75 per cent cover) and dense (>75 per cent cover). Percentages of the total original area in the Western Cape are given in parentheses.

Source: Based on GIS information supplied by the CSIR (Environmentek).

It is important to note that because Fynbos ecosystems are dynamic and are driven by fire, this means that the yields of goods and services generated per unit area, and hence their values, fluctuate in space and time. There is frequently an increase, or decrease, in Fynbos services and products with increased biomass, until the next fire regenerates the growth cycle. To account for this, mean-aged Fynbos is usually used in models, or data are collected from a number of areas of different post-fire age.

4.1 Direct Use Values

4.1.1 The value of harvested Fynbos products

Although there is evidence that some medicines and foods have been harvested from Fynbos in the past by the Khoi-khoi, the Fynbos has never been rich in these products, and few food or medicinal plants are harvested from the Fynbos today (Cowling and Richardson, 1995). The most important foods harvested are sour figs (*Carpobrotus* spp.) and honeybush tea (*Cyclopia* spp.). Buchu (*Agathosma* spp.) is exploited for essential oils used in flavouring, perfumery, medicine and brandy (ibid.). Thatching reed (*Thamnochortus* spp.) is harvested in substantial quantities from the wild, even today. Currently the most important species harvested in the wild are flowers and other products for the ornamental industry.

It should also be noted, however, that there is also a trend towards cultivation of many of the products currently harvested from Fynbos, including flowers, buchu, honeybush tea and thatching grass. Indeed, another Fynbos product, rooibos tea (*Aspalathus linearis*), is no longer harvested in the wild. Cultivation usually yields superior products and much higher values per ha, and this trend may eventually decrease the use value of the products in the wild.

The consumptive use of flowers, sour figs, honeybush tea, buchu and thatch is described in more detail below. In all cases, we consider only yields from the natural veld, and not from cultivated stands. There have been no attempts at a comprehensive quantification of the harvest of Fynbos products, and the following estimates are based almost entirely on key-informant interviews and on farm surveys from the Agulhas Plain region (which contains all but Sand Plain Fynbos). The area of each vegetation type on each farm was ascertained with the aid of a GIS coverage of the area.

It is important to note that the amounts of most Fynbos products available for harvesting are highly dependent on the age of the Fynbos, or in other words, the length of time the veld has had to recover after fire. In the following analyses, we have attempted to use a range of values where possible to include harvest rates from veld of differing ages. Actual harvest rates will, of course, differ from area to area, depending on age as well as other factors. Where only one or two estimates were available, caution is needed in extrapolating the results over larger areas and over time.

In estimating consumptive use values of Fynbos, we have assumed that current levels of use are sustainable. Fynbos veld from which wildflowers, thatching reed, honeybush tea and buchu are harvested are all managed in some way or other, such as by altered fire regimes, bush-cutting shrubs to encourage growth of thatch and pruning plants to stimulate new growth and enhance harvest potential. There is very little information as to how sustainable these activities are either in terms of the utilized plants themselves, or in terms of the non-target species with which they grow. Certain farms admit to having overharvested flowers in the past which led to local extinctions and where contract pickers are picking flowers, there are some instances where overharvesting may occur. In addition, the practice to remove shrubs to allow for better growth of thatching reed, is negatively affecting endemic members of the Proteaceae in certain regions. Also, a too-frequent fire cycle, which may be optimal for wild populations of resprouting buchu species (5–6 years), could negatively affect the growth of other Fynbos plants. This is a key area where more research needs to be done.

Flowers The wildflower industry has two components: a fresh flower and a dried flower industry, both of which depend to a large extent on harvesting from the wild. Products comprise flowers (Proteaceae) and greens (comprising many taxa including *Leucadendron* foliage, ericas, and so on for use as filler material) for the fresh industry, and flowers, including *Leucadendron* cones and other products, for the dried flower industry.

At least 100 species are used in the wildflower industry (Cowling and Richardson, 1995), although numbers and species fluctuate, following local and overseas fashions. In order to place a value on the flower harvest, we used interview data on farming activities in the Agulhas Plain, which incorporates four types of Fynbos vegetation, but not Sand Plain Fynbos, which is not considered viable for flower harvesting. The net income of farmers was calculated on the basis of supplier prices, labour and transport costs. It was estimated that flower picking yields a net income of nearly R10 million at the farm gate level in the Aguhas Plain alone (Table 9.3). Yields in other areas are unknown, but are likely to be comparatively small. The total value added to the economy from this industry was estimated as follows. The flower industry generates a gross income of R149.3 million per year, of which R86 million is from natural vegetation and the remainder is from cultivation. This yields an estimated value added of R55.9 million attributable to natural vegetation. Attributing this value to all privately-owned Fynbos areas, this value is assumed to be spread among the vegetation types in the same ratios as their

Table 9.3 *Average annual net income per ha and total net income to landowners (on harvested and unharvested land) from Proteaceae flowers and cones (f/c) and from other Fynbos flowers and greens in the four different types of Fynbos on the Agulhas Plain*

Vegetation type	Area (ha) on Agulhas Plain	Type of product	n (species used)	Average income/ha currently realized on Agulhas Plain	Total net income on Agulhas Plain (R/y)	Estimated total averge VAD/ha (national level)
Mountain Fynbos	48 646	Proteacae f/c	13	93.79		
		Other	42	47.76		
				141.55	6 885 826	17.22
Laterite Fynbos	12 953	Proteacae f/c	3	8.04		
		Other	7	57.75		
				65.79	852 161	175.27
Limestone Fynbos	13 593	Proteacae f/c	5	111.39		
		Other	17	27.04		
				138.43	1 881 613	52.34
Strandveld	19 398	Other	5	11.39	220 971	6.29
Total	94 590		70		9 840 570	

Note: Values are based on mean yields per ha, and value added at farmgate level, for each species in the area. Average VAD/ha for the industry as a whole is taken as total VAD attributed to vegetation types in the same ratios as relative farmgate values.

Source: Turpie et al. (forthcoming).

161

respective yields, and resultant estimates of value added per ha are summarized in Table 9.3.

Buchu   Buchu, mainly from *Agathosma crenulata* and *A. betulina*, is collected from Mountain Fynbos, mainly from a region of roughly 600 000 ha along the north–south spine of the Cape Fold belt mountains from Paarl to Niewoudtville. In addition to a small local market for medicinal use and buchu brandy, the buchu industry has a large export component where the essential oils are used in the flavour and fragrance industries. The export industry is estimated to be worth R12 million per annum. However, the demand for natural essential oil products is decreasing as cheaper, synthetic products are being utilized. Approximately 50 per cent of the buchu harvest comes from the wild. Thus Mountain Fynbos yields a value added of R1.72 per ha on average.

Sour figs   Sour figs, *Carpobrotus acinaciformis*, *C. deliciosus* and *C. edulis*, are harvested throughout the Strandveld, especially in the southeast (Cowling and Richardson, 1995). Harvest levels of 2.6 kg/ha and 3.3 kg/ha have been reported from two nature reserves in this area, with an overall harvest of 3.0 kg/ha. Sour figs are sold for approximately R7 per kg, which, with an estimated 75 per cent value added share, yields a mean value added of R15.1/ha for Strandveld vegetation.

Honeybush tea   Honeybush tea is made from at least nine of the 20 species of *Cyclopia*, but mainly *C. intermedia*, *C. subternata*, and *C. sessiliflora*. It is currently harvested from the wild, but will be cultivated in the future. About 25 tonnes of dried and processed honeybush is produced by farmers per year. At R12/kg, this yields a value added (assuming 25 per cent intermediate inputs) of R225 000 annually. Most honeybush tea is currently collected from a Mountain Fynbos area of perhaps 200 000 ha in the Kouga–Langkloof region, which thus yields approximately R11.25 value added per ha, or R0.10 per ha on average for all Mountain Fynbos.

Thatch   The most important thatching reed obtained from Fynbos is *Thamnochortus insignis* (mannetjiesriet), which occurs on deep sandy limestone-derived soils between Cape Agulhas and Albertinia. This species makes up about 98 per cent of the total thatch harvest. Other species harvested in small quantities are *T. erectus* (wyfie-riet), along the southern Cape coast, and *T. spicigerus*, along the west coast from Table Bay to Langebaan (Cowling and Richardson, 1995). In addition, *Chondropetalum tectorum* (pannetjiesriet) is harvested in small quantities throughout the Fynbos region, and is currently popular in the wildflower industry.

A total of about 5.6 million bundles are estimated to be harvested annually in the region, which, at a unit price of R1 per bundle, is valued at R5.6 million. The entire industry is reported to be worth about R10 million (ibid.), thus having an estimated value added of about R6.5 million (assuming 35 per cent input costs for the industry), and this translates to an average of R31.85 per ha in Limestone Fynbos.

Honey   The Cape Honeybee *Apis mellifera capensis* is endemic to the Fynbos region, where it is naturally limited in population size by available nesting sites (Rebelo, 1987). At least 58 000 hives are kept on farms throughout most of the Fynbos region (Table 9.4), both for the production of honey and for providing a pollination service to fruit farmers. While some are kept solely in Fynbos vegetation, most are kept in or near *Eucalyptus* plantations, where the bees spend 20 per cent of their time foraging, the remaining time being spent in Fynbos. The *Eucalyptus* serve to boost honey production, while the diversity of flowering Fynbos plants ensures that honeybees can overwinter in the natural vegetation where they build up their reserves and strengthen their colonies. It is estimated that about 50 per cent of honey production is attributable to Fynbos vegetation.

Table 9.4   *Estimated density of hives in different Fynbos types, and the part of gross income per ha generated by beekeeping attributed to each vegetation type (accounting for the partial role of* Eucalyptus *spp. and other forage crops), and net income per ha (VAD) at the farmgate level*

Fynbos type	Total hives	Hives/ha	Gross income from honey per ha (R)	Total VAD at farm gate per ha
Mountain Fynbos*	15 000	0.007	0.49	0.34
Laterite Fynbos	1 000	0.036	2.52	1.76
Limestone Fynbos	20 000	0.098	6.86	4.80
Sand Plain Fynbos	10 000	0.064	4.48	3.14
Strandveld	12 000	0.061	4.27	2.99

Note: Most of the bees are kept at low altitudes within the Mountain Fynbos vegetation type, so the values are not evenly spread.

On average, hives yield 20 kg of honey per year, yielding a total wholesale value of honey of R11.6 million, and a retail value in the region of R29 million per annum. Fynbos is accountable for an average value added of R70

per hive per year in terms of honey production, yielding value added of
between R0.34 and R4.80 per ha, depending on vegetation type (Table 9.4).

4.1.2   Effects of alien invasives on Fynbos yields and direct consumptive values

While little research has been undertaken on Fynbos yields in general, even
less has been done to investigate the effect of degradation of Fynbos areas by
the invasion of alien plants. At best we can only make reasoned assumptions
as to the effect this might have on yields, and hence, value of the vegetation,
and further research will be needed to verify our estimates. If it is assumed
that the potential yield of Fynbos products harvested from the veld is not
affected in any way by the aliens other than through a reduction of the area in
which the indigenous species can grow, then the losses in productivity can be
estimated to be roughly equivalent to the loss of cover of natural vegetation
(for example, negligible loss under light infestation, 12.5 per cent loss in
scattered infestations, 50 per cent loss under medium infestation and 87.5 per
cent loss in densely infested areas). In actual fact it is likely that the costs of
invasion will be disproportionately higher than the level of invasion, due to
increasing problems of access to resources. Given these assumptions, the
effect of alien invasion on Fynbos consumptive use values is estimated in
Table 9.5.

Table 9.5   *Potential direct consumptive use value of pristine Fynbos and value of current harvesting from the natural veld under different degrees of infestation by aliens (VAD in R/ha, 1997 prices)*

Vegetation type	Overall mean	Pristine or little infestation	Scattered infestation	Medium infestation	Dense infestation
Mountain Fynbos	19.04	20.16	17.64	10.08	2.52
Laterite Fynbos	175.27	368.48	322.42	184.24	46.06
Limestone Fynbos	71.55	116.00	101.5	58.00	14.50
Sand Plain Fynbos	0	0	0	0	0
Strandveld	6.86	8.77	7.67	4.39	1.10

There are also some gains, in terms of consumptive use values of invasive
aliens, which cannot be ignored. Due to lack of suitable resources in natural
Fynbos, certain alien species have become a valuable source of firewood,
especially where they occur in dense stands. Rooikrans *A. cyclops* is the main
source of firewood, although inferior firewood sources such as Port Jackson
Willow *A. saligna* are used to a small extent in areas where Rooikrans is scarce.

Landowners cut Rooikrans at a cost of R75 per thousand pieces, and sell it loose for R140 per thousand pieces. It thus has a net value to landowners of at least R65 per thousand pieces. Packaged (in 10-kg bags containing about 18 pieces), the wood retails for about R220 per thousand pieces locally, and up to R400 per thousand pieces in Cape Town. Depending on exact density and age of an *A. cyclops* stand, a mature, dense stand produces up to 30 000 pieces/ha (C. Martens, Cape Nature Conservation, personal communication) We estimate that an eight-year old (that is, suitable sized) stand can yield 11 250 pieces per hectare. Assuming that all trees reaching eight years of age are cut, densely infested stands of *A. cyclops* probably yield (11 250 × R0.065)/8 = R91.ha^{-1}.y^{-1}. This mainly affects Limestone Fynbos and Strandveld values. In Limestone Fynbos, dense infestations are estimated to comprise about 90 per cent *A. cyclops* and fuelwood value can thus be estimated to be about R82/ha. In Strandveld, any dense infestations are likely to be 100 per cent *A. cyclops*. It is unknown what the total harvested area is, however.

4.1.3 Non-consumptive use value

Fynbos provides non-consumptive use value in the form of recreation, such as hiking and ecotourism. Already 20 per cent of the total Fynbos area is in protected areas and is used for recreation, and recreational facilities on privately owned lands are becoming increasingly common. Much of this value is uncaptured by markets, however, and in the case of ecotourism, the potential of Fynbos is yet to be exploited on a significant level. Very little work has been done on estimating the recreational use value of Fynbos, and no attempts have been made to ascribe different values to different types and qualities of Fynbos.

A preliminary study was recently carried out on the recreational use value of the De Hoop Nature Reserve within the Fynbos biome (Turpie, 1996). The 36 000 ha De Hoop Nature Reserve, dominated by Limestone Fynbos as well as wetland and coastal features, receives about 9000 visitors per year, or 0.25 visitors.ha^{-1}.y^{-1}. Using the travel-cost method, the recreational use value of the reserve was estimated in terms of visitors' travel and on-site costs to use the reserve plus their consumer surplus. Using conservative assumptions, this study estimates an average consumer surplus of R19 per visitor, or approximately R5.ha^{-1}.y^{-1}. Total recreational use value of the reserve was estimated as R16.ha^{-1}.y^{-1}, which is substantially lower than the estimated potential value of R365.ha^{-1}.y^{-1} used by Higgins et al. (1997) and Costanza et al. (1997). Their estimate of one visitor per 100 ha per day far exceeds the current user densities of most large protected areas in the region. Indeed, most Fynbos reserves, with the exception of the Cape of Good Hope Nature Reserve which boasts the southwestern tip of Africa and purported meeting place of two oceans, provide an experience of 'getting away from it all.' For example, the maximum capacity of visitors to the Cederberg Wilderness Area has been set at one visitor per 500 ha per day (Deacon, 1993), and the average density at De Hoop Nature Reserve is one visitor per 1460 ha per day (Turpie, 1996). Not all of De Hoop Nature Reserve is accessible to visitors, however, and the effective area used by visitors is probably much smaller. Thus we estimate that the effective visitor density is about one per 500 ha, having a recreational value of $R47.ha^{-1}.y^{-1}$.

No empirical research has been carried out to test the reactions of people to decreased quality of Fynbos areas through alien invasion. In some cases, even medium-level infestation of vegetation may not negatively affect levels of recreational use. Indeed, alien plants can even enhance the recreational use value for some people (pines provide shade, and flowering acacias are attractive). However, it is likely that dense infestations, which are both monotonous and relatively impenetrable, will have a strongly negative effect on recreational use value (Higgins et al., 1997). These relationships can at present only be guessed at, however, and we make the conservative assumption that recreational use value will be negatively affected in direct proportion to the level of invasion by aliens (Table 9.6).

Table 9.6   Estimates of recreational use values for different quality categories of vegetation within protected areas (assuming zero public recreational value for unconserved Fynbos), and average values for all Fynbos (R/ha, 1997 prices)

	Pristine or little infestation	Scattered infestation	Medium infestation	Dense infestation
Protected areas	57.98	50.73	28.99	7.25
Mean for all Fynbos	12.61	11.03	6.31	1.58

4.2   Indirect Use Values

4.2.1   The value of ecosystem functioning and water supply

Fynbos invaders generally reach a much higher biomass than the plants that they outcompete (Table 9.7). The greater biomass of invading plants has led to up to tenfold increases in the fuel load in Fynbos areas (Van Wilgen and Richardson, 1985). The resultant more-frequent and high-intensity fires affect indigenous plant community structure, kill indigenous seeds and lead to markedly increased levels of erosion after fire (Scott et al., 1998). Riverbank erosion is also accelerated and even coastal sediment movement patterns are

Table 9.7 Relationship between above-ground biomass (B) and post-fire age (a) in years for different vegetation categories, and the calculated above-ground biomass for a 7.5-year old (roughly average aged, assuming a 15-year fire cycle) stand of each

Vegetation category	Relationship between post-fire age (a, yrs) and biomass (B, g.m^{-2})	Biomass (g.m^{-2}) at 7.5 years
Short ericoid-restioid Fynbos	B = 932 log a – 108	708
Tall moist Fynbos	B = 9541 log a – 636	7 713
Tall alien trees	B = 20025 log a – 7064	10 459

Source: Kruger (1977) and van Laar and van Lill (1978), in Le Maitre et al. (1996).

affected (Richardson et al., 1992). Although the costs of soil erosion are extremely difficult to estimate in economic terms, part of it is exhibited by the high expenditure by the City of Cape Town on clearing sediment from stormwater drains, roads and houses below heavily invaded parts of Table Mountain (Van Wilgen et al., 1996).

The high biomass of aliens relative to the indigenous flora also leads to increased transpiration losses, and thus reduction in the proportion of annual precipitation entering stream flow and groundwater supplies. This is something which is of particular ecological and economic concern in South Africa, a semi-arid country which suffers water shortages throughout.

The effects on stream flow of increased biomass in catchment areas planted to various degrees with pines have been relatively well quantified through experimental and monitoring studies of catchments in the Western Cape since the 1930s (van Wilgen et al., 1998). Analysis of these long-term data series have produced predictable relationships between biomass and streamflow, and have allowed simulation modelling of the effects of catchment invasion (Le Maitre et al., 1996). Le Maitre et al.'s catchment model predicted dire consequences of a lack of management of aliens in terms of water losses, with more than 30 per cent of the water supply from a 10 000 ha catchment being lost over 100 years.

The rainfall equivalent, or streamflow from an area with minimal vegetation cover, can be calculated as

$$MAR = -367.6 + 0.74 \, MAP,$$

where *MAR* and *MAP* are mean annual runoff and precipitation (Chapman et al., 1995, Le Maitre et al. 1996). Thus, with minimal vegetation cover, and with the *MAP* for the Western Cape Fynbos region of about 1200 mm, the *MAR* for the Fynbos biome would be 520 mm for an average rainfall year. However, with increased biomass in catchment areas due to invasive alien vegetation, this runoff can be decreased considerably.

For a 10 000 ha catchment, the loss of available water attributed to alien vegetation can be estimated using the equation

$$Q = 0.0238^*B,$$

where Q is the reduction in annual streamflow (mm) and B is the above-ground biomass (g.m^{-2}; Van Wilgen et al., 1997). A reduction in streamflow of 100 mm is equivalent to reduction in water yield of 10 Mm^3 (million cubic metres) of water per year.

The biomass of a 7.5-year stand of Fynbos comprising 70 per cent short ericoidrestioid Fynbos and 30 per cent tall moist Fynbos (after Van Wilgen et al., 1996), and of a 7.5-year old stand of alien trees would be roughly 2810g.m^{-2} and 10 459g.m^{-2}, respectively. A heavily invaded area thus has an additional biomass of 7649 g.m^{-2} with respect to a pristine catchment. The additional biomass created by aliens in heavily infested areas results in a reduction of streamflow by 182 mm, reducing overall catchment yield by 18.2 Mm^3 from 52 to 33.8 Mm^3 per year. The impact of different degrees of invasion on water yields are illustrated in Table 9.8.

Using these relationships, it has been estimated that the country loses 7 per cent of runoff, or 3300 Mm^3 water annually to alien vegetation, a third of which (1036.83 Mm^3) is lost from the mountain catchments of the Western Cape, reducing runoff from the latter catchments by some 25 per cent (Versveld et al., 1998).

Table 9.8   *Estimated mean above-ground biomass, loss of mean annual runoff in Fynbos for a 10 000 ha catchment of different categories of infestation level, and resultant water yield per ha of Fynbos of different levels of infestation, and the value of water runoff*

Infestation level	Mean % cover	Water yield (m^3/ha/year)	Water loss (m^3) (% of total 2310m^3)	Value of loss (R/ha/year)
Zero/Light	2.5	2260	50 (2.2%)	36.00
Scattered	15	2040	270 (11.7%)	194.40
Medium	50	1400	910 (39.4%)	655.20
Dense	87.5	721	1590 (68.8%)	1140.80

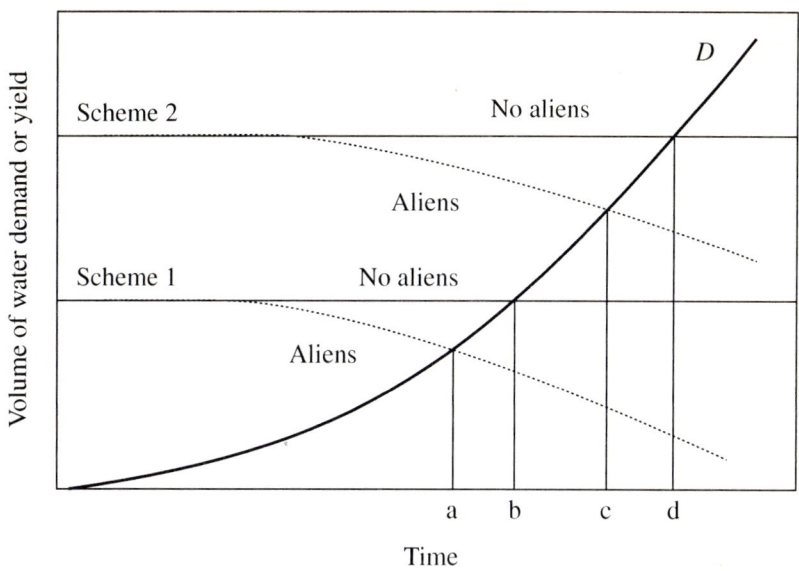

Source: Van Wilgen et al. (1997).

Figure 9.2   *Effect of aliens on water supply and the temporal implications*
                 for water supply schemes meeting consumer demands

Are these losses important? In the Western Cape, the mountain catchment areas cover 9 per cent of the province, but deliver 60 per cent of the water resources (Burgers et al., 1995). With a rapidly growing population, the province's water demand is projected to increase from 243 Mm^3 in 1996 to 456 Mm^3 in 2010. Current supplies are already low, and new schemes will soon go ahead. Thus the immediate consequence of these water losses to aliens is that fact that supplies from existing water schemes are outstripped by demands sooner than would be the case if the catchments were free of aliens (Figure 9.2). The fact that additional supply schemes have to be built sooner, obviously increases the supply cost of water.

What is the value of these water losses? In South Africa, there is no market price for water *per se*. The price paid for water by municipalities is based on the historical price of dam construction and the operation and distribution costs. It does not take the price of new schemes into account, and no value is allotted to the water itself, yielding a serious price distortion in terms of its effect on demand and ultimately upon the environment. Underpriced water has led to inefficient domestic and industrial use and unsustainable agricultural practices, the latter having been further exacerbated by government subsidies. To allocate a value to water, we take a minimum value as the average value of water production through future supply schemes. The average capital costs for the construction of water supply schemes in the 20 remaining sites in the Western Cape is R3.87, and the average operating costs are R0.074/m^3 of annual capacity, yielding an average supply cost of R0.48/m^3 (DWAF, 1994; Burgers et al., 1995). Taking this value to be a proxy value for water, value of water lost due to different degrees of alien invasion is given in Table 9.8. The unit value for water is higher than the conservative estimate (R0.15 to R0.45) used by Higgins et al. (1997), but, in fact, the total economic value of water is likely to be substantially greater than supply costs. Marais (1998) used a slightly higher value of R0.59. To add further perspective, the operation cost, alone, of desalination would be R1.87/m^3 (DWAF, 1994; Burgers et al., 1995). These estimates do not take into account the value added by the use of water as an intermediate input in the economy. All activities in the Western Cape are reliant on water which relies to a large extent on good-quality Fynbos mountain catchments. This service thus plays a vital role in the economy of the Western Cape, which was estimated to contribute a GDP of US$15.3 billion in 1992 (Bridgeman et al., 1992).

To date, however, the economic consequence of alien infestation in terms of the value of water has been considered in mountain catchment areas only. Lowland invaders, such as *A. cyclops* on coastal dune areas, are not considered particularly relevant in terms of water (van Wilgen et al., 1998). However, no-one has examined the effect of aliens on groundwater supplies, farm dams and lower reaches of rivers in lowland Fynbos areas. Although Fynbos mountain catchments have been estimated to fulfil about two-thirds of the Western Cape's water requirements (van Wilgen et al., 1996), many towns and farms in the lowland regions utilize groundwater resources. The importance of the groundwater aquifers is often missed, however, because little is known of the magnitude of the resource. It could be assumed that if increased demand for water leads to a shortage of lowland water resources, then the users will place additional demands on the already-high demands for water from large dam schemes.

4.2.2 Pollination by Fynbos bees

Approximately 15 000 hives are used for pollination of fruit orchards. The entire fruit-producing region depends to a large degree on this service (van der Merwe and Eloff, 1995). Hives are used for two pollination cycles per year, for which beekeepers are paid R147 per hive per cycle by fruit farmers, amounting to a total income of R4.41 million. Eighty per cent of this value (R3.53 million) can be attributed to Fynbos, as the bees spend about 80 per cent of their time foraging in this vegetation. This yields an average value added of R42.58 per hive per year (assuming 30 per cent input costs) in terms of pollination services, and these values are estimated per ha at the farm gate level for each vegetation type in Table 9.9. Taken a step further, R800 million of the R1.2 billion turnover of fruit farms in the Western Cape (1992 values) is attributed to bees, calculated on the basis of the level of dependence of different crops on bee pollination. This translates to an estimated total value added of R482 million in 1997 rands, and the total value added per ha attributed to each vegetation type is thus given in the last column of Table 9.9. Since the hive population is considered to be close to carrying capacity, the loss of Fynbos to alien invasives is likely to have a negative impact on this service, but the relationship to fruit industry values is difficult to predict.

Table 9.9   *Value added at the farmgate and fruit industry levels by Fynbos bees*

Fynbos type	Income from pollination/ha	Total VAD at farm gate per ha	Total VAD per ha
Mountain Fynbos*	0.30	0.21	57.19
Laterite Fynbos	1.59	1.11	295.31
Limestone Fynbos	4.17	2.92	802.74
Sand Plain Fynbos	2.73	1.91	524.06
Strandveld	2.60	1.82	500.15

Note: * Most of the bees are kept at low altitudes within the Mountain Fynbos vegetation type, so the values are not evenly spread.

4.3   Option and Existence Value

4.3.1   Future use (option) value – the value of biodiversity
Only a fraction of Fynbos species are actually used at present, but the maintenance of genetic diversity is important for many industries. For example, wild genetic resources are very important to the wildflower industry in order to maintain South Africa's competitive edge in international markets, because the industry is subject to fashion trends which dictate which species are marketed. Within-species genetic variation is also important. The Rooibos tea industry is based exclusively on the cultivation of a single strain of *Aspalathus linearis* (Van Wyk and Van der Bank, 1996). In 1993, the approximately 15 000 ha under cultivation yielded 3300 tonnes, of which 18 per cent was exported, realizing R7.5 million in foreign exchange (Cowling and Richardson, 1995). The reliance on a single genetic strain places some risk on the industry (for example, vulnerability to disease), but there is a large amount of variation within *A. linearis*, which offers a large gene pool from which favourable

cultivars can be selected if necessary (Van Wyk and Van der Bank, 1996). The cultivation of honeybush tea, set to be an important industry in future, is still in an experimental stage, and there is still a very strong reliance on genetic material from the wild. There is thus an incentive (and accordingly some value) in conserving these plant species in their natural habitat.

Local and overseas flower industries also rely to a large extent on the *ex-situ* conservation of Fynbos biodiversity. The Agricultural Research Council's Fynbos Genebank maintains more than 2350 variants of more than 140 species (Middelmann, 1995). Fynbos-based industries overseas include the window box 'geranium' industry in Europe – from *Pelargonium* spp., and the *Gladiolus* cut-flower industry (Scott, 1993). The Dutch have developed 136 forms of *Freesia*, with a value of R300 million at Dutch flower auctions in 1991 (Cowling and Richardson, 1995). The same trend is applicable to cultivars of other bulbous species as well as certain *Erica* species, succulents and members of the Proteaceae. The value of these products is now almost exclusively overseas where most of the commercial genetic material is utilized. However, new genetic material is constantly being sought and there is most likely a large amount of 'bio-prospecting' taking place in the Fynbos biome, both legally and illegally.

It is extremely difficult, however, to predict what uses may be found for the remaining species in future, or what their value might be. One study suggested that the cost of producing a new floricultural variety (about R100 000) could be equated to the value of an endemic plant species (Higgins et al., 1997). This would translate into R584.7 million if the number of endemics in the Cape Floral Kingdom (5847) was used. Similarly, although the value of Fynbos plants for medicinal purposes has not been very well researched (Fourie et al., 1992), Scott (1993) suggests that there is potential in certain plant families that are well represented in Fynbos for extraction of medicinally important compounds. Scott cites a prediction of an economist that the projected loss of 50 000 species in the world by the turn of the century would mean the loss to the pharmaceutical industry of some 25 prescription drugs with a market value of US$25 billion. The Fynbos has more than 1400 species of plants with Red Data Book status (Cowling and Richardson, 1995). If these plants were to become extinct, the proportional loss to the future pharmaceutical industry based on the above assumption could be as much as US$700 million.

4.3.2   Existence value

Two studies have been carried out to estimate the existence value of Fynbos areas, one concerning the De Hoop Nature Reserve (Turpie, 1996), and the other, the privately owned lands of the Agulhas Plain (Turpie et al., 1997). These studies use the contingent valuation method (CVM), which uses questionnaire surveys to elicit people's willingness to pay (WTP), in this case to ensure the conservation of Fynbos areas. This is a somewhat controversial technique, because it is open to much bias, but it is one of the only ways in which existence value can be estimated. In both studies, the WTP was estimated for people living within 50 km of the area and in Cape Town, some 150–250 km away.

Total WTP by these populations for De Hoop, which conserves 36 000 ha of coastal lowlands dominated by Limestone Fynbos, was R14 million annually (1996 rands). If we assume that half of this value is attributed to the marine component of the reserve, then the existence value elicited for the terrestrial Fynbos area was $R194.ha^{-1}.y^{-1}$, or $R213.ha^{-1}.y^{-1}$ in 1997 rands.

In a similar study of the highly floristically diverse coastal Agulhas Plain area, people allocated 44–47 per cent of their total WTP for conservation in the area to the terrestrial Fynbos area, yielding a total WTP for the terrestrial area of R33.5 million. Taking the area of natural veld only, about 120 000 ha of the total area of 160 000 ha, the total existence value of this area to residents of the Cape Peninsula and the Agulhas Plain is $R279.ha^{-1}.y^{-1}$ (1997 rands).

These values do not include the WTP for conservation of these areas by the rest of the province, and indeed, the rest of the world. It is also important to note that these values cannot be extrapolated to the Fynbos region as a whole: people's marginal WTP is likely to decrease dramatically as the total area conserved changes. At best, one could estimate the minimum average WTP per ha as the larger of the two values averaged over the total area of Fynbos. This provides a very conservative minimum estimate of $R9.50.ha^{-1}.y^{-1}$ as the average existence value per ha of Fynbos.

4.3.3   Effects of alien infestation on option and non-use values

As alien plants displace native species, converting species-rich vegetation to single-species stands of trees (van Wilgen et al., 1998), they pose a significant threat to the endemic flora. Invasive trees and shrubs threaten about 750 species in the Fynbos biome, a globally unequalled and significant figure (Richardson et al., 1992).

If existence value has most of its basis in species diversity, then alien invasion may only affect this value inasmuch as it affects species richness. However, it is more likely that existence value of Fynbos is also based on existence of pristine stretches of vegetation which retain their ecosystem functions and integrity, in which case even minor levels of infestation may erode this value significantly.

4.4   Net Losses in Fynbos Values due to Alien Invasion

Net depreciation in Fynbos resources was calculated as the reduction in value flows due to quality degradation caused by alien invasion minus economic gains from the alien vegetation. Multiplied by respective areas of various Fynbos vegetation and infestation class, a total loss of R455 million was derived to reflect net depletion of Fynbos stock values. This is about 60 per cent of the total value added derived from Fynbos vegetation in its current state, which means that the resource has been reduced to less than 50 per cent of its potential economic value as a result of degradation caused by alien invasion alone. In other words, this meant that if Fynbos ecosystems are restored to their original pristine state the resource would yield a total annual value of about R1.24 billion at the 1997 prices (R786 million + R455 million). This value is equivalent to about the total value added in plantation forestry and amounts to about 6 per cent of total value added in agriculture, forestry and fisheries combined (Turpie et al., forthcoming).

5   CONTROLLING INVASIVE ALIENS: COSTS, BENEFITS AND STRATEGIES

5.1   Control Methods, Costs and Strategies

Clearing of aliens in Fynbos is generally costly, particularly in mountainous areas where access is difficult and teams sometimes have to be flown in with helicopters. In order to clear the serotinous invaders (pines and hakeas) they have to be felled, after which seeds are released, germinate and are then burnt about a year later. Further follow-up operations are required about 2.5 and 10 years after burning to eliminate 'escapees' (Macdonald et al., 1985 in van Wilgen et al., 1996). Acacias, which produce large seed stocks in the soil, require more intensive follow-up measures to remove seedlings by hand (van Wilgen et al., 1996). Furthermore, resprouting trees, such as *A. saligna*, need to be individually poisoned with herbicide after felling.

  Early efforts at clearing aliens, as a result of concern about the loss of Fynbos biodiversity, failed to be effective, as they did not take the biology of the invaders into account and did not include follow up clearing to remove new seedlings (van Wilgen et al., 1997). Clearing efforts were stepped up in the 1970s, following the realization that alien invasion of catchments could lead to substantial water losses. At the same time, research was initiated into finding biological control agents. The resultant integrated control programmes petered out in the late 1980s with a decline in funding (ibid.). In the meantime, the biocontrol measures that were introduced have started to have a significant impact on several species, including *A. saligna*, *A. longifolia* and *Hakea* (Versveld et al., 1998), although it is a slow process (Dean, 1998).

Following improved understanding of the effects of catchment invasion on water supplies (Le Maitre et al., 1996), and the recognition that the time for which existing water supply schemes could meet demand could be significantly lengthened by keeping catchments clear of aliens, the government's Working for Water Project was initiated in 1995. This was a renewed campaign to clear alien vegetation in catchment areas, and the Fynbos Working for Water Project forms the largest subsector of this project. With its intensive monitoring, this project has yielded comprehensive data on the financial costs of alien clearing (Table 9.10). It has been estimated that clearing the country of aliens would cost about $2 billion, or $100 million per year for 20 years, if biological control is not taken into account (van Wilgen et al., 1998).

Table 9.10   Costs including clearing, two follow-ups and burning, for three broad levels of infestation (Rands per ha)

	Light	Medium	Dense
Pinus	1034	2943	6081
Hakea	357	2215	6280
Acacia mearnsii	965	3979	5110
Lowland acacias	260	1750	5500

Sources: Versveld et al. (1998) and South African National Parks for control of lowlands (mainly acacias).

Because of these high clearing costs, it is necessary to devise efficient control strategies. Biological control, while effective and cheap, is slow relative to the rates of invasion (Dean, 1998). Indeed, biocontrol and integrated management of aliens is seldom (if ever) incorporated into models (ibid.). Complex models are currently being developed by government which incorporate rates of spread of alien trees, impact on water yields, cost of clearing and follow-up operations, and even the loss of firewood to local communities (ibid.).

Modelling of control strategies includes determining whether to clear sparse outlier stands first and then dense stands or vice versa, but beyond a certain threshold invasion rate, these tactics are irrelevant (ibid.). If clearing effort cannot keep up with the rate of invasion, then it is a wasted effort (Higgins et al., 1997).

Because aliens spread exponentially, and control costs increase with levels of infestation, it can be expected that delay in clearing is costly in financial

terms. If it is assumed that infestation levels move to the next density category after each fire event, which would occur on average every 12–15 years,
then the cost of delay is high, before discounting is taken into account (Table
9.11). Higher discount rates soon erode this effect, however, such that at
discount rates of about 3–4 per cent the decision is ambivalent, and above
that it does not pay to clear earlier. Similarly, if an area is to be cleared, then
it does not make sense to delay clearing activity if the rate of invasion
exceeds the interest rate. These calculations do not consider the damage costs
incurred by alien spread during these delays, however.

*Table 9.11   Present value of financial costs (1996 R millions) of immediate
and delayed action in clearing Fynbos*

Discount rate (%)	Immediate action	12-year delay	24-year delay
0	45.9	75.3	104.7
3.5	42.0	45.7	42.0
4	41.5	42.6	37.0
8	37.8	24.7	13.7

Source: Based on Turpie (1996).

5.2   Justifying the High Costs of Clearing

Higgins et al. (1997) modelled a hypothetical catchment and calculated that
the present value of such an area could be increased by 37–89 per cent if it
were kept free of aliens. However, the incorporation of a full range of possible types of Fynbos values into their hypothetical area is unrealistic in many
respects, and cannot be used to make generalizations about the benefits of
clearing alien invasives from Fynbos. Costs and benefits of alien invasion and
control differ depending on type of area and on land ownership. Most attention has been focused on publicly owned mountain catchment areas, where
the main economic impact of alien invasion is due to water loss. These
wilderness areas are used for recreation, but little or no consumptive use
takes place. The economic impacts of alien invasion are quite different in
publicly owned lands in the lowlands, where water is not such a big issue,
and on privately owned lands, where consumptive use takes place. These
issues are examined further below.

5.2.1   Publicly and privately owned mountain catchment areas
Much attention has been paid to the consequences of alien infestation in
mountain catchment areas, which contain about half the area of mountain

Fynbos. These areas are mostly publicly owned, but also include some privately owned areas which also receive some level of state protection under the Mountain Catchment Areas Act. State-run alien-clearing programmes run on both public and private lands, as they protect a state resource – water.

It has been relatively easy to justify expensive alien-clearing programmes in these mountain catchment areas, in terms of the value of water saved. Higgins et al.'s (1997) hypothetical catchment model, suggested that costs of clearing aliens from mountain catchments would be justified in terms of the water savings alone. This has now been verified in a model using accurate cost data and rigorous analysis, at least for the main, higher-rainfall Fynbos catchments (Marais, 1998). Marais' cost data were based on the labour time required to clear different density classes of aliens, then priced at the Fynbos Working for Water Project (WWP) rate of R100 per day, inclusive of overheads and transport costs. Examining a number of scenarios, Marais found that clearing projects in water-rich mountain catchments were always justified in terms of the net present value of the water run-off, with internal rate of return (IRR) estimates of more than 10 per cent, no matter how long the clearing activity continues. Return rates are higher if clearing takes longer, but, with a discount rate of 8 per cent, net present values were higher if catchments were cleared more quickly (ibid.). Although Marais worked with a water value of R0.59/m^3, his results were still positive when a lower value of R0.35/m^3 was used.

Marais was not able to demonstrate the same positive results for drier catchment areas further inland, unless water values exceeded R0.47. In these catchments, positive net present values as a result of clearing were seen only over the very long term, and he suggested that it may be necessary to consider other economic benefits of clearing, such as biodiversity values (Dean, 1998). However, this may have been partly due to the lack of empirical hydrological and other relevant data from these areas (Marais, 1998).

5.2.2 Privately owned lands

A large proportion of Fynbos, particularly lowland Fynbos, falls outside of mountain catchment areas and within privately owned lands. Because they have no influence on the major existing or future water schemes, these areas have received considerably less attention in the fight against alien invasives. Indeed, it has even been suggested that the above-mentioned clearing costs for the country could be reduced by ignoring species such as *A. cyclops*, which occur in lowlands. This would potentially reduce required expenditures to about $800 million, or $40 million per year (van Wilgen *et al.*, 1998), which is somewhat closer to the budget of $50 million currently allocated to clearing aliens under the Working for Water Project. However, in many of these areas, aliens probably do have a significant impact on the region's groundwater resources.

Ignoring the water costs that will ultimately be seen by the state, Fynbos landowners largely suffer costs of invasion in the form of losses of consumptive use value, as well as aesthetic value. The onus is on these landowners to clear their own lands. The question is whether these losses create sufficient incentive for farmers to carry out expensive control programmes.

The Agulhas Plain is a centre of immense biodiversity importance within the Fynbos region (Cowling and Holmes, 1992), most of which is under private ownership. A typical farmer in the Agulhas Plain region might own about 500 ha of Fynbos, in addition to a similar area of cultivated lands. The average farmer's Fynbos area comprises about 60 per cent Mountain Fynbos, 10 per cent Laterite Fynbos and 30 per cent Limestone Fynbos, and such an area currently generates about R66 500 net income per year from flower harvesting for the farmer under the current average level of invasion. However, kept free of aliens, the same land would generate an income of R83 700, which means that current incomes are depressed by an average of 21 per cent due to aliens. Does this loss justify the implementation of a clearing programme, say over ten years? A simple spreadsheet model indicates that such action is not easy to justify in private financial terms at current clearing costs: if clearing costs are spread over ten years, with minimal follow-up costs continued thereafter, benefits in terms of increased production are only realized after several years, and the net present values over 20 years (a farmers' time horizon?) of cleared land is lower (R1.1 million) than that of unmanaged land (R1.2 million) at a zero discount rate. Higher discount rates obviously widen this gap, because the costs of clearing are borne up front and the benefits are realized later, and South Africans face relatively high real interest rates. Thus at present, unless farmers gain other values, for example, aesthetic values, from clearing their lands, they are unlikely to do it for financial reasons unless they are extremely far-sighted (and sufficiently wealthy).

Thus it is clear that as long as costs and interest rates remain high, the state will need to provide an incentive for farmers to clear aliens from privately owned Fynbos. In turn, it may be necessary to provide an argument, possibly again based on water, as to why the state should provide such an incentive. At present, state aid in clearing private lands is being meted out (as of last year) only to landowners who will be contracting in to a new national park in the Agulhas Plain. Perhaps this, in itself will provide an incentive for more farmers to contract into the park!

In some areas, benefits are obtained from cutting aliens on private lands. Unfortunately, however, the cutting of aliens for firewood is apparently incompatible with conservation objectives. Firewood cutting does not effectively clear aliens: only suitable trees are removed, and there is no follow-up management. Indeed, it is thought that these activities may increase their spread, for example, by spreading seeds. This produces another interesting conflict, as the introduction of a biological control agent for *A. cyclops* was a concern because of the disadvantaged communities who make a living from selling firewood. Thus the control of *A. cyclops*, in particular, poses a rather unique problem of equity consideration.

5.2.3 Publicly owned lowland Fynbos

Although the protected areas of the Fynbos lowlands have also not received the attention of the mountain catchment areas, they have received somewhat more attention than private lands, by virtue of the fact that alien control is a part of conservation management. However, budgets for alien clearing have been pathetic compared to the costs needed to remove this threat (Turpie, 1996).

It has thus become clear that in the case of lowland Fynbos areas, where clearing of alien vegetation often cannot be justified in terms of water savings, it would be helpful to demonstrate other economic benefits of clearing. In publicly owned lands, however, these benefits sometimes appear to be relatively limited: use is usually almost entirely restricted to non-consumptive activities, and with a tendency towards providing visitors with a unique wilderness experience, numbers of users are generally low, and existence value is limited by levels of awareness. Nevertheless, for the 36 000 ha De Hoop Nature Reserve in lowland Fynbos, which is invaded by alien vegetation to a serious degree (ibid.), it can be demonstrated that the benefits to society can justify clearing costs.

Based on Turpie's (1996) findings, the costs and benefits of clearing the reserve of aliens are compared over a 50 year period, applying a discount rate of 8 per cent. It was estimated that the costs, in 1996 rands, to clear the reserve over two years and continue with four follow-up programmes over two years each, would amount to a net present value of about R37.8 million (in 1996 rands). If existing recreational and existence values have their basis in unspoilt Fynbos, then it can be assumed that these values would increase with increased quality of the reserve. Thus if it is assumed that recreational values are proportionally weighted by percentage cover of aliens, and that expressed existence values only apply to lightly infested parts of the reserve, the restoration of the reserve to its pristine state would yield benefits in the order of R285 million, in present terms. This is much greater than the clearing cost, although unlike in the case of mountain catchments, most of this benefit would not actually be reflected in the national economy, so it is more difficult to defend politically.

5.2.4 The Working for Water Project: turning a problem to its best advantage

In South Africa, the government has made use of a unique opportunity to link environmental conservation with development and job creation. This unique solution, in the form of the Working for Water Project, has mobilized enough funding to make a huge difference, not only in mountain catchment areas, but recently also in lowland areas, in which clearing was difficult to justify on economic grounds. In the latter areas, poverty relief alone probably provides sufficient justification to attract donor funding. Initially creating 7000 jobs in 1995, the nationwide programme had created more than 35 000 jobs by March 1998 (van Wilgen et al., 1998). The Fynbos Working for Water Project spent R40 million on clearing in 1996/97, of which R25 million went on the salaries of nearly 3000 people. Clearing is done by contracting out jobs to previously unemployed people. But the benefits have gone beyond job creation, with emphasis on training programmes and empowerment, in activities such as clearing, team management and transport. In this way, the high cost of clearing has been turned into an internationally-sponsored socioeconomic development programme benefiting thousands of people throughout the country: a justification for clearing aliens in itself.

NOTE

*   This chapter was inspired by Charles Perrings and benefited from discussion with Tony Leiman. Council for Scientific and Industrial Research (CSIR) Environmentek in Pretoria kindly performed the GIS analysis.

REFERENCES

Bridgeman, D.H.M., I. Palmer and W.H. Thomas (1992), *South Africa's Leading Edge: A Guide to the Western Cape Economy*, Cape Town: Wesgro.
Burgers, C.J., C. Marais and S.J. Bekker (1995), 'The importance of mountain catchments for maintaining the water resources of the Western Cape Province and the need for optimal management', in C. Boucher and C. Marais (eds), *Managing Fynbos Catchments for Water*, Pretoria: FRD Programmes Report 24: 99–123.
Chapman, R.A., D.F. Scott and D. le Maitre (1995), 'Hydrological impacts of aliens in Fynbos catchments', in C. Boucher and C. Marais (eds), *Managing Fynbos Catchments for Water*, Pretoria: FRD Programmes Report 24: 40–43.
Costanza, R., R. d'Arge, R. de Groot, S. Farber, M. Grasso, B. Hannon, K. Limbug, S. Naeem, R.V. O'Neill, J. Paruelo, R.G. Raskin, P. Sutton, and M. van den Belt (1997), 'The value of the world's ecosystem services and natural capital', *Nature*, **387**: 253–60.
Cowling, R.M and P.M. Holmes (1992), 'Endemism and speciation in a lowland flora from the Cape Floristic Region', *Botanical Journal of the Linnean Society*, **47**: 367–83.
Cowling, R.M. and D.M. Richardson (1995), *Fynbos: South Africa's Unique Floral Kingdom*, Cape Town: Fernwood Press.
Deacon, J. (1993), *Management Guidelines for Rock Art Sites in Two Wilderness*

Areas in the Western Cape, Pretoria: Department of Environment Affairs and Tourism Report.

Dean, W.R. (1998), 'Space invaders: modelling the distribution, impacts and control of alien organisms', *Trends in Ecology and Evolution*, **13**: 256–8.

Department of Water Affairs and Forestry (DWAF) (1994), *Western Cape Systems Analysis: A Study Overview*, DWAF, City of Cape Town, Ninham Shand Consulting Engineers and BKS Incorporated, South Africa.

Forestek, Council for Scientific and Industrial Research (CSIR) (1994), 'Field Manual for mapping populations of invasive plants for use with the catchment management system', Stellenbosch: Unpublished report of the CSIR.

Fourie, T.G., I. Swart and O. Snyckers (1992), 'Folk Medicine: a viable starting point for pharmaceutical research', *South African Journal of Science*, **88**:190–92.

Higgins, S.I. (1998), 'Predicting rates and patterns of alien plant spread', PhD Thesis, University of Cape Town.

Higgins, S.I., J.K. Turpie, R. Costanza, R.M. Cowling, D.C. Le Maitre, C. Marais and G. Midgley (1997), 'An ecological economic simulation model of mountain Fynbos ecosystems: dynamics, valuation and management', *Ecological Economics*, **22**: 155–69.

Hilton-Taylor, C. and A. Le Roux (1989), 'Conservation status of the Fynbos and Karoo biomes', in, B.J. Huntley (ed.), *Biotic Diversity in Southern Africa: Concepts and Conservation*, Cape Town: Oxford University Press: 202–23.

Le Maitre, D.C., B.W. van Wilgen, R.A. Chapman and D. McKelly (1996), 'Invasive plants and water resources in the Western Cape Province, South Africa: modeling the consequences of a lack of management', *Journal of Applied Ecology*, **33**: 161–72.

Low, A.B. and A.G. Rebelo (1996), *Vegetation of South Africa, Lesotho and Swaziland: A Companion to the Vegetation Map of South Africa, Lesotho and Swaziland*, Pretoria: Department of Environmental Affairs and Tourism.

Malan, D.G. (1996), *The Fynbos Ornamental Industry 1993–1995*, Cape Town: SAPPEX Report.

Marais, C. (1998), 'An economic evaluation of invasive alien plant control programmes in the mountain catchment areas of the Western Cape Province, South Africa', PhD Thesis, University of Stellenbosch.

McDowell, C. and E.J. Moll (1992), 'The influence of agriculture on the decline of West Coast Renosterveld, Southwestern Cape, South Africa', *Journal of Environmental Management*, **35**: 173–92.

Middelmann, M. (1995), 'The Fynbos industry, the indigenous plant use', *Newsletter*, **3**(2): 6.

Moll, E.J. and E.L. Bossi (1984), *Vegetation Map of the Fynbos Biome*, Pretoria: Government Printer.

Munasinghe, M. (1994), 'Economic and policy issues in natural habitats and protected areas', in M. Munasinghe and J. McNeely (eds), *Protected Area Economics and Policy: Linking Conservation and Sustainable Development*, Washington, DC: World Bank and IUCN: 15–49.

Myers, N. (1990), 'The biodiversity challenge: expended hot-spots analysis', *The Environmentalist*, **10**: 243–55.

Plant Protection Research Institute (1992), *Die Kaapse Indringerbye en hulp aan Byeboere. Bylae A: Die waarde van bye as bestuiwers van landbougewasse in die RSA*, Pretoria: Taakspanverslag, Navorsingsinstituut vir Planbeskerming.

Rebelo, A.G. (1987), 'Management implications', in A.G. Rebelo (ed.), *A Prelimi-*

nary Synthesis of Pollination Biology in the Cape Flora, Pretoria: South African National Scientific Programmes Report No. 141: 193–211.

Richardson, D.M., I.A.W. Macdonald, P.M. Holmes and R.M. Cowling (1992), 'Plant and animal invasions', in R.M. Cowling (ed.), *The Ecology of Fynbos – Nutrients, Fire and Diversity*, Cape Town: Oxford University Press: 271–308.

Scott, D.F., D.B. Versfeld and W. Lesch (1998), 'Erosion and sediment yield in relation to afforestation and fire in the mountains of the Western Cape Province, South Africa', *South African Geographical Journal*, **80**: 52–9.

Scott, G. (1993), 'Medicinal and aromatic plants – healthcare, economics and conservation in South Africa', *Veld and Flora*, **79**: 84–7.

Turpie, J.K. (1996), 'A preliminary economic assessment of De Hoop Nature Reserve', Cape Town: Unpublished report, University of Cape Town.

Turpie, J.K., B.J. Heydenrych, S.L. Lamberth and B. Smith (1997), 'The establishment of a national park on the Agulhas Plain: economic implications of conservation scenarios for terrestrial and marine resources', Cape Town: Unpublished report, FitzPatrick Institute, University of Cape Town.

Turpie, J.K., B.J. Heydenrych and R. Hassan (forthcoming), 'Accounting for Fynbos: a preliminary assessment of the status and economic value of Fynbos vegetation in the Western Cape', in R. Hassan (ed.), *Accounting for Stock and Flow Values of Woody Land Resources: Methods and Results from South Africa*, Nairobi: EENESA Working Paper Series.

Van der Merwe, W.J. and P.J. Eloff (1995), 'Byeboerdery in Wes-Kaapland', *South African Bee Journal*, **67**: 105–14.

Van Wilgen, B.W., R.M. Cowling and C.J. Burgers (1996), 'Valuation of ecosystem services: a case study from South African Fynbos ecosystems', *BioScience*, **46**: 184–9.

Van Wilgen, B.W., D.C. le Maitre and R.M. Cowling (1998), 'Ecosystem services, efficiency, sustainability and equity: South Africa's Working for Water programme', *Trends in Ecology and Evolution*, **13**: 378.

Van Wilgen, B.W., P.R. Little, R.A. Chapman, A.H.M. Görgens, T. Willems and C. Marais (1997), 'The sustainable development of water resources: history, costs and benefits of alien plant control programmes', *South African Journal of Science*, **93**: 404–11.

Van Wilgen, B.W. and D.M. Richardson (1985), 'The effects of alien shrub invasions on vegetation structure and fire behaviour in South African Fynbos shrublands: a simulation study', *Journal of Applied Ecology*, **22**: 955–96.

Van Wyk, B.E. and M. Van der Bank (1996), 'Variation studies in *Aspalathus linearis* (Rooibos Tea), Program and Abstracts', 22nd Annual Congress of the South African Association of Botanists (SAAB), University of Stellenbosch, Stellenbosch.

Versveld, D.B., D.C. le Maitre and R.A. Chapman (1998), *Alien Invading Plants and Water Resources in South Africa: A Preliminary Assessment*, Pretoria: Water Research Commission Report No. TT99/98.

10. The impact of invasive species in African lakes

Victor Kasulo

---

1 INTRODUCTION

Analysis of the impact of invasive species in African lakes and rivers has focused particularly on the role of exotic fish species. This can be illustrated by the controversy over the impact of the introduction of the Nile perch (*Lates niloticus*) into Lake Victoria. However, the analysis can be extended to other fish species and water weeds. This chapter analyses the physical and economic impacts of the introduction and establishment of Nile perch, Tilapiine species, Tanganyika sardines and water hyacinth (*Eichhornia crassipes*) into African lakes and rivers. The Nile perch and Tilapiine species were introduced into Lakes Victoria, Kyoga and Nabugabo, while the Tanganyika sardines were introduced into Lakes Kariba, Kivu and Itezhi-tezhi. Water hyacinth is spreading very fast throughout Africa and is a threat to the river and lake systems of the continent (Figure 10.1).

2 FISH INTRODUCTIONS

The extent of fish introductions can be analysed from the Food and Agriculture Organization's Database on Introductions of Aquatic Species (DIAS).[1] The database was initiated in the early 1980s, and originally considered only freshwater species of fish. The database has been expanded to include additional taxa, such as molluscs, crustaceans, algae and higher plants, vertebrates and invertebrates. It does not, however, include movements of organisms within the same country. To date, the database contains 2870 records of introductions, of which 2377 are fish. Africa has experienced 430 introductions representing about 15 per cent of the total.

Source: Modified from Pitcher (1995).

Figure 10.1   Major lakes and rivers in Africa

2.1   Determinants of Fish Introductions

The main goals behind the intentional introduction of exotic fish species include aquaculture, sport fishing, creation of a new fishery, control of pests and ornament. Unintentional introductions arise from cases where exotic pond fish are washed away to rivers and lakes through flooding. The culture of carp in fish ponds in Malawi, for example, was stopped in preference to indigenous species to avoid accidental transfer to rivers and lakes (DREA, 1994). Contemporary justifications for the introduction of fish to improve or create fisheries have generally been formulated in ecological terms, although never on the basis of informed detailed knowledge of the environment. The overall principle seems to be that a component of the ecosystem is perceived to be underutilized by the endemic fauna. The perception that there is an excess of underutilized food is common to many introductions, but this is often unquantified and based on casual observations that ignore the reality of the aquatic ecosystem. In Lake Malawi, for example, the presence of fly swarms compared with Lake Tanganyika suggested to Turner (1982) that they may be cropped more efficiently by clupeid planktivores than by the indigenous cyprinids or cichlids. Although Degnbol (1993) supported the view that most of Lake Malawi's production goes into flies, not fish, that conclusion was based on old and uncertain data that did not properly cover the large planktonic fish community. A detailed survey of the whole pelagic zone of Lake Malawi showed that planktonic production is not underutilized by fish (Menz, 1995).

2.2   General Effects of Fish Introduction

There is a supposition that introduction of exotic fish species can shift the nature of the ecosystem through competition, predation and hybridization. It is believed that introduced fish occasionally replace native species in natural habitats through competition for food or predation. Most replacements occur in altered environments that give the introduced fish an ecological advantage. In addition to trophic alterations through competition for food, predation and hybridization with endemic species, exotic fish are said to have several other harmful effects. These include habitat alterations, introduction of parasites and diseases, and spatial alterations as a result of aggressive actions and overcrowding (Bruton, 1990; Moyle and Leidy, 1992; Pitcher, 1995; Williamson, 1996).

On the other hand, introduction of exotic species may increase the amount of commercially harvestable fish, leading to other socioeconomic gains such as increased employment, foreign exchange earnings and nutrients. That is, there are benefits as well as costs. Whether an introduction is considered beneficial or harmful depends on a wide range of direct and indirect effects. It also depends on the sector of society one is looking at (Reynolds and Gréboval, 1988; Reynolds et al., 1995; Williamson, 1996). The best cases in African lakes to illustrate the complexity of the problem are the Nile perch, *Lates niloticus*, the tilapiines, *Oreochromis niloticus*, *Oreochromis leucostictus*, *Tilapia zilli* and *Tilapia melanopleura*, and the sardine *Limnothrissa miodon*.

2.3   Nile Perch and the Tilapiine Species

The Nile perch was introduced into Lakes Victoria, Kyoga and Nabugabo in the late 1950s and early 1960s to feed on haplochromines and to convert them into a larger fish of greater food and recreational value. This was done amid the fear that the Nile perch would deplete stocks of other fish and reduce species diversity in the lakes (Oguta-Ohwayo, 1995). The tilapiines were introduced into Lakes Victoria, Kyoga and Nabugabo, prior to the Nile perch (Kudhongania and Chitamwemba, 1995).

The traditional fishery of Lake Victoria concentrated on *Oreochromis esculentus*, *Bagrus docmac* and *Labeo victorianus* (ibid.). It was exploited by traditional equipment causing low fishing mortality. However, increases in demand together with gear improvements and lack of management measures, increased the fish mortality and brought new species into the fishery. Four exotic tilapiines (*O. niloticus*, *O. leucostictus*, *Tilapia zilli* and *T. melanopleura*) were introduced into Lake Victoria during the early 1950s. The establishment of these four exotic tilapiines in the lake introduced interspecific competition with two indigenous species. It also enhanced the likelihood of genetic dilution through hybridization (ibid.). Nile perch were introduced into the lake during the early 1960s. Their catch became significant only from 1975, 1977 and 1978 on the Ugandan, Kenyan and Tanzanian sectors of the lake, respectively. Predation by Nile perch had considerable impact on the haplochromine stocks of Lake Victoria. It was observed that haplochromines constituted 80 per cent by weight of its food. The fishery is now dominated by the Nile perch, *Lates niloticus*, Nile tilapia, *Oreochromis niloticus* and an endemic species, *Rastrineobola argentea* (ibid.).

Fish species composition of Lake Kyoga prior to the establishment of introduced species was similar to that of Lake Victoria. The Nile perch and the non-native tilapiine species were introduced earlier and spread faster in Lake Kyoga than in Lake Victoria. Stocks of the introduced species in Lake Kyoga increased rapidly from 1963 onwards. These increases were due to the contribution of the Nile perch and of the introduced tilapiines, especially the Nile tilapia. The yield of the native tilapiines, which had dominated the fishery since its development, and that of the other native species declined (Oguta-Ohwayo, 1995).

In Lake Nabugabo, the most important fish species among commercial catches, prior to the introductions, were similar to those of Lakes Victoria and Kyoga. There are no commercial catch statistics for Lake Nabugabo, but experimental catches from the lake between 1991 and 1992 showed that the catches are dominated by Nile perch, Nile tilapia, *R. argentea* and *T. rendalli*. As in Lakes Victoria and Kyoga, other species which dominated the catches prior to the introductions are now caught in very small quantities (ibid.).

2.3.1 The impact of tilapiine species and Nile perch

Several studies on the life history of indigenous tilapiine in Lakes Victoria, Kyoga and Nabugabo put the availability of suitable spawning sites as the most important factor limiting populations. The native tilapiines were spatially segregated, with the smaller *O. variabilis* being more inshore than *O. esculentus*. When *T. zilli* and *O. leucosticus* became established, they occupied the same habitat as *O. variabilis*. Direct competition was observed for nursery grounds between *O. variabilis* and *T. zilli*. Adult *O. niloticus* competed for breeding grounds with *O. variabilis*. This competition was followed by a decline in *O. variabilis* catches. Competition for food among the indigenous tilapiines was not thought to be significant. However, *O. esculentus*, feeding only on planktonic diatoms, was at a competitive disadvantage to *O. niloticus*. The latter species ingests phytoplankton, planktonic deposits and epiphytic algae, and is capable of utilizing the bluegreen algae which are abundant in the lakes (Kudhongania and Chitamwemba, 1995; Twongo, 1995; Welcomme, 1966).

Hybridization also appears to have led to the restructuring of the tilapiine communities in Lakes Victoria, Kyoga and Nabugabo. Hybrids between *O. niloticus* and *O. variabilis*, and between *T. zilli* and *T. melanopleura* were identified. Possible hybridization between *O. niloticus* and *O. esculentus* was also reported. In crosses involving *O. niloticus*, the morphological characters of the hybrids were apparently dominated by features of *O. niloticus*. It is probable that over time, the stocks lumped as *O. niloticus* could be a mixed population of such hybrids. The apparent dominance of this species could result from its abilities as a competitor. It grows to a larger size, has a faster growth rate, is more fecund, has a longer life span, has a wider food spectrum and is less habitat restricted than any of the other tilapiine species (Kudhongania and Chitamwemba, 1995; Welcomme, 1966; Twongo, 1995).

The most decisive impact is attributed to the introduction of Nile perch, *Lates niloticus*, and Nile tilapia, *Oreochromis niloticus*. Nile perch are believed to have consumed many native fish, eliminating them from the ecosystem and bringing them to commercial extinction. In the northwest portion of Lake Victoria, a progressive decline in the experimental trawl catch rates of haplochromines following the establishment of *Lates* in the area was noted. In the Kenyan part of Lake Victoria, a decline and eventual collapse of the haplochromine fishery between 1977 and 1983 were related to continuous increases in the *Lates* population (Table 10.1). Heavy predation pressure by *Lates* was considered more responsible for the decline in haplochromine stocks in the southern part of Lake Victoria. This evidence appeared to be in line with the feeding habits of *Lates*, which selects the most abundant prey (Kudhongania and Chitamwemba, 1995). The Nile tilapia outcompeted other tilapiine species, changing their feeding habit from phytoplankton to benthic organisms (Ochumba, 1995). However, it is often argued that the presence of Nile perch was not the only factor influencing species change in the lakes. Most of the Nile perch's predation appeared to pertain to years prior to its upsurge, suggesting that other factors such as fishing pressure and environmental changes may have had as large effects as the introduction of Nile perch. For instance, where some recovery of haplochromine was observed, this was often attributed to a decrease of Nile perch in those areas. An alternative explanation is that the haplochromines had recovered due to the use of larger meshes in nets directed at the Nile perch and therefore a decrease in haplochromine fishing mortality. It has also been suggested that eutrophication may have led to increased numbers of the shrimp *Caridina nilotica*, which in turn enabled the Nile perch to increase in number. This theory seems to explain the upsurge of the Nile perch many years after its establishment (Bunday and Pitcher, 1995).

In general, the disappearance of the haplochromines is assumed to have allowed the increase of its former main food sources. Changes were also observed in the behaviour of birds and mammals. The pied kingfisher, *Ceryle rudis*, changed its diet from one consisting mainly of haplochromines to one that consists almost exclusively of *Rastrineobola*. A similar shift in diet was found for the greater cormorant, *Phalacrocorax carbo*, and to a lesser extent, for the more inshore-feeding longtailed cormorant *P. africanus*. Spotted-necked otters, *Lutra maculicollis*, which formerly fed mainly on small haplochromines, currently include *Oreochromis niloticus* in their diet. It is concluded that the replacement of haplochromines cichlids as primary and secondary consumers by the Nile perch and *R. argentea* as secondary and tertiary consumers has changed the relative importance of the main food chains significantly (Witte et al., 1995).

The change in fish composition and yield as a result of the introduced species has also been associated with a decline in fish species diversity. In Lake Victoria, for example, the introduction of the Nile perch is linked with the loss of some species of haplochromine cichlids. Oguta-Ohwayo (1995) studied the changes in fishery yield and fish species diversity in Lakes Victoria, Kyoga and Nabugabo after the introduction of the Nile perch. Changes

*Table 10.1 Catch composition (%) of major fish species and total landings (Tonnes * 1000) in the Kenyan part of Lake Victoria*

Year	Tilapiines	Clarias	Haplochromis spp.	Bagrus	R. argentea	Protopterus	L. Niloticus	Total landings
1968	14.8	10.6	22.8	7.0	4.5	17.2	0.0	16.0
1969	26.6	7.6	36.8	5.5	2.9	9.3	0.1	17.0
1970	27.5	9.7	32.7	6.7	3.2	11.0	0.2	16.0
1971	21.1	12.5	32.0	7.1	5.1	12.3	0.3	15.0
1972	14.3	17.0	29.0	5.4	7.8	12.7	0.2	16.0
1973	10.1	15.7	33.2	8.6	10.5	13.0	0.9	17.0
1974	5.6	12.9	35.0	6.4	21.8	8.6	0.5	17.0
1975	3.9	15.6	27.9	8.4	27.4	1.1	0.1	17.0
1976	5.4	13.0	34.1	5.5	30.3	5.0	0.5	19.0
1977	7.4	9.1	32.4	6.0	34.7	4.0	1.1	19.0
1978	10.9	7.2	27.8	5.9	36.5	2.6	4.5	24.0
1979	9.0	10.0	21.6	5.8	30.5	1.5	14.0	31.0
1980	18.6	4.5	13.5	2.4	35.1	1.4	16.0	27.0
1981	10.2	2.6	2.1	1.1	20.1	0.5	59.7	46.0
1982	7.3	3.4	4.2	4.2	17.1	0.4	54.4	61.0
1983	5.5	2.7	0.8	3.1	21.3	0.3	67.7	77.0
1984	10.4	1.1	0.0	0.1	27.1	0.1	57.5	72.0
1985	10.7	0.6	0.0	0.1	29.2	0.2	56.5	90.0
1986	2.7	0.3	0.6	0.1	30.5	0.2	63.5	103.0
1987	2.8	0.6	0.3	0.0	24.5	0.2	69.1	113.0
1988	2.4	0.6	0.3	0.0	36.5	0.1	59.3	123.0
1989	2.3	1.4	1.5	0.1	38.5	0.1	54.3	225.0
1990	2.2	0.2	1.1	0.1	39.6	0.1	56.7	185.0
1991	2.4	0.2	0.5	0.0	39.2	0.0	57.3	175.0

Source: Ochumba (1995).

in species diversity were examined using the Shannon–Weiner index of diversity.[2] The study found that since the introduction and establishment of Nile perch and several tilapiine species, total yields increased but fish species diversity declined drastically. It was noted that before the increase in stocks of the introduced species, fish species diversity in Lake Victoria was higher than that of Lake Albert, the original habitat of the introduced species. But after the establishment of the introduced species, fish species diversity in Lake Victoria decreased to significantly lower levels than that of Lake Albert. Similar declines occurred in Lakes Kyoga and Nabugabo (ibid.).

Overall, it can be concluded that the introduction of exotic species into Lakes Victoria, Kyoga and Nabugabo led to an increase in total catches but has had a negative impact on the diversity, distribution and abundance of the indigenous fishes. The economic implications of these changes are examined later.

2.4   The Tanganyika cluiped, *Limnothrissa miodon*

The Tanganyika small pelagic cluiped, *Limnothrissa miodon* (kapenta), was introduced into Lakes Kariba, Kivu and Itezhi-tezhi to fill an unoccupied niche and increase the productivity of the lakes (Karenge and Kolding, 1995; de Iongh et al., 1995; Cowx and Kapasa, 1995).

Lake Kariba is a manmade lake constructed on the Zambezi River for the generation of hydro-electricity. The dam wall was completed in 1960 and the filling phase lasted from December 1958 to September 1963 when the water reached the mean operational level. Artisanal inshore gill netting began in 1962 on the Zimbabwean side and catches rose to a peak of some 2500 tonnes in 1964. From then catches declined almost linearly to about 1000 tonnes in 1970 (Karenge and Kolding, 1995).

Karenge and Kolding outlined the introduction and establishment of *Limnothrissa miodon* in Lake Kariba. They noted that Jackson (1961) predicted that the pelagic habitat of Lake Kariba would remain empty because the species present in the Zambezi evolved in a riverine habitat and would, therefore, only inhabit the shallow littoral zones. Following Jackson's recommendation, kapenta was introduced into Lake Kariba between 1967 and 1969 from Lake Tanganyika.

The introduction was a success and kapenta fishing began in 1973 with a single purse-seiner. Effort grew rapidly and the fishery developed into a big industry, with more than 30 000 tonnes landed annually, and with some potential for further expansion. Thus, with the introduction of the pelagic fishery, Lake Kariba has lived up to even the most optimistic pre-impoundment predictions, that the lake might produce as much as 30 000 tonnes per year (Karenge and Kolding, 1995).

Lake Kivu forms a natural border of more than 100 km between the Democratic Republic of Congo (Zaire) to the west and Rwanda to the east. The lake was formed after volcanic eruptions gave rise to the formation of a new volcanic range, and the waters of Lake Kivu that used to flow north towards Lake Albert were blocked. After a considerable rise in the water level, the water flow was reversed towards the south into Lake Tanganyika through the Ruzizi River (de Iongh et al., 1995).

In the case of Lake Kivu, de Iongh et al. note that the interesting aspects of the lake are its ecological immaturity and the relative low fish diversity. As an ecosystem the lake had low species diversity and production so that traditional fishing practices were at a low level. Verbeke (1957) suggested the introduction of a suitable species like the Tanganyika sardine to fill this niche in Lake Kivu, in the hope that more organic matter would be converted into edible fish and less lost into mud. In the period between 1958 and 1960, thousands of two species of sardine, *Stolothrissa* and *Limnothrissa*, were transported from Lake Tanganyika to Lake Kivu. In 1974, the presence of *Limnothrissa* in the southern part of the lake was noted and in 1976 an expedition recorded it over the whole lake. *Stolothrissa* was never encountered in experimental catches, so it was assumed that this species did not succeed in invading the lake (de Iongh et al., 1995).

Another seemingly successful story for the sardine *Limnothrissa miodon* is its introduction into Lake Itezhi-tezhi in Zambia. The lake was built as an upstream storage reservoir for the Kafue Gorge Upper Hydropower Scheme. It was completed in 1977. Prior to any impoundment, the Kafue fishery system had more than 56 species. However, since inundation only 24 species have been recorded from Lake Itezhi-tezhi. The decline in species diversity was primarily due to members of the families Cyprinidae, Mormyridae and Schilbeidae being unable to adapt to the new lacustrine environment, particularly in relation to spawning and feeding grounds, and being unable to cope with fluctuating water levels in the lake (Cowx and Kapasa, 1995).

Once the fish community had become established in Lake Itezhi-tezhi, it was apparent that no indigenous plankton-feeding species was present to exploit the open-water pelagic zone. Following the experiences in Lakes Kariba and Kivu, and in an attempt to increase the sustainable fish yield from Lake Itezhi-tezhi, *Limnothrissa* was introduced in early 1992, and now appears to be well established throughout the lake (ibid.).

2.4.1 The impact of the Tanganyika cluiped, *Limnothrissa miodon*
The successful introduction of the sardine *Limnothrissa miodon* is believed to have had ecological effects on competitors and predators, on plankton and on nutrient cycling. The introduction of *Limnothrissa miodon* led to considerable increases in its predators. In Lake Kariba, for instance, the abundance of

the tigerfish, *Hydrocynus vittatus*, rose from 5 per cent to 10 per cent of the gillnet catch after the arrival of the sardines (Marshall, 1995). The introduced sardine constitute at least 70 per cent of the food intake of tigerfish. Situation studies have shown that predation mortalities on kapenta from tigerfish nevertheless account for less than 15 per cent of total sardine mortality (Karenge and Kolding, 1995).

Despite the increased amount of food (kapenta) available for the adult population, there has been a significant decline in the number of small tigerfish, suggesting that density-dependent processes are operating mainly on the young and juvenile part of the population. This might be a result of competition rather than predation. Most inshore fish species, when very small, feed on zooplankton as does the introduced sardine, hence competition for food at juvenile stages should exist. Karenge and Kolding point out that predation pressure is now less important than interspecific competition, particularly at the lower trophic levels. Against this, Marshall (1984) attributed the rapid decline in small tigerfish biomass to commercial purse seining for sardines where they occurred as bycatch.

Little is known about population dynamics and biology of the other fish species in the lakes, but many are believed to eat fish to some extent. They can probably feed on juvenile sardines in shallow water and could, therefore, have benefited from the introduction of *Limnothrissa*. The survival of their fry could be enhanced because *Hydrocynus* would prey on the sardines instead.

Other sardine predators are piscivorous birds. On Lake Kariba, the white-winged black-tern, *Chlidonias leucoptera*, which feeds on sardines, has learned to hunt at night around the fishing boats. The gray-headed gull, *Larus cirrocephalus*, has also taken advantage of the sardines by scavenging fish from the racks on which they are sun-dried. This gull was once a vagrant to the lake but there is now a considerable resident population which has begun to breed on small islands (Marshall, 1995).

The effect of planktivorous fishes on plankton populations is that larger species decrease or even disappear while smaller species become dominant. *Limnothrissa* has brought about changes of this nature in the lakes into which it was introduced. In Lake Kariba for instance, diaptomids and larger cladocerans decreased rapidly after the sardines were introduced and *Chaoborus* apparently disappeared. Rotifers and nauplii larvae became increasingly important constituents of the zooplankton, while the mean biomass decreased. In Lake Kivu, comparison of plankton samples in 1953, before the introduction of *Limnothrissa*, with those taken in 1981 after the introduction indicated a strong decrease in size of cyclopoid species and a significant drop in standing crop. The larger planktonic species declined, leading to the almost complete disappearance of *Daphnia* and an increase of ciliates and other protozoa. These changes are indicative of size-selective predation on the plankton by the sardine (de Iongh et al., 1995; Marshall, 1995).

Not much is known about the effect of *Limnothrissa* on nutrient cycling. However, in Lake Kariba, it has been suggested that *Limnothrissa* contributed to the decline of the fern *Salvinia molesta*. The floating mats of this plant retained large quantities of nutrients, which were evidently released when they collapsed between 1970 and 1975. There was a considerable increase in the relative abundance of several fish species at the time. If the sardines were responsible for the collapse of *Salvinia* then they clearly have the capacity to influence nutrient cycling in a lake. But the effects of such changes are unpredictable (Marshall, 1995).

2.5   Economic Implications of Exotic Fish Species

The different cases outlined above do not clearly state whether the benefits in terms of fish yield outweigh the damage to endemic species following the different introductions. Since the benefits of introductions are sensitive to fish prices, which change on a month-to-month basis, it has been argued that evaluation of the benefits should be subject to continuous review (Pitcher, 1995).

Different conclusions have been reached regarding the socioeconomic impact of introduced species in the different African lakes. In Lake Victoria, for instance, it has been difficult to evaluate the actual cost of the damage caused by the introduction of exotic species. It is not possible to come up with a value for the haplochromine species that are no longer extant. One argument regarding the cost of damage caused by Nile perch is that its upsurge forced Lake Victoria's fishery to forgo yields of haplochromines. The sustainable yield of Lake Victoria's haplochromine fishery without the introduced Nile perch is estimated at between 266 000 tonnes and 550 000 tonnes per annum. The presence of the Nile perch, whose sustainable yield is in the order of 280 000 tonnes, has meant that up to 270 000 tonnes of sustainable yield from Lake Victoria may have been forgone (ibid.). The value of the forgone alternative can be obtained using market prices. However, the unreliability of both the estimation method and market prices would lead to a poor estimate of the value of the opportunity cost. The above argument is also weak in that it assumes that the Nile perch acted alone in the depletion of haplochromines.

Several attempts have been made to estimate the economic benefits from Nile perch. The benefits include increased production, (marketing) employment, nutrition and other indirect benefits. Reynolds et al. (1995) estimated that the production gains in ex-vessel value over the period 1975–89 amounted to about US$280 million (at 1989 prices). The number of fishers (primary and secondary) and their dependents were estimated at 475 000 in 1975 but

1 266 000 in 1989: an increase of 267 per cent. The increase in fish production meant that greater numbers of people were able to eat high-quality
animal protein in the form of fish. The export of the Nile perch from Lake
Victoria also provided a new source of foreign exchange to Kenya, Uganda
and Tanzania. Between 5 and 10 per cent of the lake's production is currently
for export (ibid.).

These estimates do not, however, take into account the distributional and
redistributional impacts. Harris et al. (1995) note that distributional impacts
may be estimated by finding out how the streams of new benefits are distributed among the users, while redistributional impacts may be estimated by
identifying changes among beneficiaries resulting from the altered ecosystem. For the case of Lake Victoria the main changes involve the level and
distribution of income, and ease of entry to the fishery. Harris et al. argue that
along with an increase in aggregate income, the new fishery has had the effect
of concentrating income in the hands of a small minority of fishers. They also
argue that although the new fishery made it possible for the separation of
ownership, management and operations, thereby making it easier for other
people to enter the industry, the increased cost of boats and nets has been a
barrier to ownership in the sector. The same is said to be true with processing
plants which are beyond the reach of most processors and have mostly been
supplied by foreign aid programmes (ibid.).

The introduction of *Limnothrissa miodon* in Lakes Kariba, Kivu and Itezhi-
tezhi is generally argued to be an economic success. *Limnothrissa miodon* is
not a major fish predator like the Nile perch and its ecological effects are
believed to be less dramatic (Marshall, 1995). In Lake Kariba, the pelagic
fishery consisting almost entirely of *Limnothrissa* produces nearly ten times
as much as the inshore fishery, which utilizes the indigenous fish species. The
1993 price of sardines from Lake Kariba was about US$1000 per tonne, and
estimated annual catches are between 27 000 and 36 000 tonnes, giving
annual earnings of between US$27 million and US$36 million (at 1993
prices). Actual figures show that the fishery is worth about US$31 million
annually to Zimbabwe and Zambia (Pitcher, 1995). The same applies to Lake
Kivu where catch has risen from a few hundred tonnes before sardines were
stocked to about 4300 tonnes per annum (Marshall, 1995). Since the early
1980s, a profitable artisanal sardine fishery has been developing on the lake.
The number of fishing units in Rwandese waters increased from six in 1980
to 144 in 1991. Recorded Rwandese catches increased from 65 tonnes in
1981 to 370 tonnes in 1987 (de Iongh, 1995). Recorded catches from Rwanda
and the Democratic Republic of Congo are about 2500 tonnes per year, and
valued at US$2.5 million (at 1993 prices).

However, the estimated potential catch of sardines in Lake Kivu is between
7000 and 10 000 tonnes per year, giving an estimated annual income (at 1993

prices) of between US$6 million and US$9 million (Pitcher, 1995). Unlike the case of Lake Victoria, no serious distributional and redistributional effects are expected, since this is a traditional fishery. There is little published information on the catch levels of Lake Itezhi-tezhi. It is estimated that the lake can produce between 18 000 and 25 000 tonnes of sardines worth between US$18 million and US$25 million (at 1993 prices) annually to Zambia (ibid.).

It follows that the net cost of the introduction of exotic species into fresh-water lakes is sensitive to the diversity and productivity of the target lakes. In lakes with low fish diversity and production, the introduction of exotic species is likely to involve relatively low ecological costs. This has been illustrated by the case of Lakes Kariba and Kivu whose production and diversity increased after the introduction and establishment of the sardine, *Limnothrissa miodon*. However, in lakes characterized by multifarious fish and high productivity, such introductions can be a disaster. This is the case in Lake Victoria, where the introduction and establishment of the Nile perch contributed towards the collapse and disappearance of the haplochromine cichlids. Although the new fishery has led to an increase in total fish production, employment and foreign exchange earnings, these benefits, which are associated with socially unfavourable distribution and redistribution effects, may not outweigh the loss in fish diversity.

3   INVASIVE WATER WEEDS

Three main water weed pests in Africa are water lettuce or Nile cabbage, *Pistia stratiotes*, water fern, *Salvinia molesta*, and water hyacinth, *Eichhornia crassipes* (Hill, 1991a). Water lettuce is indigenous and has a very wide distribution. It is less aggressive than the other two and is only a pest under highly eutrophic conditions. In Africa, native insects are believed to exert an acceptable level of control most of the time. In addition, a weevil specific to *Pistia stratiotes* was found and can be used as an effective control. The other two water weeds are of South American origin. The water fern *Salvinia molesta* has been controlled very successfully in several African countries by the weevil *Cyrtobagous salviniae*. The countries include South Africa, Namibia, Zambia, Zimbabwe and Kenya (Room, 1990; Hill, 1991a; Williamson, 1996). In this chapter the focus is on the water hyacinth because, unlike the other two water weeds which are under control, it remains a threat.

Water hyacinth is a member of the plant family *Pontederiaceae*. Two growth forms representing the same species exist: small plants with swollen petioles, common in nutrient-poor situations, which flower prolifically; and large plants up to a metre or more in height, without swollen petioles, common in nutrient-rich situations, which flower only rarely (Thompson, 1991a). There are three reasons why water hyacinth has potential as a weed in Africa. The first is its very high growth rate. The second is the lack of specific parasites and grazers. The third is the relative stability of most African lakes.

Water hyacinth grows readily on any open muddy surface or sheltered water. Its growth rate is extremely rapid. Under favourable environmental conditions, the population of water hyacinth is said to double every five to 15 days. Its reproduction is by horizontal stems and seeds. One plant is said to be capable of producing up to 140 million vegetative daughter plants in one year if neither space nor nutrients are limiting. Seeds form an important source of reinfestation in cleared areas because they can survive up to 30 years in anaerobic mud (Twongo, 1991; Thompson, 1991a).

In its native habitat in South America, water hyacinth is part of a complex ecosystem, which includes various parasites, grazers and diseases. So insects, fungi and bacteria which have evolved with the water hyacinth over many millions of years exploit it as a food source and, in the process, reduce its rate of growth and spread. In Africa on the other hand, water hyacinth does not appear to have effective natural enemies. Again, in its native range, water bodies are not usually permanent, so that populations of the plant die back each year and re-establish from seed after the next inundation. The plant is only a problem in permanent water bodies where its phenomenal growth rate is unchecked by seasonal drought (Thompson, 1991a).

3.1   Distribution in Africa

There are three possible ways in which water hyacinth may be transported from one location to another: water-borne dispersal, diving birds and through people. Water-borne dispersal demands connections between water bodies. Most of the water systems in Africa are well connected, making this one of the potential dispersal methods. Diving waterbirds could theoretically swallow seeds as they sift mud for food, then pass them through the gut after they have flown to a new water body. There is no evidence for bird-mediated dispersal, however, and if it occurs, it is probably on a small scale. The other vector is people. The weed produces attractive blue flowers and is therefore in great demand for aquaria and ornamental ponds. It is believed that this is how it was introduced and then spread in Africa (Thompson, 1991a). Taylor (1991) notes that at one point the plant was reported to be on sale at a duty free shop in the departure lounge of Entebbe International Airport in Uganda.

Water hyacinth was introduced to Egypt in the early part of the twentieth century and remains a cause of very serious problems there, particularly to irrigation systems. It was also introduced into the Democratic Republic of Congo (Zaire) at Kisangani in about 1952. The weed appeared in the Upper

Nile (Sudd) swamps of Central Sudan in about 1958, and was firmly established there by 1960. Soon more than 100 square km of hyacinth were seasonally building up behind the Jebel Aulia Dam. Infestations in Nigeria and Benin date only from 1985, in Ghana from 1980, and in Malawi from 1968 (Thompson, 1991a). Table 10.2 shows some of the African countries infested by the weed and the associated water bodies. The weed is still spreading throughout Africa including the river and lagoon systems of West Africa, the Great Lakes Region and river systems in the southern and northern parts of the continent (Joffe and Cooke, 1997).

Table 10.2   Main water bodies infested by water hyacinth in Africa

Country	Water bodies
Angola	Kwanza River and related irrigation network
Benin	So and Queme Rivers, Lake Nokoue
Burundi	Kagera River
Democratic Republic of Congo	Congo River, Lake Albert
Egypt	Nile River and related irrigation network, and northern lakes
Ghana	Tano Lagoon and Accra/Tema water areas
Ivory Coast	Tano Lagoon, Comoe River, Ono Lake
Kenya	Lakes Victoria and Naivasha
Malawi	Lake Malawi, Shire River
Mali	Niger River
Mozambique	Zambezi River
Niger	Niger River
Nigeria	Niger River
Rwanda	Kagera River
Sudan	Nile River
Tanzania	Lake Victoria, Pangani, Kagera and Sigi Rivers
Uganda	Lakes Victoria, Kyoga and Kwania
Zambia	Kafue Dam
Zimbabwe	Lake Chivero and Manyame River

Source: Joffe and Cooke (1997).

3.2   Physical Impacts of Water Hyacinth

Water hyacinth is in isolation a harmless plant, being non-poisonous. As an invasive it causes problems such as reduction in production, diversity and quality of fish; obstruction of waterways and prevention of boat movement; damage to water supply and hydro-electric machinery, pumps and intakes; spread of water-borne diseases; and increased water loss through evapotranspiration (Bikangaga et al., 1998; Taylor, 1991; Twongo, 1991).

Although specific studies to establish the exact impact of water hyacinth on fish productivity, diversity and quality are hard to come by, most empirical work indicates negative consequences. In particular, spawning and nursery grounds for fish may be smothered by the hyacinth mats. Low oxygen levels associated with extensive mats of the weed make these environments unsuitable for high oxygen-demanding fish species. Light shading and oxygen depletion by the hyacinth mats lead to lower primary productivity and suppression of phytoplankton growth. In the case of limited nutrient supply, infestation interferes with nutrient dynamics and lake productivity, including fishery productivity, since the extremely high growth rate of the water hyacinth makes it a very important nutrient sink (Thompson, 1991a; Taylor, 1991). In addition, the roots of water hyacinth trap waste material and contaminate the fish, leading to poor-quality fish (Bikangaga et al., 1998).

Water hyacinth obstructs the flow of water in waterways and canals thereby reducing hydraulic efficiency in irrigation. It also obstructs boat movement by blocking access channels. In ship docking bays, ships entering the dock in the presence of the weed are slowed down, sometimes being delayed up to two hours before docking. The weed can choke the engine filters of the ship thus increasing the frequency of their clearing and breakage. This obstruction also affects fisheries' operations.

As far as generation of hydro-electric power is concerned, water hyacinth is known to block screens causing regular stoppages of generators for cleaning. The weed also causes breakage of the screens and reduces the rate of flow of the water. All these lead to a reduction in the amount of energy produced. In water supply, the weed causes blockages of valves and water filters, causing resistance in or complete stoppage of water-pumping operations.

Water hyacinth also has negative effects on the health of the people who live along the infested water bodies. It provides a habitat for agents of malaria and bilharzia and harbours snakes. It is also believed to transmit amoebic dysentery, typhoid fever and is said to cause severe skin rashes when in contact with the skin (ibid.).

A further physical impact is due to the fact that water hyacinth loses water rapidly through its leaves. It is estimated that the average loss of water due to evapotranspiration by the weed is about 3.5 times that from a free water surface. The effect of such massive loss of water due to evapotranspiration is likely to be more striking in wetlands with limited quantities of water (Twongo, 1991).

Positive ecological impacts of the establishment and spread of water hya-cinth are limited. Points which suggest that it might be beneficial include the observations that it forms a substrate for invertebrate food organisms, and that its roots provide shelter for juvenile fish (Willoughby et al., 1993). The recovery in haplochromine stocks in Lake Kyoga, for example, coincided with its invasion and spread. The hyacinth invaded Lake Kyoga in 1988 and became established between 1991 and 1992. Its floating beds provided cover, thereby allowing haplochromines which had taken cover in marginal macrophytes to recolonize the lake and multiply. Hence it was concluded that the hyacinth provided a valuable habitat for some species (Oguta-Ohwayo, 1995). However, an empirical study on the effects of water hyacinth on the abundance and diversity of fish and invertebrate species in Lake Victoria did not fully support these observations. The study showed that the only fish species which are able to inhabit areas under the mat and to penetrate more than a few metres from its edges are those having accessory breathing organs such as *Protopterus* or *Clarias*. But the study showed that water hyacinth is capable of supporting a large and diverse community of macroinvertebrates, most of which were abundant at the mat edges (Willoughby et al., 1993). It follows that although the weed is not able to support a large diversity of fish, it provides a valuable habitat for invertebrates and some fish species.

3.3 Control of Water Hyacinth

Because there is no natural control of water hyacinth in Africa, artificial eradication methods have to be considered. These fall into four groups: manual and mechanical methods, chemical methods, biological control and environmental manipulation. Manual and mechanical methods for the weed involve physical removal from the water using nets, booms and barrages. Once removed, the plant can be killed by exposing it to the sun, on dry land away from the possibility of water flushing. This method is direct but is only feasible in very small and well-defined water bodies (Taylor, 1991). In other cases, booms and barrages have been used to prevent hyacinth drifting down rivers. However these do not really work, first because only one or two plants need to escape the traps to start downstream infestations, and second because booms are frequently put in place too late. Booms also need to be regularly cleared by mechanical dredges (Thompson, 1991b).

Chemical methods involve the use of herbicides. Many herbicides work very quickly, but the side-effects upon the environment can be serious. Some herbicides are toxic to fish. Others are slow to degrade and so build up in the environment. Herbicides are typically used when the extent of infestation is very large. However, it could also be justified where there are large but localized mats of the weed (Taylor, 1991). The main external effects of herbicides appear to lie with fisheries and with non-target plant communities. For instance 2,4-D is temporarily effective on water hyacinth, but has adverse side-effects. It affects non-target plant species as well as animals. In addition, 2,4-D, though probably the best option, is poorly translocated from plant to plant along stolons, so multiple spraying is almost always necessary. A common feature of chemically treated water hyacinth populations is the mass death of vegetation mats. As it rots, it removes oxygen from the water and creates temporary anoxic conditions that are toxic to most fish species. The dead mat usually sinks, but rises to the surface again due to buoyancy of gases such as methane produced by anaerobic decomposition of the dead hyacinth material. As the mats re-surface, seeds start to germinate and re-establish the hyacinth population. It is often counterproductive because it can increase seed production and, because spraying must be repeated, does not allow the area to recover ecologically (Thompson, 1991b).

Biological control has concentrated upon the search for an insect, fungus or other organism that specifically attacks water hyacinth and preferably nothing else (Taylor, 1991). In 1961, intensive field research in Amazonia identified the first specific predator/parasite of water hyacinth: weevils of the genus *Neochetina*. After extensive screening over many years, it was found that *Neochetina bruchi* and *Neochetina eichhorniae* are absolutely specific to water hyacinth. Now at least five species of insects are believed to be hyacinth specific, and two species of fungi have potential for use (Thompson, 1991b). Although several African countries have begun to use biological control, there is a common local perception that control brought about by the water hyacinth weevil *Neochetina spp.*, is too slow and that faster action is required. The scientific consensus, driven by public perception, appears to be that the water hyacinth biological control system, as currently implemented, should be made more effective (Joffe and Cooke, 1997).

Environmental manipulation involves water-level control and watershed management. For example, flooding is used to control weeds in rice paddies, since exposure and drying can kill plants that have a constant demand for water. Water hyacinth is very susceptible to drying out – a habitat factor which keeps the plant under control in the highly seasonal wetlands of the Brazilian Pantanal. Thus, if water-level manipulation is possible, as is sometimes the case in reservoirs, some control may be achieved by this method. Erosion, sedimentation, nutrient inputs and other factors can encourage undesirable weed growth. Weed control through catchment management avoids conditions which encourage weed growth and other deleterious side-effects of eutrophication (Thompson, 1991b).

3.4   Economic Implications of Water Hyacinth Control

The economics of water hyacinth control can be analysed by comparing the costs and benefits of eradication or management and utilization. Water weeds can, in general be utilized for livestock food, potash production, fertilizer, activated carbon, compost, mulch, paper, energy (briquettes or biogas), and wastewater treatment. However, water hyacinth has little potential for any economic utilization. It is a very poor source of livestock food, in terms of nutrient content and palatability. It is 95 per cent water, and what remains after burning off the carbon is 50 per cent silica and 30 per cent potassium. The high potassium level is a problem for livestock unless the hyacinth feed is mixed with something more palatable. Only 1.5 per cent of the dry matter is accounted for by nitrogen. This means that less than 0.5 per cent of the fresh plant is protein. Even though the protein is said to be well balanced, there is too much silica, calcium oxalate and potassium for animals to find it palatable. In addition, undiluted hyacinth feed is also acidic (Thompson, 1991b).

Fibre length is very short so only low-quality paper can be produced without adding wood pulp. Papyrus is a better feedstock for paper and particleboard. As a fertilizer, water hyacinth contains too much carbon. Decomposing bacteria use all the nitrogen and there is nothing left for crop plants. As mulch, hyacinth is good, but nitrogen fertilizer applications are necessary to prevent nutrient starvation. It makes good compost and can be compressed into fuel briquettes or used in biogas generators, but harvesting for these purposes is much more highly labour intensive than for other feedstocks available. For example, Hill (1991b) reports that control of water hyacinth on the Nile yielded insufficient weed to maintain a biogas plant set up to convert the weed into methane. Hyacinth is used for wastewater treatment in some countries, but papyrus would be more appropriate for African countries (Thompson, 1991b). In other words the opportunity cost of control is low.

Given that water hyacinth has low use value, the analysis can be reduced to one of valuing the costs and benefits of eradication or control. The economic costs imposed by water hyacinth can be defined by the willingness of the affected parties to pay to avoid detrimental effects, and the benefits of a control programme can be defined by willingness of the affected parties to pay for the programme so as to gain its positive effect. In practice, estimates of water hyacinth-related benefits and costs use simple methods that estimate the direct benefit and cost of control (Joffe and Cooke, 1997). The benefits of control comprise the damage avoided. There are few cases where the damage caused by water hyacinth infestation has been valued.

In Uganda, for example, Bikangaga et al. (1998) are trying to quantify in monetary terms how much various sectors have lost out or benefited due to the presence of the weed. The major sectors involved include fisheries, hydro-power, water transport and water supply. In fisheries, a 10 per cent decline of fish catch is reported. Delays in catch delivery times have increased on average by two to three hours a day. Delayed landing of fish leads to deterioration of the fish quality. This reduces the price of the fish. For example, the price of Nile perch declines by 70 per cent when boats are delayed by three hours. In addition during periods of weed attack, boat operators must carry additional fuel of 20–30 litres of petrol per trip, which is about 30 per cent above the normal requirement, to take care of the delay encountered and extra power required to push their way through the weed. They also carry additional ice amounting to about one-third of their usual supply in order to prevent their fish from getting spoiled due to delayed landing. Sometimes boats are unable to go out to fish for several weeks because of blockages to their routes. In extreme cases the whole landing site is closed and activities shift to other centres. In addition to obstruction, the weed entangles fishing nets causing damage. At times fleets of gear are carried away by mats of the weed and have to be replaced. The choking out of boat engines results in increased breakdowns and a rise in maintenance costs.

In hydro-power generation, Bikangaga et al. (ibid.) report considerable losses of output due to the stoppage of the generators made necessary for cleaning. In one month for instance, the Ugandan Electricity Board lost a total of 1.2682 gigabite hours due to water hyacinth alone, losing earnings worth US\$91 313. In the water supply, water hyacinth damages water pumps and filters. Blockages of water filters cause resistance to water pumping and leads to the use of more electricity both during pumping and cleaning of filters. Cleaning of filters has increased by 200 per cent in the presence of water hyacinth and water pumps are overhauled frequently. However, water hyacinth has reduced the amount of total nitrogen and phosphorous in the water, thereby contributing to the cleaning-up process. This means that water treatment costs have not increased due to the invasion of water hyacinth in the pumping sites.

In a different valuation analysis, the Lake Victoria Environmental Management Project estimated annual losses of US\$0.2 million in local fisheries, US\$0.35 million in beaches and water supply for domestic, stock and agricultural purposes and US\$1.5 million in urban water supply due to blocked intakes (Joffe and Cooke, 1997). These estimates represent the direct benefits of control.

The cost of controlling water hyacinth depends on the method of control. Alimi and Akinyemiju (1990) compared the direct cost of manual, mechanical and chemical control methods for some sites in Nigeria. Costs to clear one square kilometre of hyacinth were US\$9500 for manual control (most of the cost being labour charges), US\$8000 for mechanical control (the main costs being machine purchase and mechanical repairs), and US$4400 for chemical control (mostly chemical and application costs). Although this analysis appeared to support chemical control, no mention was made of its environmental effects on non-target species. Nor was it stated that these costs would be recurring indefinitely, and there was no comparison with the costs of biological control methods. One estimate of the cost of biological control found that a total cost of US$60000 could completely control water hyacinth over areas very much larger than one square kilometre (Thompson, 1991b), but there is no estimate of the direct costs of biological control per square kilometre.

In Uganda, mechanical operations around Owen Falls dam required the purchase of three harvesters at a total cost of US$2.5 million. Variable costs are estimated at US$19 000 per month. For chemical control, the use of a boat would cost US$246 per hectare for glyphosate and US$118 per hectare for 2,4-D. Spraying by aircraft would cost US$187 per hectare for glyphosate and US$59 per hectare for 2,4-D. For biological control it is estimated that US$95 000 would be spent annually mainly for monitoring. In most cases, manual, mechanical and chemical control options have high recurrent cost implications. Manual and mechanical operations may be required continuously while chemical spray will need to be repeated periodically. A biological control method is regarded as the most desirable long-term management option (Joffe and Cooke, 1997).

Experience from different countries and water bodies shows that control of water hyacinth can be quite costly. In Nigeria a defensive expenditure approach has been used to generate a preliminary estimate of US$50 million annual economic costs associated with water hyacinth infestation of the Niger River system. The Lake Victoria Environmental Management Project allocated US$8.31 million to water hyacinth control to defend against estimated direct costs of US$6–10 million per annum in the absence of control (ibid.). In Uganda, the government allocated US$3.09 million for the control of water hyacinth in Lake Victoria between 1991/92 and 1997/98 (Muramira, 1998), in addition to US$4.5 million from a variety of donors. Additional costs for a medium-term programme covering other main affected lakes and waterways are estimated at US$19.5 million. In Egypt, manual and mechanical control expenditures are currently running at about US$7 million per annum. In Malawi the total project costs for a three-year biological control programme in the Lower Shire Valley are US$400 000. Zimbabwe has spent US$215 000 on physical and chemical control of water hyacinth on Lake Chivero (Joffe and Cooke, 1997). Table 10.3 gives the estimated annual expenditures associated with the control of water hyacinth in the different countries and water bodies. These figures are rough estimates and provide a very incomplete perspective on the problem, but they support the conclusion

*Table 10.3   Economic costs and control expenditures (per annum)
associated with water hyacinth*

Country/Water body	Amount (US$ '000)
Nigeria	50 000
Lake Victoria	9 660
Uganda	4 560
Egypt	7 000
Malawi	133
Zimbabwe	43
Total	71 396

Source: Joffe and Cooke (1997).

that the invasion and proliferation of aquatic weeds in general and water hyacinth in particular are associated with significant economic costs for the affected African countries.

4   SUMMARY

The physical and economic impact of invasive species in African lakes and rivers is mixed. This is specifically the case in exotic fish introductions where increased fish productivity is often accompanied by negative ecological effects. The difficulties in evaluating the cost and benefit of different introduced species have led to controversy over whether such introductions are beneficial. In the case of the Nile perch the increase in catch is believed to have contributed towards the extinction of numerous endemic species in the target lakes – a cost which may outweigh the benefits.

However, the introduction of the Tanganyika sardine into some African lakes increased productivity with less dramatic impact on the lakes' ecosystem. In this case the benefits may outweigh the costs. The introduction of exotic fish species into African lakes is sensitive to the diversity and productivity of the target lakes. In lakes with low fish diversity and production, introduced fish species can increase productivity with less ecological damage. But in lakes with high fish diversity and productivity, such introductions can be costly.

The impact of introduced species also depends on the feeding habits of the species being introduced. Predator species such as the Nile perch can cause more damage than planktivores like the Tanganyika sardine, whose effect may mostly be on the plankton community.

Invasive water weeds are in general associated with less utilization value and high cost of damage and control. The water hyacinth, for example, has a low use value but high economic costs.

NOTES

1. The database can be accessed on the Internet at http://www.fao.org/fi/statist/fisoft/dias/mainpage.htm
2. The Shannon–Weiner diversity index is estimated using the formula: $H = -\Sigma(p_i \ln p_i)$ where p_i is the proportion of each species i in the sample.

REFERENCES

Alimi, T. and O.A. Akinyemiju (1990), 'An economic analysis of water hyacinth control methods in Nigeria', *Journal of Aquatic Plant Management*, **28**: 105–7.

Bikangaga, S., E. Rukunya and J. Alinaitwe (1998), 'Report on economic valuation of water hyacinth as an environmental problem on Uganda's fresh water resources and its effects on key economic activities', Economic Network for Eastern and Southern Africa (ENESA).

Bruton, M.N. (1990), 'The conservation of the fishes of Lake Victoria, Africa: an ecological perspective', *Environmental Biology of Fishes*, **27**: 161–75.

Bunday, A. and T.J. Pitcher (1995), 'An analysis of species changes in Lake Victoria: did the Nile perch act alone?', in T.J. Pitcher and P.J.B. Hart (eds), *The Impact of Species Changes in African Lakes*, London: Chapman & Hall: 111–35.

Cowx, I.G. and C.K. Kapasa (1995), 'Species changes in reservoir fisheries following impoundment: the case of Lake Itezhi-tezhi, Zambia', in T.J. Pitcher and P.J.B. Hart (eds), *The Impact of Species Changes in African Lakes*, London: Chapman & Hall: 321–33.

de Iongh, H.H., P.C. Spliethoff and F. Roest (1995), 'The impact of an introduction of sardine into Lake Kivu', in T.J. Pitcher and P.J.B. Hart (eds), *The Impact of Species Changes in African Lakes*, London: Chapman & Hall: 277–97.

Degnbol, P. (1993), 'The pelagic zone of Central Lake Malawi – a trophic box model', in V. Christensen and D. Pauly (eds), *Trophic Models of Aquatic Ecosystems*, Manila: International Center for Living Aquatic Resources Management (ICLARM): 110–15.

Department of Research and Environmental Affairs (DREA), (1994), *Malawi: National Environmental Action Plan*, Lilongwe: Malawi Government.

Harris, C.K., D.S. Wiley and D.C. Wilson (1995), 'Socio-economic impacts of introduced species in Lake Victoria fisheries', in T.J. Pitcher and P.J.B. Hart (eds), *The Impact of Species Changes in African Lakes*, London: Chapman & Hall: pp. 215–42.

Hill, G. (1991a), 'Waterweeds biological control in East Africa', in K. Thompson (ed.), *The Water Hyacinth in Uganda, Ecology, Distribution, Problems and Strategies for Control*, Rome: FAO TEP/UGA/9153/A: 60–65.

Hill, G. (1991b), 'Biological control of water weeds', in K. Thompson (ed.), *The Water Hyacinth in Uganda, Ecology, Distribution, Problems and Strategies for Control*, Rome: FAO TEP/UGA/9153/A.

Jackson, P.B.N. (1961), 'Ichthyology. The fish of the Middle Zambezi', National Museums and Monuments of Zimbabwe, Kariba Studies, 1: 1–36.

Joffe, S. and S. Cooke (1997), 'Management of the water hyacinth and other invasive aquatic weeds: issues for the World Bank', Global IPM Facility, CAB Bioscience.

Karenge, L. and J. Kolding (1995), 'Inshore fish population and species changes in Lake Kariba, Zimbabwe', in T.J. Pitcher and P.J.B. Hart (eds), *The Impact of Species Changes in African Lakes*, London: Chapman & Hall: 245–75.

Kudhongania, A.W. and D.B.R. Chitamwemba (1995), 'Impact of environmental change, species introductions and ecological interactions on the fish stocks of Lake Victoria', in T.J. Pitcher and P.J.B. Hart (eds), *The Impact of Species Changes in African Lakes*, London: Chapman & Hall: 19–32.

Marshall, B.E. (1984), 'Kariba (Zimbabwe/Zambia)', in J.M. Kapetsky and T. Petr (eds), *Status of African Reservoir Fisheries*, Committee for Inland Fisheries of Africa (CIFA) Technical Paper No.10: 105–53.

Marshall, B.E. (1995), 'Why is *Limnothrissa miodon* such a successful introduced species and is there anywhere else we should put it?', in T.J. Pitcher and P.J.B. Hart (eds), *The Impact of Species Changes in African Lakes*, London: Chapman & Hall: 527–46.

Menz, A. (ed.) (1995), *The Fishery Potential and Productivity of the Pelagic Zone of Lake Malawi/Niassa*, Chatham, UK: Natural Resources Institute.

Moyle, C. and R.A. Leidy (1992), 'Loss of biodiversity in aquatic ecosystems', in P.C. Fiedler and K.S. Jain (eds), *Conservation Biology*, New York: Chapman & Hall: 127–95.

Muramira, T.U. (1998), 'The impact of market liberalisation on the Lake Victoria Fishery', Paper presented at the Beijer Research Seminar, Zambia, 26–28 May.

Ochumba, P.B.O. (1995), 'Limnological changes in Lake Victoria since the Nile perch introduction', in T.J. Pitcher and P.J.B. Hart (eds), *The Impact of Species Changes in African Lakes*, London: Chapman & Hall: 33–43.

Oguta-Ohwayo, R. (1995), 'Diversity and stability of fish stocks in Lakes Victoria, Kyoga and Nabugabo after establishment of introduced species', in T.J. Pitcher and P.J.B. Hart (eds), *The Impact of Species Changes in African Lakes*, London: Chapman & Hall: 59–81.

Pitcher, T.J. (1995), 'Species changes and fisheries in African lakes: outline of issues', in T.J. Pitcher and P.J.B. Hart (eds), *The Impact of Species Changes in African Lakes*, London: Chapman & Hall: 1–16.

Reynolds, J.E. and D.F. Gréboval (1988), 'Socio-economic effects of the evolution of Nile perch fisheries in Lake Victoria: a review', Committee for Inland Fisheries in Africa (CIFA) Technical Paper No. 17, FAO, Rome.

Reynolds, J.E., D.F. Gréboval and P. Mannini (1995), 'Thirty years on: the development of the Nile perch fishery in Lake Victoria', in T.J. Pitcher and P.J.B. Hart (eds), *The Impact of Species Changes in African Lakes*, London: Chapman & Hall: 181–214.

Room, P. (1990), 'Ecology of a simple plant-herbivore system: biological control of *Salvinia*', *Trends in Ecology and Evolution*, 5: 74–9.

Taylor, A.R.D. (1991), 'Water hyacinth in Lake Victoria – the problem and solutions', in K. Thompson (ed.), *The Water Hyacinth in Uganda, Ecology, Distribution, Problems and Strategies for Control*, Rome: FAO TEP/UGA/9153/A: 123–5.

Thompson, K. (1991a), 'The ecology of the water hyacinth and its distribution in Uganda', in K. Thompson (ed.), *The Water Hyacinth in Uganda, Ecology, Distribution, Problems and Strategies for Control*, Rome: FAO TEP/UGA/9153/A: 24–8.

Thompson, K. (1991b), 'The options available in Uganda for water hyacinth control', in K. Thompson (ed.), *The Water Hyacinth in Uganda, Ecology, Distribution, Problems and Strategies for Control*, Rome: FAO TEP/UGA/9153/A: 45–52.

Turner, J. (ed.) (1982), 'Biological studies on the pelagic ecosystem of Lake Malawi', FI:DP/MLW/75/019 Technical Report 1, FAO, Rome.

Twongo, T. (1991), 'Implications of the water hyacinth infestation in Uganda for fisheries, with particular reference to Lake Kyoga', in K. Thompson (ed.), *The Water Hyacinth in Uganda, Ecology, Distribution, Problems and Strategies for Control*, Rome: FAO TEP/UGA/9153/A: 19–23.

Twongo, T. (1995), 'Impact of fish species introductions on the Tilapia of Lakes Victoria and Kyoga', in T.J. Pitcher and P.J.B. Hart (eds), *The Impact of Species Changes in African Lakes*, London: Chapman & Hall: 45–57.

Verbeke, J. (1957), 'Chaoboridae (Diptera, Nemotocera) stades immatures et adulters', in *Exploration Hydrobiologiques des Lacs Kivu, Edouard et Albert*, Tervuren, Belgium: Inst. R. Sci. Nat. Belge: 185–202.

Welcomme, R.L. (1966), 'Recent changes in the stocks of Tilapia in Lake Victoria', *Nature*, **212**: 52–4.

Williamson, M. (1996), *Biological Invasions*, London: Chapman & Hall.

Willoughby, N.G., I.G. Watson, S. Lauer and I.F. Grant (1993), 'An investigation into the effects of water hyacinth on the biodiversity and abundance of fish and invertebrates in Lake Victoria, Uganda', Technical Report, Natural Resources Institute, Overseas Development Administration, UK.

Witte, F., T. Goldschmidt and J.H. Wanink (1995), 'Dynamics of the Haplochromine Cichlid fauna and other ecological changes in the Mwanza Gulf of Lake Victoria', in T.J. Pitcher and P.J.B. Hart (eds), *The Impact of Species Changes in African Lakes*, London: Chapman & Hall: 83–110.

11. Economic evaluation in classical biological control

Garry Hill and David Greathead

1 INTRODUCTION

Classical biological control is the purposeful introduction and permanent establishment of exotic natural enemies of pests and weeds, with a view to permanently suppressing their abundance within a prescribed region or country. The first successful introductions of insect natural enemies were made in 1888, and of weed natural enemies in 1902. To date, more than 5000 natural enemies of insects and mites have been introduced for classical biological control, and more than 900 introductions of natural enemies of weeds (Greathead and Greathead, 1992; Julien and Griffiths, 1998; authors' unpublished records (BIOCAT database)). The rate of permanent establishment of introduced natural enemies against arthropod targets is about 25 per cent, with complete control of pest populations achieved in about 10–15 per cent of cases. For weeds, the success rate is higher and more thoroughly evaluated. A detailed analysis of results of weed biological control projects up to 1980 revealed the following statistics (Julien and White, 1997): from a total of 729 releases of weed biocontrol agents, 64 per cent established and 28 per cent of them were involved in successful control of a weed. Thirty-nine per cent of the 179 reviewed weed biocontrol projects were successful, and 48 per cent of the 101 species of weeds targeted were controlled. The analysis revealed a total of 178 species of biological control agent were used, 71 per cent of which established and 34 per cent of which were successful in at least one location.

Classical biological control of pests and weeds is carried out almost entirely by public sector organizations. The provision of classical biological control services is normally regarded as a public good as its benefits are usually distributed throughout a community and cannot normally be captured by individual companies. This chapter reviews the literature on economic analyses of biological control and discusses the need for improved economic tools for decision making prior to the implementation of control programmes.

2   RESULTS OF BENEFIT–COST ANALYSES

Biologists rather than economists carried out most of the early economic evaluations of biological control projects. In most cases their analyses consisted of summing non-discounted cost savings to producers accruing from the successful biological control of pests over an arbitrary time period (Simmonds, 1967; Greathead, 1995). The first major evaluation of economic benefits and costs of biological control was carried out by DeBach (1964) who reviewed biological control successes within the state of California over the period 1923–59. He concluded that the net savings accruing from five successful biological control projects (citrophilus mealybug, *Pseudococcus calceolariae*; black scale, *Saissetia oleae*; klamath weed, *Hypericum perforatum*; grape leaf skeletoniser, *Harrisina brillians*; and spotted alfalfa aphid, *Therioaphis maculata*) amounted over this period to US$115 million, for an outlay in biological control research of approximately US$4.3 million. He made no attempt to discount costs or benefits. Another similar analysis published by a biological control practitioner (Simmonds, 1967) set out to demonstrate that a handful of highly successful biological control implementation projects provided cost savings far in excess of the costs of running the organization responsible for the implementation (the Commonwealth Institute of Biological Control). An evaluation of the biological control of the coffee mealybug (*Planococcus kenyae* (Le Pelley)) estimated total accumulated benefits to the Kenya coffee industry of £10 million over the period 1940–59 compared with costs of £30 000 (Melville, 1959).

More rigorous treatment of economic evaluation of biological control has been carried out since the 1980s by economists, mostly from Australia, using economic surplus techniques (Tisdell and Auld, 1990; Lubulwa and McMeniman, 1998). The approach of social cost–benefit analysis (SCBA) has been adopted and widely applied in Australia (Lubulwa and McMeniman, 1998).

Most biological control programmes have escaped rigorous evaluation, either from a technical or economic perspective. Clearly, given the substantial failure rate of natural enemy introductions in classical biological control programmes, most will yield a negative benefit: cost ratio. A survey of published *ex-post* economic assessments of biological control programmes found 27 such examples where benefit–cost ratios could be calculated (Table 11.1).

The examples given in Table 11.1 are a mixture of ratios which have been calculated by professional economists using various forms of SCBA, and less rigorous examples where biologists have performed discounted cash flow analyses which usually only take into account producer surpluses. Several of the benefit:cost ratios calculated in Table 11.1 (those indicated by an asterisk) have been calculated for this chapter by the authors by manipulating data

Table 11.1 Summary of published cost–benefit analyses or other attempted economic evaluations of biological control projects

Pest	Country	Year	Currency	Costs (C)	Benefits (B)	Ratio: B/C	Methods	Source
Alfalfa weevil (*Hypera postica* (Gillenhal))	USA	1987	US$ mill.	22.00	677.00	31	CBA discounted @4% for 16 years	White et al., 1995
* Armyworm (*Mythimna separata* (Walker))	New Zealand	1974	NZ$ mill.	0.02	93.70	4462	CBA discounted @10% for 30 years	CAB, 1980; Mohyuddin and Shah, 1977
Banana skipper (*Erionota thrax* (Linnaeus))	Aus/SE Asia	1990	Aus $ mill.	0.27	22.50	83	CBA discounted @8% for 30 years	Lubulwa and McMeniman, 1998
Breadfruit mealybug (*Icerya aegyptiaca* (Douglas))	Aus/SE Asia	1990	Aus $ mill.	0.63	2.57	4	CBA discounted @8% for 30 years	Lubulwa and McMeniman, 1998
Cassava mealybug (*Phenacoccus manihoti* (Matile-Ferrero))	Africa (34 cos.)	1977	US$ mill.	14.80	2 205.00	149	CBA discounted @10% for 25 years	Norgaard, 1988
* Coconut scale (*Aspidiotus destructor* (Signoret))	Trinidad	1955	£ sterling	3 630.00	609 157.00	168	CBA discounted @10% for 30 years	Simmonds, 1967
Coconut chrysomelid (*Brontispa longissima* (Gestro))	Samoa	1981	Dmark	797 061.00	3 969 136.00	5	CBA discounted @10% for 10 years	Voegele et al., 1989
Coconut leafminer (*Promecotheca cumingii* (Baly))	Sri Lanka	1971	£ sterling	20 500.00	2 184 495.00	107	CBA discounted @10% for 30 years	CAB 1980; Dharmadikari et al., 1977
* Black sage (*Cordia curassavica* (Roemer and Schultes))	Mauritius	1952	£ sterling	9 545.00	763 407.00	80	CBA discounted @10% for 30 years	Simmonds, 1967
* Cottony cushion scale (*Icerya purchasi* (Maskell))	Caribbean	1966	£ sterling	2 570.00	23 424.00	9	CBA discounted @10% for 30 years	Simmonds, 1967
Fruit piercing moth (*Eudocima fullonia* (Clerck))	Aus/SE Asia	1990	Aus $ mill.	0.67	0.66	0.99	CBA discounted @8% for 30 years	Lubulwa and McMeniman, 1998
* Mango mealybug (*Rastrococcus invadens* (Williams))[1]	Togo	1986	US$ mill.	137.61	111 206.00	808	CBA discounted @10% for 30 years	Voegele et al., 1991
Giant sensitive plant (*Mimosa pigra* (Linnaeus))	Aus/SE Asia	1990	Aus $ mill.	1.30	23.06	18	CBA discounted @8% for 30 years	Lubulwa and McMeniman, 1998
Potato tuber moth (*Phthorimaea*	Zambia	1972	£ sterling	15 363.00	235 380.00	15	CBA discounted	CAB, 1980; Cruickshank

operculella (Zeller))

Species	Location	Year	Currency	Cost	Benefit	Ratio	CBA	Source
* Prickly pear (*Opuntia fs* spp.)	Nevis	1960	£ sterling	500.00	76 341.00	126	@10% for 10 years CBA discounted @10% for 30 years	and Ahmed, 1973 Simmonds, 1967
* Rhodes grass scale (*Antonina graminis* (Maskell))	Texas	1978	US$ mill.	0.20	1 481.01	7405	CBA discounted @10% for 30 years	Dean et al., 1979
* Rose grain aphid (*Metopolophium dirhodum* (Walker))	New Zealand	1988	NZ $ mill.	1.32	2.81	2	CBA discounted @10% for 30 years	Grundy, 1990: lowest estimate given; highest is 35.4
* Rufous scale (*Selenaspidus articulatus* (Morgan))	Peru	1977	£ sterling	1 025.00	992 429.00	968	CBA discounted @10% for 30 years	CAB, 1980: Beingolia, 1977
Water fern (*Salvinia molesta* (Mitchell))	Aus/SE Asia	1990	Aus $ mill.	0.70	27.72	40	CBA discounted @8% for 30 years	Lubulwa and McMeniman, 1998
Wood wasp (*Sirex noctilio* (Fabricius))	Australia	1979	Aus $ mill.	5.21	12.80	2	CBA discounted @10% for 40 years	Tisdell, 1990: Marsden et al., 1980
Skeleton weed (*Chondrilla juncea* (Linnaeus))	Australia	1976	Aus $ mill.	2.33	261.20	112	CBA discounted @10% for 40 years	Tisdell, 1990, Marsden et al., 1980
* European spruce sawfly (*Gilpinia hercyniae* (Hartig))	Canada	1932	Can $ mill.	0.30	5.73	19	CBA discounted @10% for 14 years	Reeks and Cameron, 1971
* Sugarcane scale (*Aulacaspis tegalensis* (Zehntner))	Tanzania	1971	£ sterling	5 120.00	900 820.00	176	CBA discounted @10% for 30 years	CAB, 1980: Williams and Greathead, 1973
* Sugarcane stem borer (*Diatraea saccharalis* (Fabricius))	Caribbean	1931	£ sterling	5 721.00	923 722.00	161	CBA discounted @10% for 30 years	Simmonds, 1967
Two-spotted mite (*Tetranychus urticae* (Koch))	Australia	1976	Aus $ mill.	0.59	14.40	24	CBA discounted @10% for 40 years	Tisdell, 1990: Marsden et al., 1980
White wax scale (*Ceroplastes destructor* (Newstead))	Australia	1976	Aus $ mill.	1.04	1.50	1	CBA discounted @10% for 40 years	Tisdell, 1990: Marsden et al., 1980
* Winter moth[2] (*Operophtera brumata* (Linnaeus))	Canada	1971	Can $ mill.	0.41	6.35	15	CBA discounted @10% for 30 years	CAB, 1980: Embree, 1977

Notes:

CBA = Cost–benefit analysis; CAB = Commonwealth Agricultural Bureau.
*   Analysis has been carried out by the authors using data from the original publication.
1. Based upon an assumed rate of spread of 1% of infested area per year throughout mango growing area of Africa, using FAO production statistics.
2. Lump-sum costs and benefits in original publication evenly spread across 8 and 10 years, respectively – see publication for further explanation.

presented in the original publication. This has been done where apparently reliable information has been published on costs of programme implementation and annual savings resulting from the biological control, but a discounted cash-flow analysis is lacking. These figures have been used to calculate net present values of costs and benefits over a 30-year time horizon assuming an annual 10 per cent discount rate.

The benefit:cost ratios produced by this process undoubtedly have many inaccuracies and omissions, and the data are of variable quality. Most of the analyses consider only producer surpluses. However, the calculation of this simple benefit:cost ratio allows the literature on the economics of biological control to be reviewed and compared using a simple standard tool.

Very few economic analyses of biological control have attempted to estimate the variability surrounding point-estimates of a benefit:cost ratio. However, it is clear that considerable uncertainty is often attached to estimates of production, consumption and price/cost estimates used in their calculation. In an exception to this usual approach, Grundy (1990) calculated that the annual savings arising from the control of the rose grain aphid (*Metopolophium dirhodum*) in New Zealand probably varied from NZ$500 000 to NZ$5 million. We would guess that this order of magnitude variation in estimates of benefits is typical of many programmes reviewed here, and this should be borne in mind when interpreting all such benefit:cost calculations. Furthermore, a feature of many of the published analyses is that authors frequently claim to have made conservative estimates of the benefits.

A histogram of the distribution of benefit:cost ratios (Figure 11.1) produced from the figures presented in Table 11.1 shows that nearly all of the successful programmes analysed are highly cost effective. Twenty-six of the 27 programmes have benefit:cost ratios greater than unity, the single exception having a ratio of 0.99. The data in Figure 11.1 suggests that there is some apparent discontinuity in the distribution of benefit:cost ratios with a cluster falling in the region of one to 40, and another cluster between 100 and 1000 though there is no obvious reason for this. Clearly, some programmes which are particularly effective, produce massive benefit:cost ratios. These programmes all have characteristics of being against pests or weeds of major economic importance over a wide geographical area, where the level of pest or weed suppression achieved by biological control was high.

This conclusion was first pointed out in an economic review of research projects carried out by the Commonwealth Scientific and Industrial Research Organization (CSIRO) Division of Entomology during the period 1960–75 in Australia (Marsden et al., 1980). This review of the economic returns to projects showed that the total investment of public funds into the Division yielded a very high economic return, but that the return was generated by relatively few projects, indeed most of the economic returns could be attrib-

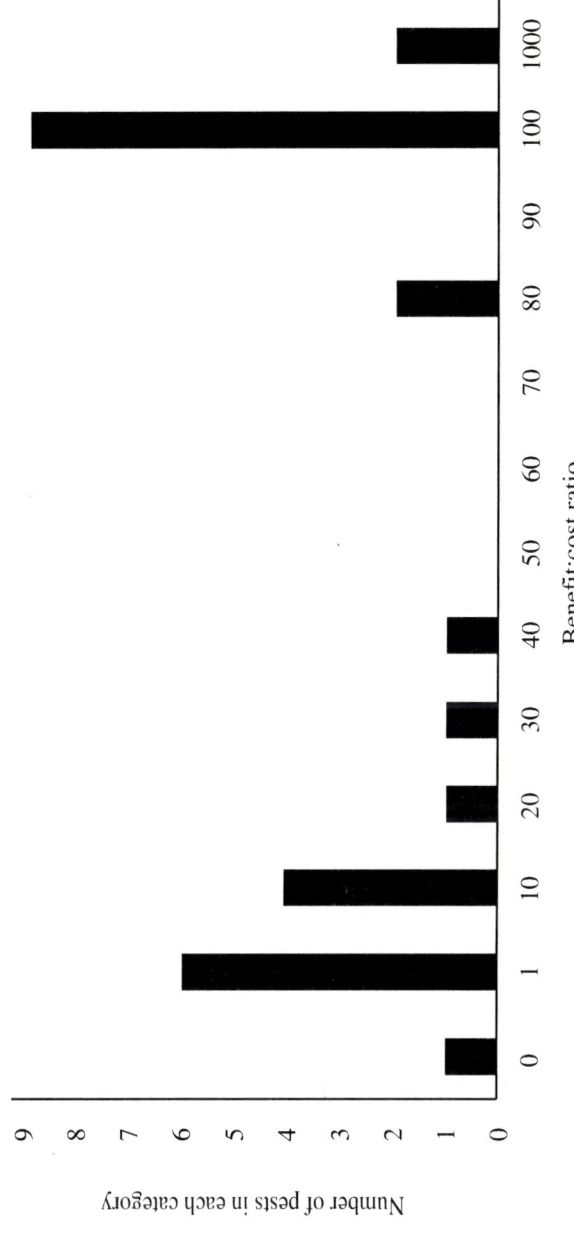

Figure 11.1   Distribution of benefit:cost ratios for 27 published analyses of classical biological control

uted to a handful of projects. A further analysis of these results showed that the four biological control programmes included in the analysis yielded a much greater return than projects on non-biological control subjects (Table 11.2; Tisdell, 1990), with one project, skeleton weed (*Chondrilla juncea*), having an overriding influence upon the outcome.

In spite of the range of assumptions and techniques used in these studies, the conclusion that successful biological control programmes usually have large, positive benefit:cost ratios appears to be robust and intuitively correct. Biological control of pests and weeds would appear to be a good public good investment, but given its modest success rate, a broad and well-selected portfolio of projects is advisable.

Table 11.2   Economic benefits and costs of research projects on biological and non-biological pest control by CSIRO Division of Entomology*

Project	Benefit (A$ million)	Cost (A$ million)	Benefit/cost ratio
Biological control			
Skeleton weed	261.2	2.33	112.1:1
Two-spotted mite	14.4	0.59	24.4:1
Sirex wasp	12.8	5.21	2.5:1
White wax scale	1.5	1.04	1.4:1
Total for biological control	289.9	9.17	31.6:1
Total for non-biological control	60.5	23.76	2.5:1
Total for all projects	350.4	32.93	10.6:1

Note: * Data are from Tables 1.1 and 1.2 of Marsden et al. (1980). Returns are estimated for the period 1960–2000 and are expressed in constant (1975 Aus$) net present values, based on an assumed 10% discount.

Source: Tisdell (1990).

3   LIMITATIONS OF SOCIAL COST–BENEFIT ANALYSIS (SCBA)

SCBA is acknowledged to have several limitations and drawbacks (Anderson and Settle, 1977; Hansen, 1986; Tisdell, 1990). It takes no account of changes in income distribution. The amount of information required for carrying out a SCBA can be considerable and hard to gather or imprecise, particularly if changes accruing to consumers surpluses are to be taken into account. It is doubtful whether all relevant net benefits or outcomes from biological control projects can be expressed solely in terms of money or by any other single measure. Thus, it has been argued that SCBA, by focusing on a single objective criterion, is too narrow a means of expressing costs and benefits, especially for environmental weed targets (Cullen and Whitten, 1995).

Conway (1987) proposed a wider characterization of benefits and costs, focusing particularly on resource-poor farmers. He proposed four factors to be considered in evaluating a new agricultural technology namely: (i) impact upon farmers yield or income; (ii) stability measures of yield or income; (iii) effects upon wealth distribution; (iv) effects upon sustainability of yield or income. There has been no attempt to-date, to implement Conway's scheme rigorously in the evaluation of biological control programmes; indeed his approach has been criticized by economists for its lack of rigour, and absence of underlying theoretical structure (Tisdell, 1990). However, a recent example of the biological control of the mango mealybug in Togo in the 1980s provides a good illustration (below) of how an evaluation of the impact of biological control may effectively include both economic and qualitative measures of impact (Voegele et al., 1991).

4   NON-ECONOMIC EFFECTS – THE EXAMPLE OF THE MANGO MEALYBUG

The example of the biological control of the mango mealybug in Togo encapsulates many of the issues of measuring non-economic effects resulting from an invading pest and its control (Voegele et al., 1991). The mango mealybug (*Rastrococcus invadens* (Williams)) was first observed in Africa, in Togo, in 1982 causing serious production losses of mango fruit. There it was estimated to be causing an annual economic loss of US$2.5 million. The pest was successfully controlled by a parasitic wasp (*Gyranusoidea tebygi* (Noyes)) introduced from India in 1987. A benefit–cost analysis taking into account only producer surpluses in Togo gave a ratio of 62:1 (rising to 808:1 when estimated benefits throughout Sub-Saharan Africa are included (Table 11.1), using data in Voegele et al., 1991). Non-economic benefits were judged to have accrued from the successful control of the pest through improved nutrition of local communities (the fruit is rich in vitamins A and C), the continued use of parts of the mango tree in local medicine (most notably the drinking of infusions to cure fevers), the widespread social use of large mango trees as a focal point of village life within many villages in Togo as a meeting place for the community, and finally the use of mango trees as places of worship by both Christian and animist religious groups (ibid.).

No attempt is made to quantify these effects in economic terms, but their qualitative description provides a broader basis for interpreting the benefits of the biological control programme beyond the bounds of economics. Further value could possibly have been added to this analysis if the authors had attempted to apply Conway's (1987) framework to their case study, addressing issues for example, of income distribution and stability. In spite of its lack of adoption and its criticism by economists (Tisdell, 1990), approaches like those suggested by Conway (1987) and Voegele et al. (1991) would give a broader perspective to evaluating the benefits of agricultural research and extension interventions which may be particularly applicable in developing countries and in cases where benefits cannot easily be captured or expressed in economic terms.

5   A SUMMARY OF *EX-POST* ECONOMIC EVALUATIONS

This review confirms the claims of pioneer biological control practitioners (DeBach, 1964; Simmonds, 1967) and the more recent and more rigorous work of others (Marsen et al., 1980; Greathead, 1995; Tisdell, 1990; Cullen and Whitten, 1995; Lubulwa and McMeniman, 1998) that successful biological control programmes are characteristically highly cost effective. Given the self-renewing nature of biological control, and the magnitude of the problems caused by invasive pests and weeds (easily the most frequent targets for a biological control intervention) this outcome is not surprising.

This review also tentatively supports the often-expressed view of biological control practitioners that the successful programmes pay for the unsuccessful ones. If we assume, conservatively, that one in ten programmes are successful, then the average benefit:cost ratio of the successful projects needs to be 10:1. The results presented here (Table 11.1, Figure 11.1), suggest that the average ratio is considerably more than this. However, this conclusion presupposes that those examples of successful biological control programmes which have been subjected to an economic evaluation are a random and unbiased sample. This may be true in some cases, for example the review presented by Lubulwa and McMeniman (1998). However, in other cases it appears more likely that the more spectacularly successful examples have been chosen for economic study and reporting.

Notwithstanding this uncertainty, this review adds support to the view that biological control programmes, considered *en masse*, are a sound and profitable investment for public good funds. However, given the relatively poor success rate for biological control programmes, investment in biological control activities needs to be made through a portfolio of projects carried out over a considerable number of years. The existence of specialized teams of biological control scientists in many national and international research organizations is evidence that public good funds are already being invested in this manner.

While the methods employed in SCBAs of biological control programmes can be debated and refined, the generally robust conclusions from *ex-post* studies suggests that further work in this area will yield little new information. On the other hand, the relatively unexplored area of *ex-ante* economic analysis could lead to improvements in investment decisions and subsequent returns in biological control funding in particular or in agricultural research funding in general. Indeed, there would seem to be a strong case for developing better *ex-ante* technical evaluations of projects to see if the success rate can be raised from its current relatively low rates of 10–15 per cent for insects and 30–40 per cent for weeds. This is discussed in the following section.

6 *EX-ANTE* ECONOMIC EVALUATIONS OF PROPOSED BIOLOGICAL CONTROL PROJECTS

Surprisingly little effort was made in carrying out *ex-ante* economic assessments of proposed biological control projects until the end of the 1970s. A pioneering study was made in Canada (Harris and Cranston, 1979) on the potential range of invading European knapweeds (*Centaurea* spp.) in Canada and the costs of control (chemical, environmental management, biological control) in order to demonstrate the potential benefits of applying biological control. The first studies carried out in Australia were made in response to conflicts of interest arising during the programme to control a pasture weed, Patterson's curse (*Echium plantagineum* (Linnaeus)). SCBA techniques were used to evaluate the likely benefit:cost ratio from the successful control of this weed. Subsequently, similar techniques were used to evaluate another programme against brambles (*Rubus* spp.) as weeds of pasture and rangeland (Cullen and Whitten, 1995; Tisdell, 1990). These techniques have proved particularly effective in providing a vehicle for resolving conflicts of interest and weighing costs and benefits.

The first *ex-ante* evaluation of a proposed biological control programme against a weed without a market valuation was that of Old Man's Beard (*Clematis vitalba*) in New Zealand (Greer and Sheppard, 1990). This study used contingent valuation techniques to elicit the community's willingness to pay for the control of the weed as a proxy for the benefits they expect to receive from it. The study was able to demonstrate that the resources currently allocated to the biological control of the weed were considerably less than the value the community attributed to its containment, and on this basis resources were allocated to a biological control programme.

The above studies are of considerable importance in showing how *ex-ante* SCBA was able to assist in resolving conflicts of interest in proposed biological control programmes, and in assisting in decision making for resource allocation to programmes addressing targets which do not have a market valuation. Risk assessment, based upon economic SCBA techniques, has now been adopted in law in Australia as the accepted way of resolving conflicts of interest in proposed biological control programmes (Cullen and Whitten, 1995).

The use of *ex-ante* economic analyses for assessing biological control programmes has wide application as a tool for assessing the actual and potential commercial and social costs of an invading species. Biological control practitioners lack the skills and more often than not, the funds, to carry out such studies. In the past, *ex-ante* studies have been carried out primarily to resolve conflicts of interest, but they could be much more widely used as a tool to allow managers to make better and more timely decisions on resource allocation.

A common problem experienced by biological control practitioners is delays to the start of projects. As noted above in the case of the biological control of the mango mealybug in Africa, considerable cost savings will accrue to the early implementation of biological control of an invading pest. But it is well documented that many problems of invasive pests and weeds in agriculture and the environment do not receive attention until they have become a very serious problem, even in situations where their invasive potential is known and where successful biological control agents have been demonstrated elsewhere. A current case in point is water hyacinth (*Eichhornia crassipes*) in Africa, where delays in biological control implementation have led to the problem escalating to huge proportions (Joffe and Cooke, 1997). We believe that biological control practitioners and their funders would benefit from a decision support tool which would allow them to assess, according to the best available criteria, the economic losses likely to occur due to a newly invading pest or weed. Such a tool would need to consider inputs of key technical parameters such as rate of spread of the pest/weed, yield losses, expected levels of control and the probability of achieving control (where appropriate based upon knowledge of previous biological control attempts).

It would also need to consider key economic inputs such as production and consumption losses, elasticities of supply and demand, and means of evaluating and incorporating non-market costs and benefits into the equation. This decision support tool, preferably computer based, could assist managers in making better decisions in questions of resource allocation to control projects, and provide a framework within which to debate assumptions and predictions. This should also improve the timeliness of implementation of biocontrol projects and contribute significantly to competent *ex-post* evaluations.

Some factors that need to be considered in such *ex-ante* studies compared with those for *ex-post* studies are listed in Table 11.3. Some of the technical information needed is straightforward and should be available from official

Table 11.3   Measuring the impact of biological control interventions before and after implementation: factors to be considered for each case

Factor	Before – potential impact	After – actual impact/benefit
Area affected	Measure area at risk of infestation Predict ultimate distribution of pest Measure rate of spread	Measure known area of infestation
Damage level	Estimate damage/yield loss from crop yield data	Yield loss assessment with and without biocontrol by field experimentation
Indirect damage	Estimate likely side-effects of pesticide applications: extent of displacement of native organisms	Assess impact on non-target organisms from before/after data on distribution and abundance
Amenity	Estimate likely effect on quality of life, human health, environment, social and cultural practices	Measured environmental, social and cultural benefits following control
Cost of biocontrol	Assess availability of natural enemies Estimate costs of exploration, importation, quarantine, release, evaluation Estimate probability of successful control	Known costs of biocontrol implementation
Economic loss/ benefits accruing	Estimate benefits/costs to producers and consumers, elasticities Undertake contingent valuation studies for non-market effects	Measure actual benefits to producers and consumers, price elasticities

statistics (for example, government or the UN Food and Agriculture Organization (FAO) production and market statistics), maps, Geographic Information
System (GIS), or aerial photographs. Other parameters such as the potential
distribution and likely abundance of the pest, or an introduced natural enemy,
and impact on non-target organisms are less easily calculated. Computer
programs which predict distribution and abundance of invading species using
life history parameters and climate data, already exist (for example, Climex
(Sutherst and Maywald, 1985)), and such methods might form the basis for a
more comprehensive decision support tool.

Costs of research into biological control agents for weeds in Canada, and
their introduction, were considered by Harris (1979). He suggested that the
cost of finding, screening and introducing an agent could usefully be calculated in scientist years (cost of employment and research expenditure) and
that on average two years were required for each agent introduced and two
agents are released before control is achieved. Methods for estimating economic and social costs have already been discussed above in relation to
ex-post evaluations. A model for estimating both economic and non-economic costs and benefits will include a mixture of technical and economic
parameters. The *ex-ante* parameters are likely to be more difficult to obtain
and accordingly less precise than *ex-post* parameters, but will none the less
provide a useful framework for assessing risk and evaluating control options.

7   DISCUSSION

In spite of their high failure rate, biological control projects have proved to be
a cost-effective use of public good funds. Thanks to its sustainable and self-
renewing nature, returns to successful biological control programmes can be
higher than those of other successful agricultural technology research programmes, and significantly higher than average returns on public good
investment projects. *Ex-post* studies for the historical evaluation of biological
control projects have proved to be a robust and useful tool in evaluating
economic benefits from implementing biological control programmes, but
the greater and largely untapped potential of economic evaluations is in *ex-
ante* studies, in particular studies which combine economic and technical
ex-ante analyses of costs and benefits. They would offer decision makers
better means of assessing the scope of problems associated with invasive
species, of making quicker and better decisions on funding biological control
or indeed other agricultural research and extension programmes, and of im-
proving further the returns on investment in biological control programmes.

Biological control practitioners, and indeed all stakeholders involved with
the control of invasive species would benefit from the development of deci-

sion support tools which would allow them to carry out *ex-ante* economic analyses more easily and more effectively.

REFERENCES

Anderson, L.G. and R.F. Settle (1977), *Benefit-cost Analysis: A Practical Guide*, New York: Lexington Books.

Beingolia, O.D. (1977), 'Culmina con éxito proyecto de control biológico de la queresa redonda de los citricos, Selenaspidus articulatus Morgan, en el Perú', *Noticiero Entomologico*, **1**: 3–4.

CAB (1980), *Biological Control Service; 25 Years of Achievement*, Farnham Royal, UK: Commonwealth Agriculture Bureaux.

Conway, G.R. (1987), 'The properties of agroecosystems', *Agricultural Systems*, **24**: 95–117.

Cruickshank, S. and F. Ahmed (1973), 'Biological control of potato tuber moth *Phthorimaea operculeua* (2ell.) (Lep.: Telechiidae) in Zambia', Technical Bulletin 16, Farnham Royal, UK: Commonwealth Institute of Biological Control, pp. 147–62.

Cullen, J.M. and M.J. Whitten (1995), 'Economics of classical biological control: a research perspective', in H.M. Hokkanen and J.M. Lynch (eds), *Biological Control Benefits and Risks*, Cambridge: Cambridge University Press: 270–76.

Dean, H.A., M.F. Schuster, J.C. Bolling, P.T. Rihard and P. DeBach (1979), 'Complete biological control of *Antonina graminis* in Texas with *Neodusmetia sangwani* (a classical example)', *Bulletin of the Entomological Society of America*, **25**: 262–7.

DeBach, P. (ed.) (1964), *Biological Control of Insect Pests and Weeds*, London: Chapman & Hall.

Dharmadikari, P.R., P.A.C.R. Perera and T.M.F. Hassen (1977), 'A short account of the biological control of *Promecotheca cummingi* (Col.: Hispidae) the coconut leaf-miner in Sri Lanka', *Entomophaga*, **22**: 3–18.

Embree, D.G. (1977), '*Operophtera brumata* (L.), winter moth (Lepidoptera: Geometridae)', in *Biological Control Programmes Against Insects and Weeds in Canada 1959–1968*, Commonwealth Institute of Biological Control, Technical Communication, No. 4 Commonwealth Agricultural Bureaux, Farnham Royal, UK: 167–75.

Greathead, D.J. (1995), 'Benefits and risks of biological control', in H.M. Hokkanen and J.M. Lynch (eds), *Biological Control Benefits and Risks*, Cambridge: Cambridge University Press: 53–63.

Greathead, D.J. and A.H. Greathead (1992), 'Biological control of insect pests by insect parasitoids and predators', BIOCAT database, *Biocontrol News and Information*, **13**: 61n–68n.

Greer, G. and R.L. Sheppard (1990), 'An economic evaluation of the benefits of research in biological control of *Clematis vitalba*', Agribusiness and Economics Research Unit, Lincoln College, Canterbury, New Zealand, Research Report No. 203.

Grundy, T.P. (1990), 'A cost–benefit analysis of the biological control of the rose-grain aphid in New Zealand', Proceedings of the 43rd New Zealand Weed and Pest Control Conference: 163–5.

Hansen, J.R. (1986), *Guide to Practical Project Appraisal: Social Cost-Benefit Analysis in Developing Countries*, Vienna: UNIDO.

Harris, P. (1979), 'Cost of biological control of weeds by insects in Canada', *Weed Science*, **27**: 242–50.

Harris, P. and R. Cranston (1979), 'An economic evaluation of control methods for diffuse and spotted knapweed in western Canada', *Canadian Journal of Plant Science*, **59**: 375–82.

Hulme, M.A. (1988), 'The recent Canadian record in applied biological control of forest pests', *Forestry Chronicle*, **6**: 27–31.

Joffe, S. and S. Cooke (1997), 'Management of water hyacinth and the invasive aquatic weeds: issues for the World Bank', World Bank consultancy report.

Julien, M.H. and M.W. Griffiths (eds) (1998), *Biological Control of Weeds, A World Catalogue of Agents and their Target Weeds*, 4th edn, Wallingford: Commonwealth Agricultural Bureau International.

Julien, M.H. and G. White (eds) (1997), *Biological Control of Weeds: Theory and Practical Application*, Australian Centre for International Agricultural Research (ACIAR) Monograph Series.

Lubulwa, G. and S. McMeniman (1998), 'ACIAR supported biological control projects in the South Pacific (1983–1996): an economic assessment', *Biocontrol News and Information*, **19**: 91n–98n.

Marsden, J.S., G.E. Martin, D.J. Parham, T.J. Ridsdill Smith and B.G. Johnson (1980), *Returns on Australian Agricultural Research*, Commonwealth Scientific and Industrial Research Organization (CSIRO), Australia.

Melville, A.R. (1959), 'The place of biological control in the modern science of entomology', *Kenya Coffee*, **24**: 81–5.

Mohyuddin, A.I. and S. Shah (1977), 'Biological control of *Mythimna separata* (Lep.: Noctuidae) in New Zealand and its bearing on biological control strategy', *Entomophaga*, **22**: 331–3.

Norgaard, R.B. (1988), 'Economics of the cassava mealybug (*Phaenococcus manihoti*; Hom.: Pseudococcidae) biological control program in Africa', *Entomophaga*, **33**: 3–6.

Reeks, W.A. and J.M Cameron (1971), 'Current approach to biological control of forest insects', in *Biological Control Programmes Against Insects and Weeds in Canada*, Commonwealth Institute of Biological Control, Technical Communication No. 4, Commonwealth Agricultural Bureau: 105–13.

Simmonds, F.J. (1967), 'The economics of biological control', *Journal of the Royal Society of Arts*, October: 880–98.

Sutherst, R.W. and G.F. Maywald (1985), 'A computerised system for matching climates in ecology', *Agricultural Ecosystems and Environment*, **13**: 281–99.

Tisdell, C.A. (1990), 'Economic impacts of biological control of weeds and insects', in M. Mackauer, L.E. Ehler and J. Roland (eds), *Critical Issues in Biological Control*, Andover: Intercept Press: 301–16.

Tisdell, C.A. and B.A. Auld (1990), 'Evaluation of biological control projects', Proceedings 7th International Symposium on Biological Control of Weeds, Rome, Italy: 93–100.

Voegele, J.M., D. Agounke and D. Moore (1991), 'Biological control of the fruit tree mealybug *Rastrococcus invadens* in Togo: a preliminary sociological and economic evaluation', *Tropical Pest Management*, **37**: 379–82.

Voegele, J.M., F. Klingauf and T. Engelhardt (1989), 'Untersuchungen zur

Wirtschaftlicheit des biologischen Pflanzenschutzes anhand eines Fallbeispiels aus West-Samoa', *Gesunde Pflanzen*, **41**: 255–8.

White, J.M., P.G. Allen, L.J. Moffitt and P.P. Kingsley (1995), 'Economic analysis of an areawide program for biological control of the alfalfa weevil', *American Journal of Alternative Agriculture*, **10**: 173–9.

Williams, J.R. and D.J. Greathead (1973), 'The sugarcane scale insect *Aulacaspis tegalensis* (Zhnt.) and its biological control in Mauritius and East Africa', *Pest Articles and News Summaries*, **19**: 353–67.

PART III

Conclusions

12. Conclusions

Charles Perrings, Mark Williamson and Silvana Dalmazzone

---

1 WHY ECONOMICS MATTERS TO THE CONTROL OF INVASIVE SPECIES

Invasive species have been found in most parts of the world, but the pattern differs from biome to biome. Within terrestrial systems, xeric (deserts, semi-deserts, tropical dry forests and woodlands) and northern arctic systems are typically least affected, while in island systems invasive species have been directly responsible for a number of documented extinctions. Lake, river and near-shore marine systems are similarly more affected than pelagic marine environments (Heywood, 1995). This pattern probably reflects differences in the susceptibility of the underlying ecosystems to invasions. The difficulties in drawing conclusions from the raw data were stressed by Lonsdale (1999) who concluded that species properties, ecosystem properties and propagule pressure (Williamson, 1996) needed more study. The pattern also undoubtedly reflects differences in human behaviour, land use, demographic, market and institutional structures, the regulatory framework and the control strategies adopted, all of which will incidentally affect propagule pressure. That is, the susceptibility of ecosystems to biological invasions seems to us to depend in large part on how those ecosystems are used, and on the measures taken to protect them against the effects of pests and pathogens.

In the existing literature, the relation between human behaviour and invasives is reflected in the focus on disturbance of ecosystems. Habitat fragmentation and clearance are both argued to have increased the susceptibility of remaining fragments to invasion (Neiring, 1990) as has agricultural disturbance. But there seem to be few general rules to be derived from a concept as coarse as 'disturbance'. As we indicated in the introduction to this book, the ecological evidence so far suggests that it is not possible to generalize much about invasions, and that what is needed are precise case studies (Williamson, 1999). Even in the most detailed case studies, however, the ecological evidence typically excludes the behaviour of the people responsible for the

227

introduction and spread of species. Disciplinary specialization has stepped in between the study of the organism and its vector.

The main implication of the chapters in this volume is that the development of an appropriate control strategy depends on an understanding of the way that human behaviour and invasive species interact. This in turn reflects the institutional and policy environment within which people make their decisions. The importance of human behaviour in the control strategy is well established in the treatment of invasive species that have direct effects on human health, such as the immuno-deficiency virus, HIV. Indeed, for such species control depends on the ability to influence the behaviour of infected and susceptible people. For other invasives, however, prohibition and/or eradication are the preferred options. The dominant control mechanisms at introduction are quarantine or the prohibition of blacklisted species.[1] These are often blunt instruments that are frequently neither efficient nor cost-effective.

The evaluation of the costs and benefits of control options depends on both the objective risks of invasions and the perception of those risks. It is very difficult to identify the probabilities attaching to different outcomes on the basis of either the characteristics of species or their habitat. This is partly because the risks are not wholly exogenous. Just as with the spread of disease, the spread of other potentially invasive species depends on people's behaviour. The pattern of spread depends not just on the control strategy, but on the use made of invasive species, their predators and competitors, on demographic patterns, on transport networks and the like.

The probability of establishment of intentionally introduced species is expected to be higher than that of unintentionally introduced species, simply because intentionally introduced species have been selected for their ability to survive in the environment where they are introduced (Williamson, 1994; Smith et al., 1999). But the probability of establishment and spread also depends on the way in which the environment is altered by human behaviour. The introduction of specific disease or pest resistant crops, for example, selects in favour of other pests and predators. Understanding the effects of human behaviour may help to improve our ability to predict the risks of invasions.

Whether or not a particular invasion is important, and to whom, depends on the expected cost of that invasion and the perceptions of those costs. This is an area where very little work has been done, and where much of what is available consists either of highly aggregated estimates of the *ex-post* cost of invasions in particular sectors, or *ex-post* cost–benefit analyses of successful control strategies – equivalent to winning lottery tickets. There is a clear need to improve the basis on which (a) control strategies are evaluated, and (b) the potential impacts of species introductions are valued.

The economics of invasive species is concerned with the interdependence between human behaviour and the introduction, establishment and spread of species from one managed or impacted ecosystem to another. It adds an extra dimension to our understanding of the process of invasions. It also adds an array of instruments to the traditional control options, and a set of decision tools with which to assess both the efficiency and cost-effectiveness of control options.

2 PREDISPOSING ECONOMIC CONDITIONS

To identify the institutional and policy conditions that predispose countries to biological invasion, Dalmazzone considers a number of measures of extroversion. These comprise measures of the openness of a country's economy and especially of its agriculture, livestock and tourism sectors, the composition of its trade flows and its regulatory regimes. There are a number of limitations to the available ecological and economic data. The complexity of ecological responses to invasives, difficulties in defining and observing appropriate variables, and discrepancies in the spatial and temporal scale of ecological and economic data are all potential sources of error both in the specification of the biological invasions model, and in measurement. Ecological data are collected by region or natural reserves, whereas economic data are typically classified by country. Economic time series are generally available, but ecological time series are not. Nevertheless, the establishment of alien plant species in 26 different countries has been shown to depend on rates of change in GDP, trade flows and their composition, land devoted to agriculture and to livestock production, land still forested and with wood cover, import duties, population density and island status.

This suggests that the economic effects associated with human activities are important determinants of the extent to which a given country will be invaded – the economic consequences hypothesis. Although all ecological communities may be susceptible to invasions at some level, economic activities appear to increase that susceptibility. Variables related to trade have a less strong although still significant impact on the share of alien species hosted by any given country.

This adds insight, for example, to the problem of biological invasions on islands (Lonsdale, 1999). Island ecosystems are generally considered highly susceptible to invasions because of a particularly vulnerable native biodiversity. But island states are also typically, on average, small open economies, often geared to the production of primary products. Dalmazzone points out, for example, that the average percentage of merchandise imports as a share of GDP in the sample considered is 43 per cent for island countries, as against

32 per cent for the whole sample, and 26.8 per cent for continental countries. Island states are not only more susceptible ecologically, they are much more open in terms of the movement of goods and services across ecological boundaries. Understanding the economic and institutional environment can improve estimates of the risk of invasions.

There are, however, a more general set of predisposing conditions. The most important of these is that the market prices of potentially invasive species do not reflect the cost they may impose on society. Invasions are typically external to the market. At the same time many existing markets have been prevented from operating efficiently by agricultural policies and institutions. Fiscal, price and incomes policies have all promoted management regimes that have increased the susceptibility of agroecosystems to invasion. Subsidies designed to promote cash cropping as a means of increasing export revenue have encouraged the use of farm inputs that lay agroecosystems open to invasion.

Part of the problem in the developing countries is that farm incomes leave little room for farmers to take a wider or longer view of their behaviour. In many cases farm income is depressed both because of adverse movements in international commodity prices, and because of the effects of national policy. In many countries administered prices have reduced producer incomes and so discouraged investment in habitat conservation. While growth has reduced poverty in some economies, poverty has been deepening in others. Between 1960 and 1990 the share of the poorest 20 per cent of countries fell from 2.3 per cent of world GNP to just 1.4 per cent, while the share of the richest 20 per cent of countries rose from 70.2 to 84.7 per cent. More importantly, the income of the poorest has become more not less variable (Human Development Report, 1998).

The liberalization of agricultural markets has implications for both the level and stability of prices. It is generally expected that average producer prices will rise, but given that most administered prices were designed to stabilize incomes, it may also be expected that producer prices will become more variable. The presumption is that administered prices impose welfare losses that significantly outweighed any welfare gains from stabilization. This may be true, but it is an empirical question that has not been resolved. Certainly, the empirical evidence is that liberalization has occurred alongside a marked increase in price risk. The coefficient of variation of detrended prices for the major food products rose sharply between the mid-1960s and the mid-1980s. In addition, these prices became positively correlated, so reducing the value both of diversification within agriculture and of export earning stabilization schemes (ibid.).

The Uruguay round of the GATT (General Agreement on Tariffs and Trade) in fact led to a worsening of the trade balance of net food importers and countries that have historically enjoyed preferential access to the European Union under the Lomé Convention (mainly in Sub-Saharan Africa). During the period 1983–93 the World Bank estimated that per capita consumption and GDP declined at, respectively, 1.8 and 0.8 per cent per year in Sub-Saharan Africa (World Bank, 1998). Under the 'Brundtland hypothesis' (for example, Pearce and Warford, 1993), countries locked in to products for which the terms of trade decline will tend to increase exports of those products just to maintain foreign exchange earnings. Consistent with this hypothesis, the response to falling real primary commodity prices in Sub-Saharan Africa has not been a reduction in primary commodity production, but an increase in the volume of exports.

The high level of indebtedness of many low-income countries has not helped. This has partly been a consequence of dependence on primary commodity production – primary commodity prices having to follow a downward secular trend. Both barter and income terms of trade have declined for many of the poorest countries despite increasing volumes of exports. That is, consistent with the Brundtland hypothesis, the volume of agricultural exports has risen but has still lost ground in terms of purchasing power.

There is not much evidence that biodiversity loss has been driven by poverty in any direct way. However, poverty does induce people to focus on their immediate needs and to ignore the longer-term consequences of their actions. Poverty also distorts people's responses to economic incentives. Incentives either may not work at all or may work in the wrong direction. Getting prices right may be a necessary condition for the efficient allocation of environmental resources, but it is not sufficient.

3   BIOLOGICAL INVASIONS AND HUMAN BEHAVIOUR

The volume includes three chapters that model the way in which economic activity and an invasive species interact. Knowler and Barbier's chapter on the role of *Mnemiopsis leidyi* in the Black Sea fishery, Delfino and Simmons's chapter on disease transmission, and Watkinson, Freckleton and Dowling's chapter on the problems of invasive weeds all consider invasive species in the context of an economic decision problem. In the first case, *Mnemiopsis leidyi* is important because of its impact on a harvested species. The chapter offers a general way of modelling the effect of predators or competitors on the optimal use of harvested species. It relies on an appropriate specification of the population dynamics of the invasive species (and the species with which it interacts). This is obviously a source of considerable uncertainty. But it is clearly a *sine qua non* for the modelling and prediction of invasives.

The general approach is helpful in developing the capacity to predict the impact of invasions on the production of economically useful goods and services. It also provides a means of estimating the value of that impact. The economically valued output in the Black Sea case is a particular species, the anchovy *Engraulis encrasicolus*, but the same method can be used to model the impact of potentially invasive species in the production of a range of ecological services. The impact of invasives in lakes or wetlands, for example, might be modelled in terms of their impact on the provision of a wide array of functions including storm and pollution buffering, flood alleviation, recreation and so on. As discussed in Turpie and Heydenrych's chapter, if an invasive species reduces the optimal level of output of some valued good or service, then it is possible to estimate the losses it involves.

The difficulty in modelling the dynamics correctly should not, however, be underestimated. The chapter by Delfino and Simmons discusses how one might model the dynamic interactions between a class of invasives (pathogens), human behaviour and economic development. It shows that while the probability of infection influences decisions in a way that is reasonably well understood, the interactions between the virulence of a disease, infected and susceptible populations, the pattern of settlement and the level of development may be very complex indeed. The relation between the level of economic development, the epidemiology of an invasive pathogen, and settlement and migration is particularly interesting. In this case the spread of the invasive species depends directly on the mobility of infected and susceptible people, and is highly sensitive to parameter values. One possible outcome, for example, is that the maximization of expected utility leads to the complete segregation of infected and susceptible people.

The chapter also highlights another property of invasives that is extremely important for the choice of control strategy. While the spread of disease is affected by the private costs and benefits of the options facing people, and so may be influenced by economic incentives, it involves external effects. People will typically ignore the impact of their decisions on the infection risks to others. There is a strong public good element in the control of disease. If it is left to the market, it will be undersupplied.

More importantly, the public good involved in the control of infectious diseases and many other invasive species is of the weakest link variety. That is, the benefits from control to a whole society depend on the level of control exercised by the least effective member (Sandler, 1997). If control over a communicable disease involves national eradication campaigns, for example, that control will only be as good as the campaign run by the least effective nation. Rich nations typically have more effective public health programmes than poor nations, and the public health programmes in the poorest of the poor are virtually non-existent.

This points to two things: (a) the scope for intervention to change the incentives to those whose behaviour determines the spread of an invasive species, and (b) the need for public investment in the control of invasives either nationally (where the potential range of the invader lies within national boundaries) or internationally (where the potential range of the invader crosses national boundaries).

4 THE BENEFIT–COST CALCULUS AND DECISION RULES

There remains the question as to how to allocate public resources between control options, discussed in detail by Shogren. Although there are reasons to believe that decision makers' perceptions and valuations of the risks posed by invaders may be biased, it is nevertheless appropriate to evaluate investment in the control of invasives through the use of benefit–cost techniques. However, there are few rigorous attempts to evaluate control strategies in this way. A number of the remaining chapters in the volume discuss the costs and benefits of invasive species in particular cases: weed species in Australian agroecosystems (Watkinson et al.), *Pinus*, *Hakea* and *Acacia* species in the South African Fynbos (Turpie and Heydenrych); plant and fish species in the African Lakes (Kasulo) and rabbits in Australia (White and Newton-Cross), and the tree *Maesopsis eminii* in the eastern arc montane forests of Tanzania (Lovett). Their findings indicate a serious problem that clearly warrants substantial public investment in control, but only Watkinson et al. offer an evaluation of current or alternative control strategies.

The variation in techniques used in Shogren, Watkinson et al., Turpie and Heydenrych, White and Newton-Cross, Hill and Greathead, and Zavaleta (1999) shows that there needs to be more comparison and discussion of the usefulness of different ways of calculating cost–benefit ratios. Invasion accounting is still rather primitive, not always distinguishing capital from income, recoverable from non-recoverable costs, and taking arbitrary and variable discount rates. In biocontrol, as Hill and Greathead state, the analysis of control options has focused on the *ex-post* calculation of discounted benefit–cost ratios for effective controls. As we have already noted, this is tantamount to calculating the value of a winning lottery ticket. It tells nothing about the efficiency of a decision to buy a lottery ticket; it cannot by itself guide *ex-ante* decisions about when to control and when not to control; nor can it guide the choice between control options. For all those, we need the probability of effective control, for which Hill and Greathead give an indication of size and variation. In biocontrol, as in other invasives situations, the probability of success varies with both type of invasive species and the type of system involved (Williamson, 1996), so that historical rates may be unsatisfactory predictors of future ones.

The decision problem reflects the fact that biological invasions fall into the category of low probability events with a high potential cost (Williamson, 1992). The probability that any one introduced species will establish and become a pest or pathogen is very low, but the costs to society if it does can be very high. Smith et al. (1999) suggest 2 per cent for the probability of plant introductions into Australia becoming pests, somewhat higher than the 0.01–1.6 per cent, mostly based on British examples, indicated by the tens rule of Williamson and Fitter (1996); though all these figures are markedly affected by the definitions of 'introduced' and 'pest' (Williamson, 1996). At the same time, as is shown throughout this book, the control and/or damage costs of species that do become significant pests or pathogens can be extremely high.

The expected utility hypothesis suggests that control options should be evaluated in terms of the expected values of outcomes with some adjustment for risk aversion. If expected values can be calculated for the net costs of control options, then an expected net present value can be estimated within the framework of cost–benefit analysis (CBA). Risk attitudes may be allowed for by either adjusting the discount rate upwards by a risk premium, or finding the certainty equivalent of the expected environmental damage (the certain damage that would yield the same disutility as the expected damage).

One complication with biological invasions is that pests or pathogens frequently involve 'dread' – a phenomenon that increases subjective risk assessments connected with certain types of health risk (McDaniels et al., 1992). It has been shown that risk rating has a higher effect on willingness to pay for risk-reduction measures in infrequent high-dread situations, than in frequent low-dread situations (Loomis and du Vair, 1993). In fact the power of the expected utility hypothesis declines as the probabilities of outcomes tend to unity or to zero. In the former case the probability of an 'almost sure' event tends to be approximated by certainty. In the latter case, people facing a 'very unlikely' event tend either to overestimate the probability or to identify it with zero. For very low probabilities the weighting function is often not defined. In the liability insurance markets it has long been established that where the probability is very low but the potential loss is very high, insurers demand a risk premium that exceeds the expected losses while the insured are willing to pay less than predicted by expected utility calculations (Katzman, 1988).

Many of the current methods for determining the effectiveness of screening, control, mitigation or eradication procedures can be cast in cost–benefit terms. Consider, for example, the method for evaluating screening procedures for potentially invasive species discussed by Smith et al. (1999). They define the expected value of the costs of control (through screening) to be the product of three factors: (a) the accuracy of the control (the screening process), (b) the probability that a species will be invasive, and (c) the expected cost of error.

The accuracy of a screening process is the proportion of species that have, *ex-post*, been found to be appropriately dealt with in the screening process: namely, the proportion of invaders assessed that are rejected by the process, and the proportion of non-invaders assessed that are accepted by the process. The first of these,

$$A_i = (I_r / I_t)$$

is the ratio of the number of invaders rejected by the process, I_r, to the number of invaders assessed by the process, I_t. The second

$$A_n = (N_t - N_r / N_t)$$

is the ratio of the number of non-invaders accepted by the process, $1 - N_r$, to the number of non-invaders assessed by the process, N_t. From this is derived a likelihood ratio for the screening process

$$LR = (I_r / I_t) / (N_r / N_t)$$

If $LR > 1$, then the screening process has some predictive ability.

The test of a particular screen is the value of the product of this likelihood ratio and the two remaining factors: the probability that an introduced species will become a pest, R, and the expected cost if it does, K. The former depends on the probability that the introduced species escapes to become a casual species, the probability that a casual species will naturalize, and the probability that the naturalized species will become a pest. In general this is very low – as the tens rule suggests – although it has been noted to be as high as 17 per cent for some weedy species from some Australian pastures (Lonsdale, 1994). The acceptance criteria according to Smith et al. (1999) is that:

$$LR \cdot R \cdot K \geq 1$$

To see the relation between a test of this sort and a standard benefit–cost rule, note first that both R and K may be expressed as ratios. R may be expressed as the ratio of the probability that an accepted invasive species will impose economic costs (will be a pest), which we denote R_i, and the probability that an accepted non-invasive species will not impose economic costs (will not be a pest), which we denote R_n. Implicitly, Smith et al. assume that $R_n = 1$. Similarly, the expected cost of pests, K, may be expressed as the ratio of the expected costs of accepting an invasive species that turns out to be a pest, which we denote K_i, and the net costs of rejecting a non-invasive species that turns out not to be a pest, which we denote K_n.

That is, staying with the notation in Smith et al. (1999), the test for the screening process to be acceptable is:

$$LR \cdot R \cdot K \cong \frac{\dfrac{I_r}{I_t} \cdot R_i \cdot K_i}{\dfrac{N_r}{N_t} \cdot R_n \cdot K_n} \geq 1$$

$LR \cdot R \cdot K$ is accordingly equivalent to the ratio between two terms. The first term is the product of the proportion of potential invasives rejected by the control, the probability of a potential invasive doing damage, and the expected costs of invasives. It is the expected cost of invasives avoided by use of the screen. The second term is the product of the proportion of potential non-invasives rejected by the control, the probability of a potentially non-invasive species yielding benefits, and the expected net benefits of non-invasives. It is the expected benefits of non-invasives lost in the screening process: the opportunities forgone by the screen.

Although the expected value of K is undiscounted in the Smith et al. formulation, and in many other conventional tests for the acceptability of measures to deal with invasive species, this should not be the case. Indeed, in the absence of discounting it is generally impossible to make intertemporal comparisons. The expected net costs of admitted invasives and the net benefits of excluded non-invasives should be discounted at some positive rate. We do not discuss the question of what the appropriate rate may be, but note that the result will often be highly sensitive to the discount rate. In this case, the test requires that the expected present value of the benefits of the screening process (the net costs avoided by the screening programme) are no less than the expected present value of the costs of control (the forgone benefits of the screening programme). In other words $LR \cdot R \cdot K$ is approximately equal to the ratio of discounted benefits and costs of the screening programme.

$$LR \cdot R \cdot K \cong E \sum_{t=0}^{T} \rho^t \left(\frac{B_{it} - C_{it}}{B_{nt} - C_{nt}} \right)$$

where $B_{it} - C_{it}$ is the expected net benefits at time t of excluding invasive species that are potential pests, $B_{nt} - C_{nt}$ is expected net costs at time t of excluding non-invasive species that are potentially valuable, and ρ is the discount factor. Each term in the net benefit–cost ratio $(B_{it} - C_{it})/(B_{nt} - C_{nt})$ depends on the way in which introduced species are used and the resources allocated to the screening process. That is, each term is contingent on the behaviour of resource users and their perceptions of the private costs and benefits of their actions. The 'dread' effect works on both private estimates of the risks that a potential invasive will become a pest, and the expected cost if it does.

To the extent that invasions are 'carried' by resource users whose responses to incentives are rather better understood, it is possible to develop model structures that can be adapted to the needs of particular cases, and may help predictions in those cases. The general point we wish to make here is that many current tests of the effectiveness of controls on invasives have at least elements of a standard test for the efficiency of investments – benefit–cost analysis. We have taken the example of one process for screening potentially invasive species, but we could have considered tests that are currently applied to quarantine, mitigation, or eradication programmes. In most cases, however, the current tests include a very partial assessment of the expected benefits and costs. They often ignore the opportunity cost of control programmes and the cost of controls that prove to be unnecessary. If the chapters in this volume encourage decision makers to adopt a more complete approach to the analysis of the benefits and costs of control measures, they will have taken us a step forward.

5 CONCLUDING REMARKS

Two processes above all else are the proximate causes of global biodiversity loss. The first is the destruction and fragmentation of habitats associated with the expansion of mining, forestry and agriculture. Habitat fragmentation and loss in areas of high endemism are considered to be the major cause of species extinction worldwide. In most terrestrial systems a high proportion of 'original' habitats have been converted to some specific economic use and much more land is indirectly affected by economic activity. Indeed, it is no longer useful to describe most of the world's habitats as 'undisturbed'. The main proximate cause of species loss is therefore better described as habitat disturbance, the effect of disturbance depending on its intensity, nature and location.

The second is the introduction of species – the problem of invasions. Some introductions consist of more or less controlled imports to support agriculture and fisheries. An important set of introductions are, however, entirely uncontrolled. These include a range of pests and pathogens that affect the health of human and non-human species alike. Only a small proportion of introduced species establish themselves and spread and not all invasive species are undesirable. However, the Global Biodiversity Assessment concluded that invasives generally have negative effects on both species and genetic diversity at local and global levels. These effects include the deletion of indigenous species through predation, browsing or competition; genetic alteration of indigenous species through hybridization; and the alteration of ecosystem structure and function including biogeochemical, hydrological and nutrient cycles, soil erosion and other geomorphological processes.

Behind these proximate causes, however, is a set of institutional and market conditions that increases the susceptibility of countries to invasive species, and encourages resource users to ignore the consequences of their actions. Markets fail to accommodate the risks posed by invasive species. While many private benefits of species introductions (or land use that increases the susceptibility of ecosystems to species introductions) are captured in market prices, many of its social costs are not. Markets for seeds, foods, fibres, pesticides and fertilizers drive specialization in agriculture, but do not signal its social costs. Any policy for biodiversity conservation accordingly has four key elements:

- a regulatory regime to protect key species, habitats and ecological services and to control the introduction of invasive species;
- an appropriate set of property rights in natural resources (along with their supporting institutions);
- a compensation mechanism; and
- a supporting structure of incentives and disincentives to induce the desired response.

In the case of biological invasions, however, there is an extra dimension. The most common justification for action to conserve biodiversity lies in the fact that the genetic information it contains is a global public good. This is the rationale both for international effort to conserve hotspots and for the incremental cost approach adopted by the Global Environment Facility. We have argued here that the main costs and benefits of actions to control biological invasions are local. However, biological invasions almost always involve two or more countries, the actions of one affecting the welfare of another. One example discussed in the book is the fishery in Lake Victoria. Since the lake is effectively a common pool resource, decisions made in respect of one national fishery, including the introduction of new species, necessarily affect the other national fisheries. They involve a transboundary externality.

Similarly, where the costs of failure to control invasives affect more than one country, the solution requires international cooperation. The fact that centres of endemism or range-size rarity can be in different locations from centres of species richness is important in the development of control strategies. Species richness is typically correlated with habitat heterogeneity, particularly in mountains, but may be associated with variation in soils and landscape, or interannual variation in rainfall. These need not coincide with centres of endemism where the vegetation is composed of rare species with small geographical ranges. Species of restricted distribution in centres of endemism would not generally be expected to be resilient to anthropogenic stress or shocks. In centres of unrestricted range species richness, however, it may be possible to alter environmental conditions without unduly adverse effects. Control strategies and international cooperation to control invasives should be sensitive to this.

Because of the public good nature of strategies to protect environmental health, all will require public investment in control. The particular difficulty in strategies to control invasive species is the uncertainty attaching to different control options. We have suggested that despite the particular difficulties with the base load problem in the case of invasive species, it is still reasonable to evaluate public investment in control options using a benefit–cost framework. However, as in other areas of environmental management where there are high levels of uncertainty, and where costs of error are potentially very high, it is important that the control protects the capacity of the system to absorb the stresses and shocks of biological invasions. While this does not favour the blanket eradication of all invaders, it does call for caution in the designation of the release area for screened species. The potential irreversibility of the costs of invasions and the uncertainty of the damages they may cause both favour a conservative approach to their management. But this has to be tempered by a realistic appraisal of the costs and benefits of the options.

NOTES

1. For example, the Australian Environment Protection and Biodiversity Conservation Act 1999, Section 301A, defines regulations for control of non-native species that:

    (a) provide for the establishment and maintenance of a list of species, other than native species, whose members:
       (i) do or may threaten biodiversity in the Australian jurisdiction; or
       (ii) would be likely to threaten biodiversity in the Australian jurisdiction if they were brought into the Australian jurisdiction; and
    (b) regulate or prohibit the bringing into the Australian jurisdiction of members of a species included in the list mentioned in paragraph (a); and
    (c) regulate or prohibit trade in members of a species included in the list mentioned in paragraph (a):
       (i) between Australia and another country; or
       (ii) between 2 States; or
       (iii) between 2 Territories; or
       (iv) between a State and a Territory; or
       (v) by a constitutional corporation; and
    (d) regulate and prohibit actions:
       (i) involving or affecting members of a species included in the list mentioned in paragraph (a); and

(ii)   whose regulation or prohibition is appropriate and adapted to give effect to Australia's obligations under an agreement with one or more other countries; and

(e)   provide for the making and implementation of plans to reduce, eliminate or prevent the impacts of members of species included in the list mentioned in paragraph (a) on biodiversity in the Australian jurisdiction.

REFERENCES

Heywood, V. (ed.) (1995), *Global Biodiversity Assessment*, Cambridge: Cambridge University Press.

Human Development Report (1998), CD ROM, United Nations Development Programme.

Katzman, M.T. (1988), 'Pollution liability insurance and catastrophic environmental risk', *Journal of Risk and Insurance*, **55**: 75–100.

Lonsdale, W.M. (1994), 'Inviting trouble: introduced pasture species in northern Australia', *Australian Journal of Ecology*, **19**: 345–54.

Loomis, J. and P. du Vair (1993), 'Evaluating the effect of alternative risk communication devices', *Land Economics*, **69**(3): 287–98.

McDaniels, T., M. Kamlet and G. Fischer (1992), 'Risk perception and the value of safety', *Risk Analysis*, **12**(4): 495–503.

Neiring, W.A. (1990), 'Human impacts on the south Florida wetlands: the Everglades and the Big Cypress Swamp', in G.M. Woodwell (ed.), *The Earth in Transition*, Cambridge: Cambridge University Press: 463–75.

Pearce, D.W. and J.J. Warford (1993), *World Without End: Economics, Environment, and Sustainable Development*, Oxford: Oxford University Press.

Sandler, T. (1997), *Global Challenges*, Cambridge: Cambridge University Press.

Smith, C.S., W.M. Lonsdale and J. Fortune (1999), 'When to ignore advice: invasion predictions and decision theory', *Biological Invasions*, **1**: 89–96.

Williamson, M. (1992), 'Environmental risks from the release of genetically modified organisms (GMOs) – the need for molecular ecology', *Molecular Ecology*, **1**: 3–8.

Williamson, M. (1994), 'Community response to transgene plant release: predictions from British experience of invasive plants and feral crop plants', *Molecular Ecology*, **3**: 75–80.

Williamson, M. (1996), *Biological Invasions*, London: Chapman & Hall.

Williamson, M. (1999), 'Invasions', *Ecography*, **22**: 5–12.

Williamson, M. and A. Fitter (1996), 'The varying success of invaders', *Ecology*, **77**: 1661–5.

World Bank (1998), *World Development Indicators 1998*. CD ROM, International Bank for Reconstruction and Development/World Bank.

Zavaleta, E. (forthcoming), 'Valuing ecosystem services lost to *Tamarix* invasion in the United States', in H.A. Mooney and R. Hobbs (eds), *Invasives Species in a Changing World*, Washington, DC: Island Press.

Index

adaptation 60, 63, 65–6
Africa
  economic decline 231
  Fynbos vegetation 6, 152–80
    characteristics 153–5
    control of invasive aliens 174–80
    ecological–economic impact of
      invasions 157–74
    invasion by alien plants 155–7
  invasive species in African lakes 183–
    205
    fish introductions 183–95, 204
    water weeds 195–204, 205, 218
  mango mealybug (*Rastrococcus*
    invadens) control 215–16, 218
  tropical rain forests 138–48
    distribution and ecology of
      Maesopsis eminii 140, 141–5
    existence values 145–7
Agee, M. 66
agriculture 230
  habitat disturbance and 23, 25
  impact of rabbits on 118, 129–30
  invasive species and 1–2
  weed invasions *see* weed invasions
    of Australian farming systems
AIDS/HIV 32, 36
Akerlof, G.A. 52
Akinyemiju, O.A. 202
Albert, Lake 190
Alimi, T. 202
Anaman, K.A. 5
anchovy fisheries, case study of
    introduction of *Mnemiopsis leidyi*
    in the Black Sea 71, 79–89, 231–2
Anderson, I. 117, 119, 120, 132
Anderson, L.G. 214
Anderson, R.M. 36
Andrew, M.H. 119
Annal, G. 94
Argentina 56

Asgari, S. 121
Auld, B.A. 94, 95, 209, 222
Auld, T.D. 119
Australia 209, 212, 218
  infectious diseases in 32
  rabbits in 117, 118–19
    myxomatosis in 119–20, 131
    rabbit calicivirus disease (RCD) as
      control agent 120–30, 131–3
  weed invasions *see* weed invasions of
    Australian farming systems
Axelrod, D.I. 142

bacteria 32
Balinsky, B.I. 141
Bangsund, D.A. 5
Barlow, N.D. 122
Becker, G. 57
bees 163–4, 170–71
Bell, N. 139
Bellingham, P.J. 139
benefit–cost analysis *see* cost–benefit
    analysis
Benin 197
Bensted-Smith, R. 145
Beverton, R.J.H. 85
Bikangaga, S. 198, 201, 202
Binggeli, P. 138, 140
biocontrol *see* control methods
biodiversity
  conservation policies 238
  Convention on Biological Diversity
    (CBD) 3, 59
  economic valuation of 4
  existence values 146–7
  Fynbos vegetation 152, 153, 171–2
  invasive species and loss of 1–2, 17, 58
  tropical rainforests 138, 139–40
Bishop, R.C. 76
Black Sea, *Mnemiopsis leidyi* case study
    71, 79–89, 231–2